Softball
Skills & Drills

Judi Garman

Human Kinetics

Library of Congress Cataloging-in-Publication Data

Garman, Judi, 1944-
    Softball skills & drills / Judi Garman.
        p. cm
    ISBN 0-7360-3364-5
        1. Softball--Training. 2. Softball--Coaching I. Title: Softball skills and drills. II. Title.

GV881.4.T72 G37 2001
796.357'8--dc21   00-054148

ISBN: 0-7360-3364-5

Developmental Editor: Julie A. Marx; **Assistant Editor:** Stephan Seyfert; **Copyeditor:** Robert Replinger; **Proofreader:** Jim Burns; **Graphic Designer:** Robert Reuther; **Graphic Artist:** Tara Welsch; **Photo Manager:** Clark Brooks; **Cover Designer:** Keith Blomberg; **Photographer (cover):** Tom Roberts; **Photographer (interior):** Tom Roberts unless otherwise noted; photos on pages 1, 37, 63, 109, 153, and 179 © Matt Brown; photos on pages 19, 81, 127, and 193 © Tom Roberts; **Art Manager:** Craig Newsom; **Illustrator:** Sharon Smith; **Printer:** United Graphics

Human Kinetics books are available at special discounts for bulk purchase. Special editions or book excerpts can also be created to specification. For details, contact the Special Sales Manager at Human Kinetics.

Printed in the United States of America   10   9   8

Human Kinetics
Web site: www.HumanKinetics.com

United States: Human Kinetics, P.O. Box 5076, Champaign, IL 61825-5076
800-747-4457
e-mail: humank@hkusa.com

Canada: Human Kinetics, 475 Devonshire Road, Unit 100, Windsor, ON N8Y 2L5
800-465-7301 (in Canada only)
e-mail: orders@hkcanada.com

Europe: Human Kinetics, 107 Bradford Road, Stanningley
Leeds LS28 6AT, United Kingdom
+44 (0) 113 255 5665
e-mail: hk@hkeurope.com

Australia: Human Kinetics, 57A Price Avenue, Lower Mitcham, South Australia 5062
08 8277 1555
e-mail: liaw@hkaustralia.com

New Zealand: Human Kinetics, Division of Sports Distributors NZ Ltd.
P.O. Box 300 226 Albany, North Shore City, Auckland
0064 9 448 1207
e-mail: blairc@hknewz.com

Contents

Preface

Catch the ball. Throw the ball to a target. Hit the ball. Run the bases.

Championship teams and successful players execute these fundamentals consistently and accurately. Their consistency is the result of understanding the fundamentals and developing the necessary skills using relevant and specific drills.

Softball Skills & Drills is a comprehensive treatment of the fundamentals of softball. Regardless of the level of play, this book provides the skills, drills, and strategies players need to reach their full potential as individuals and as a team. It provides valuable information for coaches, players, and players' parents. The book can also be used as a textbook for softball coaching theory classes.

Everyone must start with the basics, but the book includes skills and techniques for the advanced player as well. Fundamentals are broken down and explained simply but in depth, and drills emphasize and teach the various components of each skill. Progressions for learning are included, as well as additional drills to provide variety and opportunity to practice and refine each skill. Skill summaries and coaching tips for coaches and players are highlighted as keys for learning and teaching. Several photos and diagrams help clarify and show the skills.

Chapter 1 begins with the care and selection of the glove and then explains how to use it to make routine and desperation catches. From gathering to scooping to backhands and diving, the goal is to catch every ball. Chapter 2 covers how to make strong, accurate throws to a target. Different situations call for quick releases and different types of throws. The player learns to be accurate whether throwing overhand, underhand, side-arm, or with various flips. Chapter 3 covers the individual techniques needed for each position and how players work together to form a successful unit. The outfield is the last line of defense, and chapter 4 covers the specific talents and skills the outfield needs.

Pitching is the name of the game because the pitcher dominates in softball. Chapter 5 covers the basics of the delivery and how to throw with accuracy and speed. Specific pitches covered are the fastball, drop, rise, curve, and change-up. The pitcher must learn where and when to throw each pitch. The difference between a pitcher and a thrower is what's upstairs. How much to practice, proper warm-up, and maintaining control in the game are important parts of this chapter. A good pitcher needs a good catcher. Skills and drills for developing the catcher are covered in chapter 6.

Softball is a team game, and all nine players must work together. Team defensive plays are covered in chapter 7. Specific plays covered include the bunt and slap defense and the ever-challenging first-and-third play. Pickoffs, relays, cutoffs, and rundowns are highlighted along with suggested defensive adjustments and strategies.

Hitting, bunting, and slapping are covered in chapters 8 and 9. These two chapters include more than 50 drills for developing fundamentals and correcting problems.

The ultimate goal of the offense is to score runs. Chapter 10 covers techniques for improving speed on the bases. Knowing when to run is the second key to base-running success.

The proper execution of fundamental skills is the key to success and winning whether playing in the local league championships or the College World Series or persuing a gold medal. Players and coaches can use this book to develop skills and understand the game of softball. Play and have fun. A wonderful world awaits you.

Acknowledgments

When you think of softball as just a bat and a ball, it's only a game—but when you realize that the game can introduce you to another world, it becomes much more. When I started this journey, never did I envision the wonderful world that lay ahead.

I grew up on the prairies of western Canada where I learned the game of softball. I had a bat and a pancake of a glove. I also had a wonderful mother who taught me to play. My first game was at a softball picnic. Dreams of being a superstar filled my head. Little did I know of the doors that softball would open for me.

I've played on two national championship softball teams and coached five national championship teams. I've been on the staff of a team that won the gold medal at the Pan American Games. I've made a career out of coaching softball, including a full-time job at Cal State Fullerton. As a player and a coach, I have had the opportunity to travel the world playing and sharing the game and my love of softball. Through a bat and a ball, dreams do come true.

I will always be grateful and want to express my sincere appreciation to:

To my mother, Ruth Garman, who passed on her love of sport to her two daughters and has always been there to encourage and support our athletic pursuits. Society and the times never allowed her the opportunity to have the athletic experiences we have had, but she made sure her daughters could experience the joy of sports competition, ultimately leading to successful careers in sport.

For the opportunity to grow up in Saskatchewan in a culture that encouraged girls to pursue their love of athletics.

To the Saskatoon Imperials Senior Women's Fastball Team and particularly to manager-coach Gail Hopkins, who gave me a start and an introduction to what lay ahead. We twice were Canadian champions and represented Canada in the second World Softball Championships in Japan in 1970.

To athletic director Dr. Fred Owens (Golden West College) and Leanne Grotke (Cal State Fullerton), who hired me and gave me the opportunity and resources to build two programs into national champions.

To colleagues who so unselfishly shared their knowledge and ideas so that we could all grow together and improve the game. Through their writings and clinic presentations and by their examples, I have learned much. I am grateful for their friendship and their help: Sharon Drysdale, Gayle Blevins, Linda Spradley, Cindy Bristow, Carol Spanks, Linda Wells, Sandi Fischer, Mike Candrea, Don Sarno, Bobby Simpson, Dr. Ken Ravizza, Gerry Mauro, and Olympians Michelle Smith, Dr. Dot Richardson, and Sheila Cornell Douty.

To the superb, talented players who have kept me on my toes and made it fun and to the wonderful assistant coaches from whom I have learned so much: Michelle Gromacki, Susie Parra, John Campbell, Mickey Davis, Melannie Roche, Marty Rubinoff, Linda Shafor and Chenita Rogers.

To JoAnn Zwanziger, whose support over the years has provided me the opportunity to pursue my dreams.

Just a bat and ball? Never! My hope is that this book helps you find success in softball. May your journey be as blessed as mine has been.

Key to Diagrams

(F) Fielder

(T) Tosser

(H) Hitter

(R) Runner

(P) Pitcher

(C) Catcher

(1B) First baseman

(2B) Second baseman

(3B) Third baseman

(SS) Shortstop

(LF) Left fielder

(CF) Center fielder

(RF) Right fielder

-----------▶ Path of hit ball

───────────▶ Path of player

···············▶ Path of throw

Catching

Defense begins with catching the ball, whether it is a throw, a ground ball, or a pop fly. A good glove can make this task easier, but proper body position and technique lead to consistency and success. It is easier for players to catch balls that come directly to them and when there is time for them to assume good body positioning. But errant throws and well-hit balls often don't permit this luxury. Add to this the game situation, the speed of the runners, and obstacles such as the wind, fences, and the sun, and the difficulty increases.

Catching is a psychological skill as well as a physical one. Players must believe they can catch everything. They need to go after every ball with all they have. By never giving up on a ball, the question will never come up about whether a player could have gotten the ball "if only she had tried." By making a total commitment to every ball, players will sometimes surprise themselves at the catches they make.

Your players should strive to make catches look easy. Often, the spectacular catch is the result of a player not getting a good jump on the ball and subsequently being in poor position to make the easy catch. This chapter describes the skills and techniques that will give your players the best chance for success in making all types of catches. Later chapters include specific drills to develop these skills for position play.

THE GLOVE

The glove is a player's defensive weapon. The player must first find a glove that fits the hand comfortably. She must be able to squeeze the pocket shut around the ball so that it will not pop out. The size of the glove should fit the player's position. Infielders need a smaller glove with a shallower pocket so that they can get the ball out quickly. To extend their reach, outfielders should use as large a glove as they can control. Catchers and first-base players want a glove with a large pocket to protect their hands from being bruised by all the hard balls they will receive. Only catchers and first basemen may use a mitt (a glove without fingers). A baseball catcher's glove does not have a pocket big enough to hold a softball, but a first baseman's baseball mitt can work well in softball. Manufacturers now make gloves specifically for softball and for a girl's smaller hand.

Comfort and workability are the keys. A player should choose a glove made of quality leather that will bend easily and soften while retaining its shape as it's broken in to fit the hand and form a pocket. To soften the leather, a player can throw a ball repeatedly into the pocket or catch balls thrown by a pitching machine. Follow the manufacturer's recommendations for the use of oil.

Players must care for their gloves if they are to remain effective tools. To maintain the pocket when storing a glove, always keep a ball in it. A strap or string wrapped around the glove and ball will secure the ball in the pocket. When placing a glove on the ground, players should lay it carefully on the fingers with the pocket down.

The player's finger position shapes the pocket, which must be large enough to hold a softball. The player should never put the index finger in the glove index finger because that is exactly where the softball will hit the hand and bruise it. Instead, find a comfortable position by putting the index finger outside the glove or doubling up the fingers with three fingers in the last glove finger and the index finger alone in the next glove finger or two fingers together in the last two glove fingers.

When fielding balls below the waist, players should point the fingers of both hands down. For balls above the waist, they point the fingers up. If possible, they should catch waist-high line drives with the fingers pointed up. If necessary, players should bend their knees to get behind the ball while keeping the hands up.

Positioning the Glove

Purpose: To practice adjusting the glove position depending on the location of the ball.

Procedure: The player starts with the glove above the head at twelve o'clock with the fingers pointed up. If the glove is on the left hand, the player makes a circle clockwise to three o'clock, then six o'clock, and continuing around while keeping the pocket open as if to catch a ball. The player keeps the elbow bent and the glove close to the body in a catching position. For right-handers, at three o'clock the fingers are still pointed up. As the hand drops below the waist, the fingers gradually rotate down until they point directly down at five o'clock. As the hand crosses the midline of the body at six o'clock, the hand rotates over to a backhand position (balls caught on the side of the body opposite the glove are caught backhanded). The player rotates the thumb down toward the ground, keeping the palm open to the ball. At nine o'clock, the fingers have again rotated to an upward position. When the player is familiar with proper positioning, a partner tosses her balls to catch in various locations.

CATCHING THROWS

To catch a throw, the receiver should wait in a ready, balanced position, facing the thrower and ready to move quickly in any direction should the ball be thrown off line (see figure 1.1). The feet are shoulder-width apart with the glove-side foot slightly forward. The knees are slightly flexed with weight on the balls of the feet. The arms extend toward the thrower with the elbows slightly flexed. The pocket is open toward the thrower to provide a chest-high target. The throwing hand is beside the pocket with the fingers of both hands pointed upward and the thumbs touching. The player should always catch with two hands to secure the ball and prepare for a quick release.

As the receiver catches the ball, she should move her feet to catch it just in front of the throwing shoulder. Because the throwing hand is already there to grip the ball, no effort is wasted in bringing the ball to the throwing position, thus reducing release time. As the thrower hurls the ball, the receiver should focus on the release point and then follow the ball all the way into the glove. The receiver should flex her arms as she catches the ball to lessen the impact. The goal is to have what are called "soft hands," which will prevent the ball from popping out of the glove. The player should begin with nearly full extension of the arms so that a greater distance is available to absorb the impact. As the ball lands in the pocket of the glove, the throwing hand closes over it and the fingers then grip the seams.

Figure 1.1 The ready position for receiving a throw.

BASIC FIELDING POSITION

Infielders and outfielders use a similar basic position for fielding, which is the athletic stance used in most sports. For every pitch, players should be balanced with weight on the balls of the feet so that they can react quickly in any direction. Fielders assume the *ready position* when the pitcher has the ball. The glove-side foot is slightly ahead of the other foot, and the feet are shoulder-width apart. The toes are turned inward (pigeon-toed) so that weight is forward on the balls of the feet. Players should feel the two big toes and be balanced. The hands can be on the knees, and the body is relaxed. Outfielders may prefer to be more upright in the ready position. The focus is on the pitcher and the batter (general focus). At this time, fielders should review mentally the play they will make if the ball comes to them.

Fielders shift into the *set position* as the pitcher begins the windup, and they narrow their focus to the hitter's contact spot. (Focus has moved from general to specific, from wide to narrow.) The hands move to a receiving position with the glove open toward the batter and the elbows outside the knees. I used to say that the corners (first and third) should have their gloves closer to the ground than other fielders because of the shorter reaction time required at those positions. But as batters have become stronger and are able to hit the ball harder, safety has become a greater concern. Therefore, many players now put the glove in front of the face to protect against hard-hit balls at such a short distance. Middle infielders usually assume a position with the hands about knee level and pointing toward the ground in preparation for ground balls (see figure 1.2). Players should never put the glove on the ground because doing so limits their ability to move quickly forward or laterally. Outfielders should hold their hands chest high with the palms toward the batter and pointed up (see figure 1.3). All should assume a relaxed, balanced, and comfortable position.

As the pitch is released, the defensive player should step into what sport psychologist Ken Ravizza calls the "circle of focus," focusing all attention on the batter. The player should take a small step forward, step into that circle, and concentrate on the contact spot where the bat meets the ball. By watching the angle and the speed by which the ball leaves the bat, the player can get a good jump on the ball. The player should not wait for the ball to reach her. She must react to the batted ball early so that there is time to get in proper position. If the batter does not hit the ball, the defensive player can step back out of the circle and relax a bit.

Figure 1.2   Middle infield set position.

Figure 1.3   Outfield set position.

MOVING TO THE BALL

The goal in fielding is to get directly behind every ball so that the body can serve as a wall to stop the ball if necessary. Players should charge the ball and attack it, not letting the ball play them! A straight line to the ball is always the fastest route. Infielders should use direct angles and avoid going around the ball. Outfielders, when they have time, may circle the ball and then move into it to gain momentum on their throws. Remind players that the sooner they get to the ball, the quicker they can throw it.

The first step toward the ball is a jab step with the throwing-side foot. The jab step is a slight hop or push off the ground to begin the motion. The fielder then uses shuffle steps to square up to the ball for fielding. On a hard-hit ball, however, there may be time for only one step, which should be a step with the glove-side foot. The sooner fielders react to the ball off the bat, the easier it is for them to anticipate where the ball is going and be there waiting for it.

Coaching Points for Moving to the Ball

- Before charging, have your feet already in motion, much as a tennis player does while waiting for a serve. Have "twinkle toes" as you do a little tap dance with your feet. Doing this will help you overcome inertia and react faster.
- Make sure your line of vision extends well out in front of you. React to the ball on the first or second bounce. The sooner you pick up the ball and react, the better your chance of getting into the proper position.
- Count the number of bounces as you field the ball. Doing this helps you focus on moving to the ball and making the play.
- Don't be lazy. The goal is to be square behind every ball. Consider a backhand or any other type of catch a desperation play.
- The approach is like an airplane going in for a landing—not a helicopter!

CATCHING GROUND BALLS

Players use three basic techniques for catching ground balls hit at them. The speed of the ball, the bounce, the player's reaction time, and the speed of the batter determine which technique the fielder should use.

Gathering the Ball

Just before receiving the ball, the fielder stops, splits or spreads the legs (going from narrow to wide in a well-balanced position), and puts the glove on the ground (see figure 1.4a on page 6). The hips are down as if sitting on a chair, but weight is forward on the toes. Players must use those thigh muscles. Both hands extend forward to almost complete extension, forming the large end of a triangle in front of the feet. The fielder turns the elbow in to get the glove open. The head is over the ball, and the glove foot is slightly ahead. The player guides the ball through the triangle to the point of the

Figure 1.4 Gathering the ball. *(a)* Receive the ball in a wide stance with the glove on the ground and *(b)* use soft hands to gather the ball to the abdomen.

a   b

Figure 1.5 Scooping the ball.

triangle that is attached to the belly button. The chin is tucked, and the eyes watch the ball all the way in. As the fielder gathers in the ball, the glove hand gives softly with the impact to cradle the ball (see figure 1.4b). The player uses the bare throwing hand to close over the ball and shifts her weight to the back foot as the ball is brought in toward the abdomen.

Scooping the Ball

Because of the short distances in softball, players don't always have time to charge and then stop to gather the ball. This is especially true on slow rollers, with fast runners, and on balls that bounce close to the fielder's feet (short hops). To scoop the ball, the player must keep the body low, hold the head down, and extend the hands. The ball is caught farther in front of the body than when gathering the ball. The glove action is a snap up instead of a gathering in. Ideally, the top hand is above the glove (see figure 1.5), and the hand and glove close together to trap the ball as jaws would (glove first and then bare hand). Beginners should keep the bare hand on the side of the glove to prevent injuries to the end of the fingers should they misjudge the ball. When a player gains confidence, she should place the throwing hand above the glove in position for a quicker release. The head is over the glove as the player snaps up.

Coaching Points for Catching Ground Balls

Gathering the Ball
- Pretend you are catching a raw egg. If you are correctly gathering the ball, you should hear no sound as you give with the ball.
- Always stay square to the ball so that you can use your body to block a bad bounce or a misplayed ball.
- Always pull the ball back to the belly button (center of the body.) A common error is to gather the ball back to the throwing side in preparing to throw. If you misplay the ball, the body will not be in position to block the ball.

Scooping the Ball
- Key ideas are to catch farther out, snap the glove up, and scoop dirt.
- Balls will pop out of the glove more easily. Use your bare hand to secure the ball quickly. If the ball pops out, use both hands to catch it again.

Running Through the Ball
- Keep the head and body down until you are certain you have made the catch. Some players, feeling they must hurry, have a tendency to lift up to look at the target and runner.
- Go hard after every ball. There is no time to decide if you can or cannot get to the ball. That involves two decisions, and you don't have time to choose. Always think "I can" and go hard, running through the ball.
- When you go all out after every ball, your teammates cannot second-guess your efforts. There is no question that you tried your best!
- Stay square to the ball. Be in a position to use your body to block a bad bounce.

What Technique to Use?
- Hard-hit balls with no time to react—gather
- Hard-hit ball to your glove side and behind you—gather
- Hard-hit ball to your glove side but in front of you—scoop or gather depending on bounce
- Hard-hit ball to the throwing side—gather using backhand technique
- Short hop—scoop
- Slow roller—scoop or run through

Running Through the Ball

Players should always charge the ball, but in this case players run through the ball as they make the catch. There is no time to stop and catch the ball. Now the body goes to the ball, rather than the ball going to the body. Infielders make the catch in front of and inside the glove-side foot and inside the body (see figure 1.6 on page 8). Outfielders may find they have better balance and are more comfortable scooping the ball outside the glove foot. With either technique, the player stays square to the ball until it is caught.

By running through the ball, players extend their reach to its maximum. When players stop and reach to catch a ball, their range is limited. Running through the ball also helps players maintain balance by allowing their momentum to continue forward. Players are then in position to throw on the run. When running full speed ahead, it is often impossible to stop and reset the feet in time to make the play. A second baseman or shortstop charging a slow roller in front of her should focus on reaching and running through the ball to extend her range and then make the play. Similarly, an outfielder should concentrate on charging a ground ball and then use her momentum to throw the runner out at home.

MAKING DESPERATION CATCHES

When a player catches a ball she could not get behind, it should be considered a desperation catch. Fielders should attempt to get behind every ball they field. Good anticipation and quick feet can make this happen. Failure to get behind the ball puts the fielder in poor throwing position and hinders the ability to block the ball when necessary. The best fielders make all plays look routine and effortless. Lazy players often make what appear to be spectacular catches because they fail to get quickly into proper position. These players cost your team games.

Figure 1.6 Running through the ball.

Forehand Catches

Catches on a player's glove side are forehand catches. For the quickest reaction time, the fielder uses a jab step followed by a cross-over step. To cross over, the player pivots on the foot closer to the ball and then steps across with the opposite foot. Keeping the body low, the fielder runs hard to the side, pumping both arms, and at the last moment extends the glove-side leg and glove (with the pocket open) to the ball. The ball is fielded in front of the glove-side foot and just inside (see figure 1.7). (The glove is closer to home than the foot.) The fielder stays low with the weight on the front foot and her eyes on the ball. Using a

Figure 1.7 The forehand catch.

crossover step as the first step is slower and commits the player to a position that is more difficult to move from if she has to adjust to the line of the ball.

Backhand Catches

Catches made on a player's throwing-arm side are backhand catches. The fielder often has time to turn and step but sometimes can only react with the glove.

- **With crossover step**—The first step is a jab step. The player then executes a crossover step just before reaching and catching. The player extends the glove-side leg to the ball, flexing the knee (see figure 1.8) and dropping the hips. This is a one-hand catch. The glove catches the ball opposite or behind the forward foot. The elbow is at a 90-degree angle when possible. Movement of the glove is up with the elbow leading and pointing to the sky. The fielder needs soft hands to keep the ball in the glove. The weight is on the forward foot, and the head is over the glove. The fielder then pushes hard off the throwing foot to attain throwing position quickly.

- **No-step backhand**—Some balls come so quickly that the fielder has no time to move the feet. She should catch the ball beside the throwing foot and emphasize lifting the elbow (see figure 1.9).

Diving

Players should attempt to catch every ball. Sometimes the only way to reach the ball may be to become airborne. By leaving the feet, players can extend their reach by at least one body length. Some coaches may not allow their pitchers to dive for fear they might injure their shoulders. But I have seen pitchers save a game by diving for and catching a popped-up bunt. Players should learn to dive and go all out to make the catch. The two basic types of dives are the headfirst dive and the bent-leg slide.

Figure 1.8 Backhand catch with a crossover step.

Figure 1.9 No-step backhand catch.

Headfirst Dive. To initiate a headfirst dive, the player keeps her body low and pushes off the balls of the feet. Both arms are extended toward the ball with the palm of the glove hand up, and the fielder stays low and parallel to the ground like a swimmer doing a racing start. The player should dive as the ball approaches its lowest point and land on the upper thighs and stomach (see figure 1.10). Players should not use a volleyball dive with an arched back because they will not slide as they do on a gym floor. Back injury is a possible result. Players should not use one hand or the elbows to support themselves on the ground because wrist and arm injuries may result. A potential problem for those who keep some fingers outside their gloves is that those fingers are unprotected and more susceptible to being jammed.

Bent-Leg Slide. A bent-leg slide allows players to go all out while protecting themselves against obstacles such as a fence. To catch a ball with the bent-leg slide, the fielder should slide under it as if she were sliding into a base (see chapter 10, page 200). The catch should be made with the hands chest or waist high (see figure 1.11). It is possible to use the body to trap the ball as well. If the player is near a fence, the bent-leg slide is preferred over the headfirst dive because the risk of injury is lower. The player should keep the extended knee bent so that it can give on contact with the fence.

Figure 1.10 Stay low to start the dive and land on the upper thighs and stomach and use the throwing hand to trap the ball in the glove.

Figure 1.11 Bent-leg slide.

CATCHING FLY BALLS AND POP-UPS

When moving toward a fly ball or pop-up, a player must always communicate that she plans to catch it. A simple "mine" will do. The player should call early and loudly so that there is no doubt that she is going for the ball. Surrounding teammates should confirm that they hear her and are giving way by a simple "take it!" A fielder should never call the ball for another player except in desperation. An example would be a fielder blinded by the sun and able to get out of the way of another player, who then might be able to make a last-ditch effort.

Players should catch the ball at nose or eye level looking over the top of the glove (see figure 1.12), using both hands when possible. The bare hand should be behind the pocket and ready to close the glove quickly so that the ball cannot bounce out. This method also keeps the throwing hand close for a quick release. The fielder should give with the ball by flexing the elbows and bringing the glove toward the body.

If a fielder must make a quick throw, the ball should be caught in front of the throwing shoulder with the body slightly sideways (see figure 1.13). She should move her feet to get her body behind the ball in this position. The fielder should also keep the ball well in front of her body so that she can move into the ball as she catches it, transferring this momentum into the throw. The fielder should give with the ball toward the throwing shoulder as she makes the catch and then grips the ball.

Figure 1.12 Catch a fly ball in the center of the body at nose or eye level when a quick throw is not necessary.

Figure 1.13 Catch a fly ball in front of the throwing shoulder with the body sideways when a quick throw is necessary.

Figure 1.14 Catching a short fly ball.

Short Fly Balls

When moving to a ball well in front of them, players must keep the body low, the head down, and their eyes on the ball as they run full speed toward it. The glove should not be extended until the last minute. When the fielder does extend the glove, she holds the palm up and the pocket open as she focuses on the ball (see figure 1.14). The elbow should be rotated in to open up the pocket. The fielder must not lift her eyes or body because doing so will tend to raise the glove. When the ball is in the pocket, the fielder should use the throwing hand to trap the ball. If the ball falls in front of her, the player should keep her chin and head down and short hop the ball. The fielder must not lift the head and body because doing so would allow the ball to get under the glove. The player should be in position to use her body to block the ball and keep it from getting by.

Long Fly Balls

On balls hit over their heads, players must go back, of course, but a backpedal should not be used for more than three or four steps. Backpedaling sacrifices speed and balance. Fielders should backpedal only on balls hit directly to them that require little change in position.

The first step on long fly balls should be a drop step. The side that the fielder thinks the ball is going determines which foot to step on. She lowers the hips, pushes them back hard, and then steps on the foot to the side that she thinks the ball will land (see figure 1.15a). The fielder pivots on that foot and pushes hard with the opposite foot (see figure 1.15b), then initiates a crossover step as she

Figure 1.15 Catching a long fly ball. (a) Drop step on the foot to the side the ball will land, then (b) pivot with that foot and push hard with the opposite foot to run full speed at the ball.

a

b

turns to run full speed on a straight angle to the place she thinks the ball will descend. The fielder tries to keep her eyes on the ball to track its flight, running on the balls of the feet so that her eyes do not bounce excessively. The player should use good running form, pumping the arms. The glove is extended only during the last four or five steps and the fielder always reaches and tries for the ball. When the fielder catches the ball, she quickly secures it with the other hand. If a throw needs to be made, the fielder braces against the front leg immediately after making the catch to stop her momentum. She regains her balance, pivots, and throws.

Some players may find it difficult to read the direction quickly and drop step to the appropriate side. Such players should drop step to the side that is most comfortable (usually the throwing-side foot) and locate the ball as they take this step. If the ball is then hit to the glove side, they can use one of two techniques:

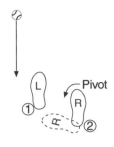

Figure 1.16 Inside or reverse roll.

- **Inside (reverse) roll**—When using the inside roll, the outfielder can keep her eyes on the ball at all times. She pushes hard off the back leg to reverse direction and pivots inward, always keeping her nose on the ball (see figure 1.16). This is a slower method than the outside roll because the player must stop and change direction. A helpful advantage for beginners is that the ball is always in sight. The inside roll should be used on fly balls that are easily within the fielder's range.

- **Outside roll**—When using the outside roll, the fielder loses sight of the ball for a moment while turning her back to it and circling around to pick it up on the other side. The move begins with the drop step to the foot farthest from the ball. The fielder pivots hard on the back foot, crosses over with the opposite leg, and sprints diagonally back (see figure 1.17). Without breaking stride the fielder picks up the ball on the opposite side. An outside roll allows the momentum of the body to continue to flow into the turn, so the fielder should use it on hard-hit balls that require a long sprint.

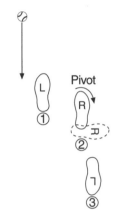

Figure 1.17 Outside roll.

Which way should players turn when the ball is directly overhead? For very deep balls, turning to the glove side gives maximum extension. The glove can reach farther from that side. For balls that aren't as deep, turning to the throwing side allows fielders to get to throwing position more easily with less movement.

Coaching Points for Catching Fly Balls

- Work on developing good balance and quick feet. Then even if you initially misjudge a ball, you can often recover in time to make the catch.
- Always catch with two hands.
- On long fly balls, a common error is to take several steps forward before judging the ball. This increases the distance the player must go when the ball is over her head. Always make sure your first step is a drop step back.

OVERCOMING OBSTACLES

Before players begin to field their positions in practice or in a game, they should familiarize themselves with all obstacles. They should count the number of steps from their position to any barriers. What materials are they made of and how will the ball and the player rebound? Is there any give? Can players climb it? Reach over it? They should check the sun, the lights, the wind, and the background. Players should use sunglasses, hats, and eye black for glare if they have any possibility of helping. Here are some tips for handling fences, the sun, and the wind.

• **Fence play**—The fielder should move quickly to the fence and find it when time permits. Not knowing where the fence is often causes a player to stop out of fear. She should find it with the hips (which are padded) or the forearm and then come back for the ball. The fielder must not run to the fence with the arms or fingers extended because injury can easily occur. If time permits, the player may have a chance to locate the fence visually, but doing this requires her to take her eyes off the ball and finding it again may be difficult. Using the bent-leg slide can provide protection when the fielder is running a long distance and doesn't have time to reach for and find the fence.

Figure 1.18 Blocking the sun.

• **Sun play**—The fielder can use the glove to shield her eyes by placing it on the sun to block the glare (see figure 1.18). She sights the ball over or under the glove and removes it from the sun at the last second to make the catch. Another solution is to approach the ball at an angle to minimize the directness of the light. Fielders must communicate with their teammates. A player in a position less bothered by the sun may be able to make the play.

• **Wind**—Players should be aware of the direction and strength of the wind and note any changes during the game. During warmups, players should observe how the wind affects the flight of the ball when hit and thrown. Depending on the strength of the wind, they may shift their positions to adjust for the effects. If the wind is blowing in toward home, they might move in four to six steps. Conversely, if the wind is behind the hitter, they might back up four to six steps, especially on "up" pitches. If the wind is blowing left or right, a normal shift is three to four steps in the direction of the wind. A strong wind can make communication difficult. Not only is it difficult to hear but what appears to be a routine ball for one fielder may drift to another fielder's area. Players should call loudly and repeatedly so that everyone can hear. Once a fielder has committed to and called for the ball, she must stay with it no matter where it blows. A ball thrown into the wind will definitely slow down, and a crosswind will blow it off line. The higher the throw, the more the wind will affect it. Fielders should keep throws down and may need to increase the number of bounces.

GROUND BALL DRILLS

Many repetitions are necessary to develop any skill, and players must practice fielding all types of ground balls every day to develop proper technique. To help players build confidence and proper skills, hit balls players can field successfully while using correct technique. Hitting hard shots that put the fielders on their heels only reinforces poor technique and does nothing for confidence.

Players can practice glove work at short distances with partners rolling the ball back and forth. This technique not only saves time and the players' arms but also allows the coach to easily observe their technique. Fielding balls and putting them in a bucket allows many repetitions in a short amount of time while saving the strain on the throwing arm. The most efficient practice is using groups of three: one fielder, one hitter, and one receiver with a bucket near her. After fielding the ground ball, the fielder tosses the receiver the ball to put in the bucket. Players rotate duties when the bucket is full.

Players should field at the correct distance for the position they play to simulate gamelike conditions. Use a variety of drills to help eliminate boredom and take care not to make the drill so long that the players are too fatigued to practice good mechanics.

Soft Hands

Purpose: To develop soft hands.

Procedure: Partners stand six feet apart and roll balls back and forth using an underhand toss. They field ground balls with their bare hands or by using flat gloves or wooden paddles. This forces players to give and gather the ball and use two hands. The hips are down, and the arms create a triangle.

Ready, Set, Go

Purpose: To practice fielding ground balls from basic "ready, set, go" positions.

Procedure: The coach faces the players, who are in a staggered position in three or four lines. On command, players assume "ready," then "set" position. On command "go," players take three steps forward to field and gather an imaginary ball. They catch and go to the throwing position with quick feet. Players don't retreat but take the ready position at that spot to continue the drill.

Variation: The coach can call for any type of catch following the command "go."

Partner Scoops

Purpose: To focus on hand action for scooping ground balls.

Procedure: Partners take positions six feet apart and roll a ball back and forth, keeping their feet still and fielding with scooping action. Players reach for the ball sooner than when gathering. They should use the top hand as a jaw to trap the ball. You may want to do this drill on grass so that loose infield dirt does not flip into your players' faces.

Line Scoops

Purpose: To practice scooping balls while running.

Procedure: A fielding line faces a tosser at a distance of 30 to 40 feet. In turn, each fielder runs hard at the tosser, who rolls or tosses a ball that must be scooped by the fielder. The fielder tosses it back to the tosser and goes to the end of the fielding line.

Variation: Rapid-fire toss is for advanced players. Players are in a line about 20 feet from the tosser. The tosser throws balls quickly at fielders' feet using an overhand throw. The tosser uses a harder throw and angles that are more difficult. The fielder moves toward the tosser, scoops the hard-thrown ball, returns it to the tosser, and goes to the end of the line. Have the fielder run back at an angle and straight back.

Explode Through the Ball

Purpose: To practice reaching and running through every ball.

Procedure: Fielders form a line about 10 feet from the tosser. One at a time they run laterally as the tosser tosses the ball low and in front of them so that they have to reach. Each player focuses on exploding through the ball as she catches it. The fielder must not stop and reach because doing so would limit her range. Each player returns the ball with a toss, waits, and forms a line that reverses the direction.

Cone Rolls

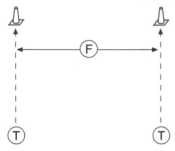

Figure 1.19 Cone rolls.

Purpose: To increase range while staying behind the ball.

Procedure: Place two cones about 12 feet apart to serve as targets and boundaries (see figure 1.19). A tosser with a ball stands about 15 feet in front of each cone. A fielder takes a position midway between the cones and several steps in front of them so that the cones will not interfere with her movement. The first tosser rolls a ball toward a cone. The fielder sidesteps to the ball, gathers it in, returns it underhand to the tosser, resets in the middle, and then goes the other way to field a ball rolled by the second tosser. The fielder must concentrate on footwork and staying square behind the ball.

Fence Range

Purpose: To emphasize running through the ball to increase range.

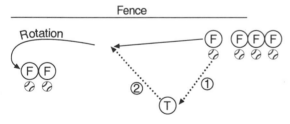

Figure 1.20 Fence range drill.

Procedure: From a single-file line, players start their turn by throwing a ball to the tosser. The fielder then sprints full speed ahead to catch a return throw that the tosser throws well ahead of her. The emphasis is on sprinting through the ball, not just reaching. The player retrieves the ball if she does not catch it and then joins a line ready to reverse direction. Do this drill with fielders running along the backstop so that players can easily retrieve any balls they miss (see figure 1.20). You can use two groups and two tossers—one group on the first-base side and one group on the third-base side.

Partner Throws

Purpose: To practice five catching techniques in a short time.

Procedure: Partners stand 12 feet apart and throw ground balls to each other to practice the following catches. The receiver stays low, keeps the glove on the ground, and uses little foot movement. The catching position is held until the ball is in the glove. The partner fields 10 balls for each of the five types of catches before players rotate.

1. Players throw balls directly to the partner to gather.
2. Using an overhand throw, players throw short hops for the fielder to scoop.
3. For forehand balls, the receiver stands sideways. The receiver should not reach with the glove, but instead let the ball come to her.

4. For backhand balls, the receiver is sideways in the crossover position.

5. For no-step backhands, the body is not sideways, and the glove is already on the backhand side.

Infield Range

Purpose: To develop greater range.

Procedure: Have a hitter at second, a hitter at home, and fielding lines at first and third, each with at least four players (see figure 1.21). The hitters hit at the same time, slapping ground balls that force the fielders to reach for them. After fielding a ball, the player puts that ball in the other hitter's hand and runs to the end of the other fielding line. Have a bucket of balls behind each hitter. If a fielder misses the hit ball, she takes one out of the bucket to give to the hitter. Halfway through the drill, reverse direction so that players must reach to the other side.

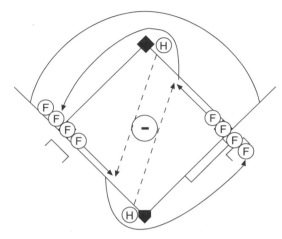

Figure 1.21 Infield range drill.

DIVING DRILLS

Coaches must work with fielders to practice diving for balls for these plays to happen successfully in a game. For both of the following drills have players start near the ground and progress to a standing start to overcome their fear of leaving their feet and hitting the ground. Use mats for a soft landing until the players are comfortable diving and to save wear and tear on their bodies.

Knee Dives

Purpose: To learn how to dive to catch the ball.

Procedure: The tosser is six feet in front of the diver, who is on her knees. Using soft safety balls, the thrower tosses balls to the side just out of reach so that the diver must dive to catch them. Players progress to starting in a squat position and then to a full standing start. When using a mat have one tosser and never more than six fielders in a line so players don't waste too much time waiting for their turn but still have time to get ready for their next attempt. I recommend using the Slide Rite sliding mat from Schutt Manufacturing to develop players' confidence as they learn to dive and to save wear and tear on their bodies. When bad weather forces you inside, this is an excellent drill if you have access to tumbling or wrestling mats.

All Out

Purpose: To practice going all out on the dive.

Procedure: A fielder faces a tosser 20 to 30 feet away. The first throw is over or to the side of the fielder's head. The fielder catches the ball and makes a good throw to the tosser. The fielder then runs hard toward the tosser, who flips a soft toss that the fielder must dive for to catch. The fielder goes to the end of the line to wait for her next turn.

FLY BALL DRILLS

Proper footwork and body positioning are the foundation for catching fly balls successfully. Use the following basic footwork drills every day to develop good balance and proper reaction to the ball. Throw balls to fielders instead of hitting them so you can place the balls exactly where they need to be to isolate each technique. Players must also practice reacting to balls hit off the bat, but hitting rather than throwing every ball takes a lot of time and creates difficulty placing the ball exactly where you'd wish.

Drop-Step Reaction

Purpose: To learn to react and drop step to the appropriate side.

Procedure: The coach faces players, who are in staggered position in three or four lines. The coach points direction with a ball. Players react with a drop step in that direction. They return to ready position and repeat. When the drop step becomes automatic, add the turn with inside and outside rolls. Then add easy tosses.

Zigzag

Purpose: To execute the inside roll emphasizing footwork, balance, and quick feet for fielding. This is a good warm-up drill.

Procedure: Players form a line side by side about 10 feet apart and face the coach. The coach points in either direction to begin the drill. Players run diagonally back using a drop step, run three steps, and then use an inside roll to change direction. They run three steps and again reverse direction. They continue zigzagging down the field.

Ball Toss for Inside and Outside Rolls

Purpose: To practice proper footwork for catching fly balls.

Procedure: Each player has a ball and lines up behind the coach or a tosser. The first fielder takes position facing the tosser about 20 feet away. All players complete one drill before they move to the next.

1. The tosser points a direction for the initial drop step and diagonal and tosses a ball to that side for the fielder to catch. The fielder catches the ball and returns to the end of the line.
2. Inside roll: The tosser points a direction for the initial drop step and diagonal, then tosses the ball to the opposite side, forcing the fielder to use an inside roll to catch the ball.
3. Outside roll: The fielder executes the previous drill but with an outside roll.
4. Ball over head: The fielder runs directly away from the tosser and turns her head to find and catch the ball.

Football Drill

Purpose: To catch fly balls with good balance, glove work, and footwork.

Procedure: Each player has a softball. The player gives the ball to the coach and then starts running straight ahead. The coach calls right or left and throws the ball in that direction. The fielder catches the ball and sprints to the end of the line behind the coach. A throw of 30 to 60 feet is sufficient and allows for more practice.

2

Throwing

Successful players can catch the ball and throw accurately to a target. These are the foundations for success! It takes much practice to develop catching and throwing skills to the point where they become automatic. Defensive practices should include time to warm up players' arms and practice throws. Players should not waste this time. They must focus on the fundamentals on every catch and throw so that correct technique becomes habit.

The overhand throw, which outfielders use almost exclusively and infielders use most of the time, is the basic throw players must master. With an overhand throw at close range, however, the ball is often out of sight of the receiver, making it difficult to track and catch. Therefore, when infielders are close to the receiver (for example, when the second baseman fields a ball in the gap and throws to first), a three-quarter or sidearm throw keeps the ball always visible to the receiver. The situation, the receiver's body position, and the speed of the runner dictate the use of other throws. Therefore, the thrower may have to use an abbreviated windup, an underhand toss, a flip, or even a throw on the run. The situation may demand quickness, but accuracy is always the primary goal. The following sections describe the basics of each of these throwing skills.

GRIP

The grip, commonly referred to as a three-finger grip, is the same for all types of throws. A softball is so much bigger than a baseball that players can't use only three fingers (as they do in baseball) and have a secure grip. Therefore, they place all fingers on the ball. The player always grips across the seams using the fingerprint part of the fingers. The middle finger is placed in the middle of the ball on one seam, and the thumb is positioned underneath on the opposite seam. The index finger and the ring finger are equally spaced on each side of the middle finger and on the same seam (see figure 2.1). The little finger is curled in a relaxed position on the side of the ball. The thumb is under the middle finger as much as possible, with the player taking care not to lock the wrist. There should be space or daylight between the ball and palm and the webbing of the thumb.

The player obtains the proper grip by rotating the ball in the glove with the throwing hand fingers until she finds the seams and can grip the ball correctly. The ball is pressed down into the glove to secure the grip and then lifted quickly from the glove with the ball pointed down and the back of the hand pointed up as the hands separate.

On a slow roller or a dead (stopped) ball, should your players pick it up with only the bare hand or should they use both hands? I believe it is essential to pick up the softball with both hands to get a firm, secure grip on the ball. By using the glove to catch the ball first, there is also less chance of not catching it. The player can then press the ball against the glove to secure the grip. Because of the large size of the softball, it is simply not possible to grip the ball firmly without using two hands. The more firmly the player grips the ball, the faster it can be thrown. Accuracy also depends on a sure grip. Are two hands slower than a one-hand pickup? Possibly, but the fielder will make up the time by throwing the ball faster and more accurately.

Figure 2.1 The three-finger grip.

Finding the Grip

Purpose: To learn to find the proper grip on the ball quickly and automatically.

Procedure: The player takes the ball out of the glove with the throwing hand, developing a sense of feel for the ball as she takes it out. This drill should be repeated until gripping the ball is smooth, secure, and fast. Beginners at first may have to look at the ball as they get the proper finger placement. With practice, speed improves and the grip becomes automatic. This is a simple drill that players can do repeatedly even while watching television, but they must remember not to throw the ball!

Two-Hand Pickup

Purpose: To practice picking up the ball with two hands to get a secure grip.

Procedure: The player places the ball on the ground in front of her, picks it up with two hands, and throws it to a partner. The partner repeats the procedure on the return throw.

OVERHAND THROW

The basic components of the overhand throw are body position, arm action, release, and follow-through. Body position (basically upright) and arm action (with the throwing-arm elbow above the shoulder) define the overhand throw. Proper body alignment keeps the ball on target. A strong release and follow-through contribute to speed and accuracy. For an accurate and strong throw, players must execute all four phases. Included later are drills to teach and develop each of these components.

Body Position

Before the throw is made, the player must turn the shoulders and hips sideways to the intended target. A throw can't be made until the feet are in place. To check alignment, draw a line between the player's feet pointing at the target (see figure 2.2). The first step after catching the ball should be with the back foot (nonglove foot), which is turned outward at a 45-degree angle and on this line. The player's weight is on the ball of the foot. She then steps toward the target with the glove-side foot, placing the arch of the stepping foot at a 45-degree angle on this line. The front knee should have some flex. The shoulders are level and sideways to the target. The front-foot touchdown is timed with the forward motion of the arm. The player pushes off with the back foot and shifts her weight forward. The backside provides the power. The hips explode open with the navel pointing toward the target. When fielding ground balls, the player should follow the sequence, "Right, left, pick ball up, right, left, throw."

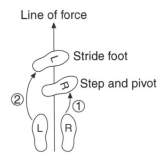

Figure 2.2 Proper foot position for the overhand throw.

Arm Action

As the player begins the throwing motion after making the catch, she extends the glove arm with the elbow slightly flexed and points it at the target while simultaneously drawing back the throwing arm so that there is a stretch across the chest (see figure 2.3a). The stretch is similar to that one might use when drawing back an arrow to shoot it. Both elbows should be lifted to shoulder height (see figure 2.3b). The throwing arm moves in a circle to reach this raised position—the ball goes from the glove down to the hip to extension backward to a point above the ear. The little finger leads the hand, and the elbow of the throwing arm points away from the body at shoulder height, bent

a

b

c

Figure 2.3 Arm action of the throwing motion. *(a)* Begin the motion by drawing back the throwing arm, *(b)* point the glove to the target and lift the ball behind the head so the back of the throwing hand is toward the body and both elbows are at shoulder height, and *(c)* start the forward motion by simultaneously leading with the elbow and pulling the glove arm down.

Coaching Points for the Overhand Throw

- Don't drop the throwing elbow below shoulder level. This will result in a sidearm throw and produce a curveball.
- Don't push the ball. Stretch your throwing shoulder back and keep your elbow above the shoulder.
- Turn sideways to the target—don't remain square. Use your whole body.
- Step with the glove-side foot. Turning sideways will help this feel natural.
- Don't palm the ball. Hold it with your fingertips and see daylight.
- If you have a sideways rotation of the ball, your thumb is rotating up at release instead of down toward the ground. Also, check that the elbow is shoulder high.

at about a 90-degree angle. If the elbow is not shoulder high, a sidearm throw results, which strains the elbow and produces a less accurate throw, that is, a curveball. At the top of the motion of the throwing arm, the wrist is cocked so that the thumb is away from the body and the back of the hand is toward the body.

To start the forward motion of the throw, the player leads with the elbow of the throwing arm while simultaneously pulling the glove arm down (see figure 2.3c). The glove arm is important for maintaining correct alignment and developing force. The arms work in opposition as they do in swimming—the harder the glove pulls down, the faster the throwing arm goes forward. The player should move the throwing arm quickly, not dragging it. The rotation is such that one shoulder replaces the other. The player snaps the wrist at release.

Release

The wrist is flexible and loose. The player cocks the wrist back in preparation to throw as she lifts the ball above the shoulder with the back of the hand facing the target. On release, the thrower snaps the wrist forward toward the target and down to provide velocity and accuracy. The thumb is pointed to the ground, and the fingers are thrown (snapped) toward the target (see figure 2.4). The index finger goes at the right eye of the receiver, and the middle finger goes at the left eye with the V bridging the nose. The last thing the thrower should feel is the ball leaving the fingerprint area of the fingers. The thrower pulls the seams sharply down. The ball comes off the middle and index fingers last, creating a vertical spin toward the thrower (backward) much like the backspin on a basketball jump shot. Placing a stripe on the ball will help players see the spin. Color a half-inch stripe or apply electrical tape across the four seams. Have players snap a handkerchief to feel wrist snap and follow-through.

Figure 2.4 Release point for the overhand throw.

Figure 2.5 Follow-through position for the overhand throw.

Follow-Through

After releasing the ball, the player throws the back (throwing) shoulder toward the target. The back leg lifts slightly off the ground with the shoelaces pointed to the ground. The fingers point toward the target as the wrist snaps and the ball is released. The player finishes with the chest over the front knee and the hand continuing down to touch the glove-side leg (see figure 2.5). The longer the throw, the more exaggerated the follow-through and the greater the bend at the waist. Infielders will generally touch their upper thighs, and outfielders will often touch their knees or lower.

LONG THROWS

The faster the ball gets to the target, the better the thrower's chance of making an out. For long throws, players must use the overhand throw, which causes less strain on the arm. By coming over the ball, the overhand throw generates a vertical spin that produces a good, accurate bounce. The thrower can increase the strength of the throw by moving into the ball and transferring the body's momentum through the ball. Outfielders use the overhand throw almost exclusively, and infielders use it whenever they have time to set up properly. The ideal choice for any long throw should be the overhand throw.

Crow Hop

To get extra strength on their throws, outfielders should use the crow hop. After catching the ball, the player hops on the throwing-side foot and pushes hard as she drives her body and momentum forward. After releasing the ball, the outfielder pushes off the back leg and steps toward the target. In simple terms, the player replaces her feet. The fingers point to the ground at the finish. See chapter 4, pages 64–65, for more details.

Long Bounce Throw

For long throws, outfielders should use the bounce throw. Rainbow throws take too long to reach the target. The path of a ball that bounces to the target more closely approximates a straight line, which is the shortest distance between two points. The bounce throw is also helpful when the sun is in the eyes of the infielders. Keeping the ball low using a bounce throw allows the ball to be tracked more easily. A low trajectory also permits the throw to be cut if necessary. Any long throw to a base should bounce approximately 15 feet from the intended receiver.

Flattening the arc of the throw also increases accuracy. For accuracy, the thrower needs to have a consistent release point. The release point is slightly in front of the throwing shoulder and at a point where the player is still able to maintain a 90-degree angle at the elbow while keeping the hand pointed up. The wrist must be able to snap forward at a release point that allows the fingers to point to the target on the follow-through. This comes with practice, and practice produces consistency.

QUICK THROWS

If the runner is very quick, the fielder may not have time for a full windup. If the ball is not hit directly to the fielder, she may not have time to get in position to make an overhand throw. When close to the receiver, the fielder must show the ball so that the receiver can see it all the way to the glove. When the throwing distance is short, a player may have sufficient arm strength that it is not necessary to use a full overhand throw.

Shortened Windup

Players may use a shortened windup when they need to be quick and can sacrifice strength and distance on the throw. A slow ground ball that requires the fielder to charge will often necessitate a shortened windup to beat the runner. Because of the longer distance to first from third and short, players at those positions must often rush their throws. Strong catchers may also use the shortened windup for a quicker release. The catcher must have the arm strength to throw without having to transfer body weight to get the ball to the base. To execute the shortened windup, the thrower pulls the ball back quickly just above the ear. The main difference is that the first movement of the throwing arm is back, not down, which shortens the arm circle. Footwork and body position are the same as those used for the overhand throw.

On the Run

When the thrower does not have time to assume a set position, she becomes a quarterback on the run. A good shortstop is able to throw on the run after fielding a slow rolling ball or a high bouncer hit by a slapper. A third baseman cutting off a bunt or slap in the hole will have a better chance of making the out using this technique.

Using an abbreviated windup, the thrower releases the ball in one continuous motion while running toward the target. She should concentrate on the follow-through of the arm with the hand pointing directly to the target. Most throwing errors are high when throwing on the run. The ball sails high because the thrower does not use a firm wrist snap. The thrower must not lob the ball. The path of the ball should be a firm straight line. The thrower must field the ball first and get a secure grip on it. Whenever possible, the chest should face directly to the target on release. After release, the fielder continues to run several steps toward the target.

Errors also occur when the fielder rushes and tries to throw before securing the ball. When the runner has clearly beaten the play, the fielder should hold onto the ball. Better that the runner get one base than to take the chance of an error giving her additional bases.

Sidearm

Also called a three-quarter throw, the sidearm throw is used when players need quickness and can sacrifice strength and distance. The second baseman and other players who are close to the receiver should throw sidearm so that the ball remains visible to the receiver and is thus easier to track, react to, and catch. This is what we call "showing the ball." Players should not throw sidearm over long distances. The weight of the softball and the increased stress on the elbow when throwing sidearm can lead to elbow injuries. The first baseman also prefers that the ball thrown across the diamond not be a curveball.

Figure 2.6   Sidearm throw.

When throwing sidearm, the elbow is below the shoulder throughout the entire arm motion and remains there when the ball is released. The sidearm throw places more emphasis on forearm and wrist movement than on the use of the shoulder. Arm movement is more horizontal. Players must be sure that the thumb rotates down on release to produce proper spin. Allowing the thumb to rotate upward will produce a curveball and increase pressure on the elbow. The glove arm still works in opposition and should point to the target for proper alignment. The footwork is the same as that used for the overhand throw, with the body remaining sideways to the target on release. When time permits, the body should be upright. When releasing the ball, the thrower should keep the shoulders level so the ball goes in a straight line. When fielding a bunt, the player often does not have time to straighten up. Still, the fielder must always take time to level the shoulders, even in a crouched position. Overthrows occur when the back shoulder is lower than the front, an alignment that produces an upward angle for the path of the ball. Alignment and follow-through are critical. The ball goes where the player throws it.

To show the ball when close to the receiver, the fielder holds the ball up in her bare hand just above the shoulder and well away from the body, maintaining a bend in the elbow of about 90 degrees. Fingers are pointed up with the thumb underneath (see figure 2.6). By using a smaller arm circle, the thrower can keep the ball always visible to the receiver. An overhand windup should not be used because the motion will cause the ball to disappear behind the body. Because the player is throwing a shorter distance, a large arm circle is not necessary.

Underhand Toss

The underhand toss is used when a quick release is required and the thrower is within 15 feet of the target. Prime examples are throws to the catcher from the corners or from the pitcher on a suicide squeeze. Other uses for the underhand toss include the short throw to a receiver covering a base for a force-out or a double play. The underhand toss is a safe and accurate throw that pitchers often use for the throw to first base after fielding a ball to the first-base side. Pitchers who have difficulty making accurate overhand throws should use this throw for balls hit to their left when they have time to run the ball close enough to first to make the play. Advanced players may use this toss to get the ball to a teammate who is in better position to make a strong throw. This might occur when the second baseman backhands a ball behind second. With her momentum carrying her away from first base, she can toss to the shortstop, who makes the throw to first.

The player should field the ball with two hands to ensure a secure grip. She then removes the glove to show the ball to the receiver. With a pendulum-like forward swing from the shoulder, the player throws the ball on a direct line with little arc, keeping the ball low (see figure 2.7a). The elbow is locked, and the wrist is stiff. The ball is guided to the target with the palm up and the fingers extended to the receiver (see figure 2.7b). The arm stops no higher than the shoulders. Backswing and body motion should be

a   b

Figure 2.7 Underhand toss. *(a)* Keep the elbow locked and wrist stiff and *(b)* release the ball with the palm up and fingers extended.

minimal. Locking the elbow and wrist helps eliminate overthrows that can occur when adrenaline is flowing. The thrower keeps the body low, flexes at the hips, and strides toward the target. If time permits, the glove can be extended toward the target so that the arms can work in opposition. But the thrower must make sure that the arms go no higher than the shoulders. Using the glove arm will aid balance and improve alignment. When a fielder needs to release the ball quickly, she should shorten the extension of the arms and rely more on the wrist action of the throwing hand.

Glove Toss

The glove toss is a desperation play used when the fielder has no chance of getting the throwing hand to the ball. The fielder cocks the wrist of the glove hand back and then snaps forward, opening the glove to release the ball. The corners and the pitcher can use this toss on suicide plays. A player chasing a rolling ball and ending up close to the base might also use the glove toss. This toss is effective up to a distance of about 10 feet. Ideally, the fielder is running toward the target, and her momentum will help the toss get there. Because this is a desperation play, however, a player may use it from any angle as a last resort. Advanced players may use the glove toss when lying on the ground to get the ball to a teammate to complete the play.

Backhand Flip

A backhand flip is sometimes necessary when the fielder doesn't have time to get her body around to face the target (the target is on the right side of a right-handed thrower).

a

b

Figure 2.8 Backhand flip. *(a)* Point the elbow of the throwing arm toward the target and bring the back of the hand in toward the chest, then *(b)* push the ball to the target simultaneously with a step in that direction while keeping the shoulders level.

A typical example occurs when a second baseman is able to stay behind a ball hit to her right near second base. Without time to turn and face the receiver, she would use a backhand flip to the shortstop covering second. To make a backhand flip, after gripping the ball the fielder points the elbow of the throwing arm toward the target and brings the back of the hand in toward the chest (see figure 2.8a). She stiffens her wrist and pushes the ball to the target simultaneously with a step in that direction. The fielder steps with the foot nearer the receiver. The side of the foot moves toward the receiver with the toes pointed straight ahead. The body stays low, rising only slightly from the fielding position. The shoulders remain square and level. Only the head turns toward the target. The fielder releases the ball as she extends her elbow. The arm stops between the waist and shoulder height with the fingers pointed toward the target (see figure 2.8b). Arm action follows a horizontal path.

WARMING UP THE ARM

Arm problems occur because of a lack of arm and shoulder strength, poor mechanics, and overuse. Players can build up their arms by weight training and gradually increasing the number of throws they make each day. They should constantly review and work on their throwing mechanics and take care not to overuse their arms. Many fielding drills can be done without throwing. Players can return the balls to a bucket to eliminate the need to throw. At any sign of soreness, players should apply ice for 20 minutes when they are finished.

Coaching Points for Long and Quick Throws

Throw	*When to use*
Overhand throw	• All long throws. • Outfielders use most of the time.
Long bounce throw	• Outfield throws to home. • Sun in receiver's eyes.
Shortened windup	• When quick release is needed. • Can sacrifice strength and distance. • Catcher throw downs, throws from third or shortstop to first.
On the run	• Third baseman cutting off ball in hole and fast runner. • Infielders charging slow rollers with fast runners. • Slap defense.
Sidearm	• Can sacrifice strength and distance for quickness. • To show ball to nearby receiver, especially second baseman throwing to first baseman. • Fielding bunts.
Underhand toss	• Suicide squeeze. • Within 15 feet of base for forces and double plays. • Pitchers who have difficulty throwing overhand.
Glove toss	• 10 feet or less from target. • No chance of getting throwing hand to ball in time. • Suicide squeeze, diving stop.
Backhand flip	• Target to right side of right-handed thrower.

Before throwing all out in practice or in a game, players must warm up their arms to prepare for full-out throwing. A proper warm-up will help strengthen the arm as well as prevent injuries.

Players should always stretch their shoulder muscles (throwing arm only) before they warm up their arms. To perform the following three exercises, players flex the knees slightly and bend forward at the waist. They stretch slowly, doing a minimum of 20 repetitions of each exercise. If a player still feels tight in the shoulder, she should increase the number of repetitions until she feels her shoulder loosen.

1. With the throwing elbow bent at 90 degrees, the player slowly swings the arm forward, lifting the hand as high as possible while maintaining a 90-degree bend at the elbow. She then swings the arm slowly back, raising the elbow as high as flexibility permits (see figure 2.9 on page 30).

Figure 2.9 Arm swing forward and back.

2. With a 90-degree elbow bend, the player swings the arm across her body as far as possible to the glove side and then back, leading with the elbow and lifting it as high as possible on the throwing side (see figure 2.10).

3. The player stirs an imaginary pot with the fingers just above the ground. She uses big, slow circles 10 times in one direction and then 10 times in the other (see figure 2.11).

Players should warm up just before full throwing. A common mistake is to warm up the arm at the beginning of practice and then do activities other than throwing, allowing the arm to cool off. If players are going to hit or the coach is going to talk a lot, the arm warm-up should be delayed until just before throwing activities. Players begin warming up at a distance that does not strain the arm, and they work up to the distance they will need to throw. In particular, outfielders should warm up with outfielders and gradually move back to a greater distance. Throwing drills to warm up the arms should take 15 to 20 minutes, a valuable chunk of practice time that players must not waste.

Players should follow several specific rules to get the most out of the throwing drills:

• Players should not talk. Instead, they should concentrate on accuracy and feeling the basics of the throw.

Figure 2.10 Arm swing side to side.

Figure 2.11 Stirring the pot.

- They should turn their bodies correctly on every throw, pretending that a camera is filming every throw for a demonstration tape.
- Players can look for feedback. Is the spin correct? Are they balanced? They should check position and alignment of the feet.
- During the warm-up, players should work on catching techniques. They should move their bodies to catch every ball with two hands in front of the throwing shoulder.
- Early in the season or any time players are experiencing throwing problems, they should review the basics and work on drills that emphasize the basic elements of the throw.

Throwing distance should be adapted to the size and abilities of the players. College-age players will usually throw at a distance of about 30 feet when warming up or doing basic throwing drills. When doing a lot of throwing, care must be taken that injuries don't occur from overuse. Decreasing the throwing distance can reduce strain on the arms. When working on technique, players need not throw at maximum speed. Using smaller (lighter) balls allows more repetitions with less strain. Young players who lack the strength to throw a regulation softball will try to push the ball. Coaches can have their teams use smaller balls (baseball, tennis) so that young players can learn proper throwing mechanics. Coaches can save wear on players' arms when working on defense by eliminating the need to throw. Players simply place the balls in buckets. In games, players must be sure that their arms stay warm and loose. Between innings, they should do warm-up throws as part of the routine. Infielders will throw to first base, returning balls that the first baseman rolls to them. Outfielders should do easy long tosses to each other. The center fielder takes a ball with her and throws to one of the other outfielders. To provide more throws, a player from the bench should go to the sideline and play catch with the third and closest outfielder.

OVERHAND THROWING DRILLS

Vary the throwing drills your players use each day to warm up their arms to continually reinforce different components of the throw. To get the most benefit from these drills, use the specific rules for throwing drills listed in the previous section. These drills can be used as part of that warm-up or at full strength following the warm-up with an emphasis on hard, strong throws and accuracy. When using a drill to emphasize a particular component, have your players throw at a shorter distance to reduce the need to throw the ball hard and to better isolate that element. Throwing distance should also be adjusted for the skill level as well as to how warm the arm is.

Quick Feet and Hands

Purpose: To develop fast feet in assuming the proper throwing position.

Procedure: The player starts with a ball in the glove and in correct fielding position with the glove on the ground and the throwing hand just outside the glove. The player takes the ball out of the glove quickly and jumps to the throwing position. She can freeze in that position or throw easily to a partner about 20 feet away.

Scarecrow

Purpose: To practice fielding and throwing techniques and check mechanics.

Procedure: The player takes two steps forward to field an imaginary ground ball. She gathers the ball in and then quickly jump turns to a throwing position with both elbows up. The player holds that position, checks alignment (sideways to the target, feet in proper position, and shoulders level), and maintains balance.

Bent Knee

Purpose: To isolate the arms to focus on the proper use of both arms and on the arms working in opposition.

Procedure: Partners take positions 15 feet apart and kneel on the leg on the throwing-arm side. The other leg is bent with the foot flat on the ground. The thrower points her glove at the target and throws using proper arm action. The receiver catches the ball and repeats the action.

Down the Barrel

Purpose: To practice full arm circle (extension) of the throwing arm and both arms working together.

Procedure: The player starts with a ball in the throwing hand and stands sideways to the target in a throwing position. The throwing arm hangs straight down with the ball touching the side of the leg. The thrower points to the target with her glove and then throws by pulling down the glove arm and raising the throwing arm, focusing on keeping the elbow up, stretching across the chest, and having one shoulder replace the other.

Release and Spin

Purpose: To develop proper release and spin.

Procedure: Partners face each other from about six feet away. One player holds the ball in her throwing hand with proper grip and puts the throwing-arm elbow in her glove at about chest height. Partners throw the ball back and forth at least 25 times. This exercise isolates the wrist action so that the players can feel this particular component. They should feel the wrist action, emphasize proper release, and check the vertical spin.

Sequence Throwing

Purpose: To force concentration so that players can work on accuracy.

Procedure: Players use this sequence when throwing to a partner. Because the numbers are not in a logical sequence, the thrower must concentrate on each throw.

1. left shoulder
2. right hip
3. right shoulder
4. left hip

Self-Toss

Purpose: To practice moving into the ball when catching a fly ball.

Procedure: The player tosses a ball to herself, catches it, and throws it to a partner, who is at throwing distance. The player should not throw the ball too high, tossing it only slightly above the head and in front of the throwing shoulder (see figure 2.12). Players work on moving into the ball when catching and using both hands to catch the ball.

Sidearm Correction

Purpose: To know if the arm drops to sidearm position.

Procedure: The player stands perpendicularly to a tall fence with the throwing arm next to the fence. The fence must be taller than the player's extended arm. With the throwing arm held at a 90-degree position, the arm should miss touching the fence by several inches. The player marks this spot and uses it every time she throws. If the arm drops to sidearm when playing catch at this position, the hand will hit the fence, providing instant feedback. Players can do this drill daily until they eliminate the sidearm throw and the overhand throw becomes automatic.

Figure 2.12 Self-toss.

Triangle Catch and Throw

Purpose: To practice correct body position when catching and throwing, with emphasis on turning the feet and body to throw.

Procedure: Three players form a triangle. The player at the right-angle corner catches the ball from the thrower in proper receiving position. After catching the ball, the player focuses on turning the feet and shoulders toward the third player (target), who is to her right, and throws to her (see figure 2.13). The receiver catches the ball and puts it in a bucket. The thrower also has a bucket, from which she takes a ball to repeat the drill. When the thrower's bucket is empty, players rotate to new positions. If the player fielding and throwing is left-handed, the receiver is to her left so that the player fielding and throwing has to turn her body.

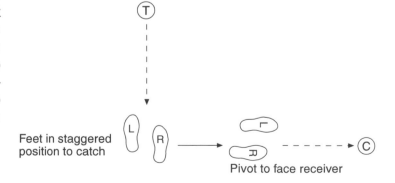

Figure 2.13 Triangle catch and throw drill.

Square Catch

Purpose: To practice turning feet in the direction of the throw.

Procedure: Four players stand in a square, positioned at throwing distance from one another. Players throw around the square 10 times in one direction, then reverse the ball. They catch the ball in proper receiving position and then turn their feet to proper throwing position.

Variation: To make sure the thrower is seeing the target before throwing the ball, have other players in the square take turns dropping to one knee. The thrower throws around the square unless the next person is kneeling. The thrower must then move her feet and realign to proper position for a throw to another receiver. Players do not use a pattern for kneeling; they just randomly kneel to keep the thrower honest. If all are kneeling, they all stand and restart the drill.

Quick Release

Purpose: To evaluate speed of release and throwing accuracy.

Procedure: Players pair up for a contest to see which pair can catch 20 balls first. The count begins with "one" on the first catch. Any partner overthrowing must run the ball back before continuing. The pair sit when finished. Reward the winners and, to make sure all teams finish the drill, penalize the last two groups by having them run an extra lap or sprint.

Timed Throws

Purpose: To measure the speed of the release and throw by timing the ball from glove to glove. This exercise demonstrates that a straight-line throw is much quicker than a rainbow throw.

Procedure: Players form a single-file line in left field. A player tosses the ball to herself, catches it, and throws to the catcher at home plate. Draw a throwing line that players must stay behind so that all are throwing the same distance. This drill is useful in tryouts.

Variations:

- Hit ground balls and fly balls to throwers. Vary the field positions.
- Place balls on the line and have players do a dead-ball pickup and throw.

Thrower in the Box

Purpose: To locate a target and use proper body alignment.

Procedure: The thrower stands in the middle of a square or in the middle of the diamond. When using the diamond, receivers should use correct positions at the bases. The coach throws or rolls a ball to the thrower and calls a position number where the throw is to be made. The receiver returns the throw quickly and accurately to the catcher so that the drill can continue. Go as fast as players' skill will allow.

Variation: The catcher throws to the number called, and the coach continues to call out numbers for subsequent throws. This drill can be done with or without a player in the middle.

Wet Ball

Purpose: To learn to throw a wet ball to prepare for soggy conditions.

Procedure: Players practice throwing with a wet ball so that they can adjust to the elements and prepare psychologically for any conditions. Many types of drills can be executed with a wet ball. Outfielders must often adjust to wet grass, so include numerous outfield ground-ball drills.

QUICK THROW DRILLS

Practice all the types of throws that are used in a game. Execute them at game speed to develop balance, proper technique, accuracy, and confidence.

Running Lap Tosses

Purpose: To develop catching and throwing skills while conditioning. This drill makes efficient use of time.

Procedure: Partners are about six feet apart and play catch as they run using underhand tosses. They can run a full lap or in a straight line down the field and back. The drill develops players' catching and throwing skills and takes their minds off running.

Throwing on the Run

Purpose: To develop throwing accuracy when throwing on the run.

Procedure: Partners in two lines face each other 60 feet apart. Make sure players are well spread apart so that an errant throw does not hit anyone. One partner does a self-toss and then runs hard at her partner for three to five steps and makes a chest-high throw. The thrower returns to her original position, and the partner repeats the drill going the opposite direction. To make the drill realistic, players should run at the speed they will use in a game.

Show the Ball

Purpose: To make sure the first baseman can see the ball.

Procedure: Fielders line up single file halfway between first base and second base. The coach or a player hits ground balls to one fielder at a time. The player fields the ball and shows it to the first baseman. The fielder cannot release the ball until the first baseman says "yes," indicating that she has clearly seen it. The first baseman catches the ball and places it in a bucket.

Variation: Execute the drill at other infield positions requiring short throws to bases.

Second Base Sidearm to First

Purpose: To practice charging ground balls and making sidearm throws from the second baseman to first base.

Procedure: Players line up in single file at the second-base fielding position. The coach or another player hits slow rollers at the fielder, who charges the ball and makes a sidearm throw to the first baseman. After throwing, the fielder goes to the end of the fielding line. The first baseman drops the ball in a bucket or returns it to the catcher feeding the hitter.

Variation: Execute the drill at other infield positions requiring short throws to bases.

Circle Backhand Flips

Purpose: To develop accuracy of backhand flips.

Procedure: Players in a tight circle pass the ball around the circle using flip tosses. Use a drill like this while players are recovering from a conditioning exercise.

Variation: With a moving circle, players can practice leading receivers with backhand flips. The player tosses the ball using a backhand flip to the player in front of her. The tosser must lead a moving player. Have the circle go both clockwise and counterclockwise. Advance to running in both directions.

Dead-Ball Backhand Flips

Purpose: To practice backhand flip to bases.

Procedure: Place three balls on the ground on the first-base side of second about 10 feet from second base. A player runs in and executes backhand flips to the shortstop standing at second base. The player flips all three balls, approaching each ball with a short run.

Variations:

- Do this drill off easy tosses or hits.
- Perform the drill from shortstop to third base.

Hit-Ball Line Flips

Purpose: To execute backhand flips off hit balls.

Procedure: Two lines of fielders stand about 10 feet apart facing the hitter. A hitter hits a ball to the first player in the fielding line. The fielder flips the ball to a teammate at the front of the opposite line, who throws to a catcher near the hitter. The catcher feeds the hitter so that the drill can continue rapidly.

3

Infield

How important is the infield? Two-thirds of the total defense, or six of nine players, play in the infield. Much of your team's success is determined by how well the infielders perform, both individually and together. Infielders must work together as a unit. They need to understand their own responsibilities and coverage as well as those of their teammates. Each player must honestly evaluate her skills as well as those of the teammate beside her. What balls should she play and which should she leave for her teammate? Who has the stronger arm? Who is in the better position to make the play? Understanding and awareness are keys to successful team play.

Communication is vital. Infielders must talk about the batter's ability, the number of outs, defensive shifting, and the speed of the runners. They should remind each other who is covering the bag and taking the throw. By working together with understanding and communication, your players can develop into a cohesive and successful unit.

BASIC POSITIONING AND COVERAGE

Infielders normally follow general rules for defensive positioning and coverage responsibilities, making adjustments from these basic positions according to the game situation and the ability of the players. Later chapters explain how pitching, hitting, and team defensive strategies influence positioning and coverage. The following basic principles explain each position and its relationship to the other positions.

The first baseman and third baseman play in front of the bag and close enough to home plate to protect against the bunt. They play as far from the foul line as possible to help cover the holes in the infield and still get anything right on the line. They must protect the line because a hit on the foul line goes for extra bases.

The shortstop and second baseman play behind the baseline and as deep as they can and still make the play. The deeper they are, the more time they have to react and the better their range. The basic position when there are no base runners and the defense is not making adjustments for the batter is midway between the two respective bases. The middle infielders will make various adjustments according to the defensive play called, the pitch being thrown, the runners on base, and the batter's abilities.

When the pitch is delivered, each player has a job to do: field the ball, act as a relay, cover a base, or be a backup. Infielders must play the ball first. Then the rule is that the player closer to the base covers it, and the other backs up the base.

Steals:	Shortstop covers second with runner on first.
	Shortstop covers third with runner on second.
Bunts:	Second baseman covers first.
	Shortstop covers second with runner on first.
	Shortstop covers third with runner on second or third.
Relays:	Ball hit to left or center field: Second baseman covers second and shortstop acts as the relay.
Ball hit to right field:	Shortstop covers second and second baseman is the relay.

FIRST BASEMAN

The first baseman will make more outs defensively than anyone on the team, so she must have a dependable glove and good agility. A first baseman who is able to catch all types of throws can make an average-throwing infield look great. Tall players have an obvious advantage because they can reach farther and offer a larger target. Many teams are hurt, however, when they put a tall player at first who cannot make the catch and the out. The first baseman should be one of the best athletes on the field. Desired characteristics of the first baseman include the following:

- Agile, flexible, and mobile
- Quick hands and feet
- Tall and left-handed
- Accurate arm to other bases

The first baseman doesn't have to be left-handed, but a left-hander has advantages. When fielding bunts, the left-handed player does not have to pivot to make throws to second and third, thus saving time. A lefty can cover the hole between first and second base more easily because the glove is on the infield side. With the glove on the inside of the diamond, a lefty can more easily give the target and make the catch.

The first baseman adjusts her position based on whether the batter is likely to hit, bunt, or slap hit. See figure 3.1 for the first baseman's positioning and coverage area.

- **Hitter**—The first baseman takes a position three to four feet in front of the base and two to three feet inside the line. One step gets her to the line.
- **Bunter**—The first baseman plays in as close as necessary to field the bunt and still have time to get back to cover the base on a hit. This distance will be from half to two-thirds the distance to home.
- **Slapper**—The first baseman plays halfway between the two previous positions while shading a little closer to the pitcher.

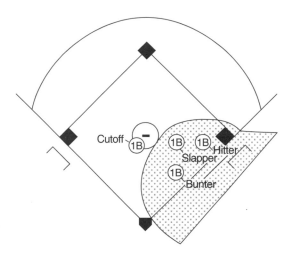

Figure 3.1 First baseman's basic positioning and coverage area.

Moving to the Base

The first baseman must get back as soon as she recognizes that fielding the ball is not her responsibility. She should always turn to her right to face toward the infield. With a quick glance to locate the base, the first baseman sprints full speed to it. If she is not far from the bag, she can sidestep to it while watching the ball. If time permits, the first baseman can kick back and feel the base so she knows where it is while waiting for the ball. The base should be directly behind the feet and in the middle of the body.

Sometimes with a fast runner, the first baseman cannot get all the way to the base to make the play. Instead of running a foot race, an option is to establish a "short position." The first baseman stops short of the base, calls out "short," gives a target, and makes the tag there. The first baseman may want to use this positioning with a fast runner at third. By setting up short, the first baseman cuts down the distance she must throw to home and may prevent the runner from scoring easily on a play to first.

Receiving Throws

The set position to receive the throw is the basic athletic position with good balance. With weight on the balls of the feet and knees slightly flexed, the first baseman can be ready to move in any direction. Arms are extended toward the thrower. The first baseman should always use her glove as a target. The first baseman should help the thrower with verbal cues, calling "Hurry, hurry, hurry" on close plays or, on routine plays, calling the fielder's name to help her locate the target. The first baseman should catch with two hands whenever possible for a sure catch and a quick release. If a stretch is required, the catch should be made with one hand to extend the reach farther. The cardinal rule is to catch the ball first and then worry about tagging the bag.

After catching the throw, the first baseman touches the base, tagging the edge of the bag with the ball of the foot rather than the heel or toe. By using the ball of the foot, the first baseman can more easily keep the foot on the bag should she lose her balance or have to extend her reach if she misplays the ball. To prevent injuries, the player must tag the inside edge of the base, keeping the foot off the middle of the bag. The following sections describe the two basic footwork techniques for touching the base.

Catch and Touch.   To use the catch-and-touch technique, the first baseman faces the throw with the heels about six inches from the edge of the base and the feet facing the thrower (see figure 3.2a). The shoulders are square to the thrower. The first baseman steps toward the ball to catch it. After the catch she steps back and touches the base with the ball of the non-glove side foot (see figure 3.2b). The sequence is step, catch, and kick back. As the player's skill level increases, this action will become almost one motion.

Which foot should the player step forward with? When the ball is straight to her, she steps with the glove side leg. When the ball is to either side, she steps with the foot closer to the ball to get behind it. An advantage of this method is that the player can quickly get the foot off the base with less chance of the runner stepping on it. To help the first baseman get in the habit, have her kick back to an imaginary base using a smooth tagging motion when playing catch with a partner during warm-ups.

a   b

Foot on Bag.   When using the foot-on-the-bag technique, the first baseman keeps one foot on the base as she steps toward the ball with the opposite foot (see figure 3.3). The foot on the bag is the foot opposite the glove. The ball of the foot is on the corner or the edge of the bag, depending on the position of the thrower. The first baseman wants to be as close to the thrower as possible, so the exact position of the foot on the bag (corner or edge) is determined by where the thrower is. The front foot is slightly ahead so that the fielder can maintain good balance and be ready to move. The shoulders

Figure 3.2   Catch-and-touch technique at first base. (a) Face the throw with the heels about six inches from the edge of the base and the feet facing the thrower. After making the catch (b) step back and touch the base with the ball of the foot on the non-glove side.

are square to the thrower. The player does not stretch and commit until she can judge the path of the ball, so she waits until the fielder throws it. The back-tagging foot turns sideways with the ankle pointing down and pushes against the base as the front foot strides toward the ball. After the tag, the player quickly removes the foot.

A disadvantage of this method is a tendency on bad throws to keep the foot on the bag and hope to reach the ball. Because catching the ball is the first priority, the first baseman should not hesitate to leave the base to make the catch. If the catch isn't made, the runner will probably advance another base.

Misthrows. Good first basemen must be able to catch all balls within their reach whether they are high, low, to the side, or the most difficult type of catch—into the runner. Successful first basemen expect to make the catch and subsequent play on any throw that they can get the glove on.

- **Low throws**—The first baseman keeps her head down to watch the ball into the glove. Balls in the dirt at the feet will require her to gather in the ball with soft hands. When the ball will bounce out in front, the first baseman stretches to reach it before it hits the ground. If that is not possible, she plays it as a short hop with a scooping motion.
- **High throws**—The player concentrates on catching the top of the ball. She stretches and maintains contact with the bag if possible. If the ball is over the bag but too high, she jumps and catches it with one hand (glove) and then lands with one foot on the bag.

Figure 3.3 Foot-on-bag technique at first base.

- **Throws to the side**—The primary goal is to catch the ball. It is better to give up the out than to have runners advance extra bases on an overthrow. If necessary, the first baseman leaves the base to make the catch, then kicks back to the bag. She does not keep her foot anchored to the base and hope she can reach the ball.
- **Throws into the runner**—If the throw is well ahead of the runner, the player makes the catch, tags the base, and lets the momentum carry her into foul territory. If the runner and ball will arrive at the same time, the first baseman moves to the inside of the base path to avoid the runner as she makes the catch. The first baseman tries to tag the runner as she goes by.

Special Plays

The first baseman must work well with several other fielders. To be successful, she must understand her responsibilities and her relationship with the second baseman, right fielder, and catcher. When balls do get by the first baseman, the right fielder can sometimes throw out the runner at first base. The second baseman covers first when the first baseman can't get back to the bag. Balls hit between the two require an understanding of who should field the ball. The catcher makes many types of throws to first, requiring the first baseman to be in different receiving positions. These four players working together control the right side of the infield.

Fielding Bunts. The first baseman's ability to field the bunt is critical to team defense. Techniques and responsibilities are covered under "Bunt Defense" in chapter 7 (page 131).

Working With the Second Baseman.   If the first baseman can field the ball and easily beat the runner to the base, she makes the play herself. This is the safe play because there is less chance of error. When the second baseman must cover the base, the first baseman uses an underhand or sidearm throw, making sure the ball is visible to the receiver.

For balls in the one-two hole, the first baseman must know her range, the range of the second baseman, and the second baseman's position on each pitch. Usually, the first baseman should go no more than two to three steps into that area. In addition, the first baseman must avoid deflecting balls so that no one can make the play. Only hard-hit balls should go between the first and second basemen. Players should call for the ball when possible and always communicate about who is covering the bag.

Any balls hit over the first baseman's head that require backpedaling of more than several steps belong to the second-base player, who has the better angle coming across on a diagonal.

Working With the Right Fielder.   On balls hit sharply to right field, the first baseman always covers the base so that the right fielder has the opportunity to throw out the runner. Because this will be a quick throw, the first baseman should assume it won't be accurate. The catcher will be backing the play.

Working With the Catcher.   On dropped third strikes, passed balls and wild pitches, pickoffs, and bunts, the catcher often throws to first base. The first baseman must be at the bag ready and in proper position to make the out.

- **Dropped third strike**—The first baseman takes an outside position at the base so that the catcher never has to throw across the base path. If the catcher has trouble finding the ball, the first baseman can help by calling out the location. The first baseman gives an outside target with the glove and calls "outside" until the ball is on its way.

- **Throwing home**—With runners at second or third, the first baseman should always expect the runner to be going home on a play to first. She makes the out and then pushes hard off the base, making sure to be well inside the base path so that the batter–base runner cannot interfere. She quickly gets her feet in position for the throw home. With fast runners and an aggressive opponent, playing a "short first base" can help the player get the ball home more quickly.

Playing Foul Balls.   To play foul balls safely and successfully, the first baseman needs to know the distance to the fence and how balls will rebound. She should study the dugouts to be aware of openings and dead-ball areas. She should imagine a line going at a 45-degree angle from first base to the foul-line fence and play any balls that will land in front of that line.

Other Responsibilities

Additional team defensive responsibilities are outlined below. Although the first responsibility is always to play first base, when no play is occurring there the first baseman should be ready to assist in other areas. The first baseman is more than just someone who stands at first base.

- Executing the cutoff. The first baseman is usually the cutoff on throws going home, assuming a position near the pitching rubber (see figure 3.1 for correct cutoff positioning). See full details of the cutoff play in chapter 7.

- Covering home on passed balls and wild pitches. Most coaches prefer that the first baseman cover home instead of the pitcher. The first baseman must react immediately to the ball, not waiting to react to the runner going home.

- Covering home on intentional walks to a left-handed batter. The first baseman should take a position close to home plate (as if fielding a bunt) and in fair territory as the rules require. The third baseman is back in regular position in case the batter hits the outside pitch.
- Helping the catcher locate foul balls. The first baseman calls the location and direction of the ball.
- Backing up the catcher on first and third play if a runner is going and backing up second base on throws from left and center field. The first baseman takes a backup position about 15 feet behind the intended receiver and in direct line with the throw. When backing up the catcher, she should be close to the fence so that she can quickly retrieve the ball off the fence.

Moving to the Base

Purpose: To improve quickness and range moving to first base.

Procedure: The first baseman takes a position halfway to home as if fielding a bunt. On the coach's command "go," she sprints to the base (turning inward to the diamond), finds the base, takes the receiving position, catches an imaginary ball, and tags the base. The player repeats the drill, moving ever closer to home to increase the distance and push herself to improve quickness in getting to the base.

Bad Hops at First

Purpose: To practice catching bad hops at first base.

Procedure: Have a thrower on the infield about 30 feet from first throwing bad hops with an overhand throw to the first baseman in receiving position at first base. The thrower has a bucket full of balls. The first baseman catches the ball, makes the out, and put the balls in a second bucket nearby. Have the first baseman do this drill every day to develop this important skill. The player gathers or short hops every ball and focuses on keeping the head down.

Three Throws From the Catcher

Purpose: To practice receiving three different throws from the catcher. The catcher is simultaneously working on the techniques involved in three plays: passed ball, bunt, and pickoff.

Procedure: The first baseman catches the following throws and places the ball in a bucket by the base (see figure 3.4).

1. The pitcher throws to the catcher, who intentionally lets the pitch get behind her. The catcher recovers the ball and throws to the outside of first base (1).

2. After catching the second pitch, the catcher throws the ball out in front of the plate to simulate a bunt. She goes after the ball and throws it to the first baseman, who is calling "inside" and giving a target there (2).

3. Last, the catcher signals for a pitchout and after receiving the pitch, throws to the inside of the bag for a pickoff (3). For a complete explanation of pickoffs, see chapter 7.

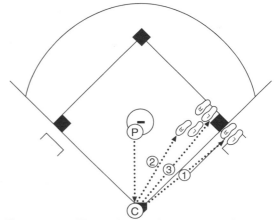

Figure 3.4 Three throws from the catcher.

Coaching Points for the First Baseman

- You can extend your reach by stretching, even going as far as doing the splits. But keep in mind that your glove must extend farther than your front foot for your stretching to be beneficial.
- On overthrows, as soon as you get the ball tag the runner if she is off the base. Chances are the runner has made some motion toward second base and is liable to be put out. Make this a habit and pick up some outs.
- Be careful not to deflect balls that should be left for the second baseman to field. When you commit to play the ground ball, the second baseman is on her way to first and no one is there to play the deflection.
- Always hustle back to cover the base even when you think there is no play. The other infielders can't make one if you're not there. If a runner is at first, you can help hold her closer to the bag by returning quickly.
- When it is obvious that you have no play, quickly remove your tagging foot and body a step or two off the base to avoid contact and the possibility of injury or interference with the runner.
- Always assume other runners are advancing on throws to first. Never be caught by surprise.

SECOND BASEMAN

Second base is one of the most difficult positions to play because of its many defensive responsibilities. The second baseman must always have her head in the game. Although the natural reaction is to go to the ball, in some instances the second baseman must go the opposite way. In bunt situations the second baseman must immediately break to cover first and then become a good first baseman.

Desired characteristics of the second baseman include the following:

- Right-handed thrower
- Quick feet and good range
- Ability to get a good jump
- Snap throw and quick release
- Good hands—plays a lot of first base
- Ability to react to the situation
- Quick release to turn double plays
- Ability to go back on pop flies

The many defensive responsibilities of the second baseman include the following:

- Covering first base on all bunts and on ground balls to the first baseman when she can't get back to first
- Backing up throws to the pitcher from the catcher
- Taking pickoffs at first and second
- Covering second base on occasion on steals when the shortstop has moved closer to third or for the element of surprise
- Taking relays from right field and from the right side of center field
- Catching foul balls behind first base

- Performing the double-play pivot at second base on throws from the shortstop or third baseman
- Working with the first baseman on grounders to the right side

The regular fielding position of the second baseman is only about six feet behind the line because she must be able to get to first to cover the base when necessary. The second baseman adjusts her position based on whether the batter is likely to hit, bunt, or slap hit. See figure 3.5 for positioning and coverage areas.

- **Hitter**—The second baseman plays as far from home as arm and quickness to first base allow. Playing deeper increases range by providing more time to get to balls up the middle and to the left.
- **Bunter**—The second baseman moves several steps closer to first to cut down the distance she must run to cover the base on the bunt. She goes to first base on every bunt attempt.
- **Slapper**—The second baseman moves in several steps and shades closer to first, just as she does when playing the bunt. This is the basic slap defense. Other options are covered in "Slap Defense" in chapter 7 (page 135).

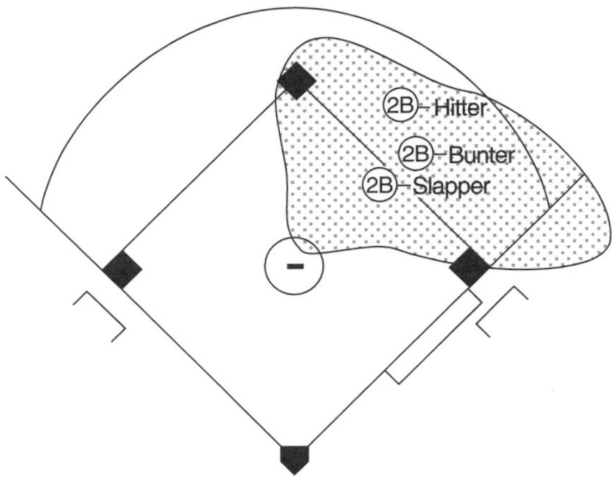

Figure 3.5 Second baseman's basic positioning and coverage area.

Special Plays

The second baseman is sometimes called the best first baseman on the team. She covers first base on bunts, slaps, and pickoffs when the first baseman can't get back. And because of her proximity to first she can take the time to block some ground balls and still make the play.

Coaching Points for the Second Baseman

- Go to first base in every bunting situation regardless of where the base runners are.
- Become a good first baseman. Practice fielding bad throws and stretching when necessary to make the out.
- When making overhand throws to first and second, use a three-quarter throw so that the ball is always visible to the receiver.
- Be comfortable and skilled using all types of throws because you will find yourself in situations that require varied throws from long and short distances as well as several kinds of double-play feeds.
- On a potential double play, look to tag the runner and then go to one.
- When fielding a ball with the runner approaching, take a charge and get an interference call.
- Use a fake pickoff (occasionally) to get the runner going the wrong way when the bunt goes down. See the section "Bunt Defense" in chapter 7 (page 131).

Figure 3.6 Second baseman's receiving position when covering first.

Blocking Ground Balls. If the second baseman can't quite catch a ball, she should at least try to knock it down. Some players, because of the short throw to first, will take the time to block hard-hit balls. If a player is more comfortable blocking hard-hit balls, she can drop to one knee like an outfielder and use her leg to block it. The second baseman is close enough to first that she can take the time to smother and block the ball and make sure it doesn't get through. When playing on uneven ground that causes bad bounces, this may be the best option.

Covering First Base. The second baseman covers first base in all bunting situations and any time the first baseman cannot get back. This play is often a footrace with the runner because the second baseman must also run a fair distance. The throw must be on the inside of the diamond to avoid hitting the base runner. Therefore, the second baseman must often take an extreme inside position on the base. She places the left foot against the nearest side of the base, faces the thrower, gives the glove for a target, catches the ball, and immediately clears out of the area by moving toward the infield (see figure 3.6). If the ball is hit sharply (i.e., to the pitcher or to a pulled-in third baseman) and the batter–base runner is not near first base, then the second baseman may use the standard first baseman's technique and footwork for tagging the base.

SHORTSTOP

The shortstop is considered the key to a good defense. She is usually the team's best player and strongest arm because she handles a large percentage of the defensive plays. The shortstop plays as deep as her arm and ability permit because a deeper position provides a better angle to the ball and more time to react. The shortstop must have the ability to charge grounders and finish the play with a quick, strong throw to first. Generally a team leader, the shortstop is in a great location to communicate and direct the defense.

Desired characteristics of the shortstop include the following:

- Right-hander with the strongest arm
- Best fielder on the team
- Consistent fielder on all types of balls
- Exceptional fielding range in all directions
- Good speed to cover both second and third
- Leadership skills

The defensive responsibilities of the shortstop include the following:

- Covering second base and third base on steals. The shortstop is in the best position to get ahead of the runner and be in position to make the tag. A runner attempting to steal second interferes with the second baseman by being in front of her. A runner going to third is behind the third baseman and out of her line of vision.

- Covering second base on first and third plays.
- Taking pickoffs at second and third. The shortstop will cover the base the majority of the time. At times second or third may take the base if the shortstop is farther from the base than normal or to provide the element of surprise.
- Taking relays from left field and center field. With the strongest arm on the infield, the shortstop will take all relays from center field that she can easily get to. The second baseman will be the relay from the right side of center field.
- Executing the double-play pivot for balls from the right side of the infield and from the pitcher.
- Catching foul balls behind third base.
- Backing up throws to the pitcher from the catcher if the second baseman is not there.

The strength of the shortstop's arm will largely determine how deep she can play. The shortstop must be strong enough to field a routine ball and throw out the majority of runners from the depth she assumes. The best shortstops play at the edge of the infield dirt, or about 10 to 12 feet behind the line. The shortstop adjusts her position according to the batter's expected type of hit. See figure 3.7 for the shortstop's positioning and coverage area.

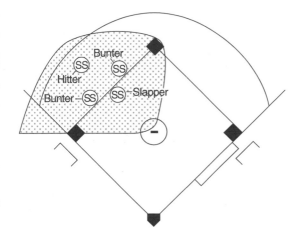

Figure 3.7 Shortstop's basic positioning and coverage area.

- **Hitter**—The shortstop plays behind the line as deep as her arm permits.
- **Bunter**—The shortstop moves several steps closer to the base she will be covering so that she can get there faster, ahead of the runner.
- **Slapper**—The shortstop moves in front of the line so that she can get to the ball more quickly.

Special Plays

Balls in the hole to the shortstop's right require the longest infield throw to first. On shallow fly balls to the left side the shortstop must work closely with the left and center fielder. Good communication is critical.

Playing Balls in the Hole.   When fielding a ball deep in the third base–shortstop hole (to the shortstop's right), the shortstop may not have enough time to plant the feet and get enough on the ball to make it all the way to first. The quickest path for a throw is a straight line, so a one- or two-bounce throw will get the ball there faster than the long rainbow throw.

Working With the Left and Center Fielders.   Going after and catching the shallow fly balls referred to as "Texas Leaguers" is difficult because of the natural fear of colliding with the outfielders who are also going for the ball. Communication is essential if those in position to go for the ball are to make a full-out effort. The shortstop must go back hard on all shallow fly balls with a resolve to catch the ball unless called off by an outfielder. Outfielders are in the best position to catch such balls because the ball is in front of them, so the shortstop must yield to any outfielder who calls for the ball. By working with the outfielders in practice catching many shallow fly balls or "tweeners," the shortstop can recognize the range of each player and work out who should catch which ball.

Coaching Points for the Shortstop

- Go to the ball and then if you are not involved, cover the nearest base.
- When there isn't a play and there are runners on, make a play. Fake a throw and catch a runner off base.
- Learn to hold the ball (eat it) and not take a chance of making an error on a play when you are too late to make an out.
- Communicate with your teammates on every play. Signal the number of outs and review who is covering the base. Don't leave anything to chance. The shortstop is usually the infield leader. Assume that leadership position.
- Work well with your pitcher. Return the ball sharply with a word of encouragement. Go to the mound when needed and appropriate.
- When shifting or adjusting your position, make sure you alert the third baseman and adjacent outfielders so that they can adjust to help plug the holes.

THIRD BASEMAN

The third baseman should have the quickest hands on the team and must be fearless. When playing in to protect against the bunt, many hard shots will come her way. Add to this the many bunt options, including the slash, slap, push, and fake, and you see why third base is called the hot corner.

Desired characteristics of the third baseman include the following:

- Right-handed thrower
- Quick and agile
- Sure hands and quick reactions
- Height to help on high bouncers
- Strong and accurate throwing arm
- Ability to throw from set and off-balance positions
- Aggressive with the ability to charge
- Good range to left to cut off balls to shortstop
- Confident, cocky, fearless

The defensive responsibilities of the third baseman include the following:

- Fielding bunts.
- Covering home when the catcher covers third on a bunt.
- Cutting off slowly hit balls between third base and the pitcher.
- Taking the relay from left field when the ball is near the foul line.
- Taking pickoffs at third base.
- Holding the runner at third.
- Covering home on intentional walks to right-handed batters. The third baseman should be in normal bunt position and in fair territory as the rules require. (The

first baseman is back in a stronger defensive position in case the batter hits the outside pitch.)

The third baseman adjusts her position based on whether the batter is likely to hit, bunt, or slap hit. See figure 3.8 for positioning and coverage area.

- **Hitter**—The third baseman takes a position three to four feet in front of the base and two to three feet inside the line so that one step gets her to the line. The deeper the third baseman can play, the more time she has to react to the ball. But the third baseman cannot let the bunt beat her. With a strong right-handed pull hitter up and no chance of a bunt, the third baseman may play even with the bag. Never in softball should the third baseman play behind the bag because she will be too deep to make the play on slow balls in front of her.

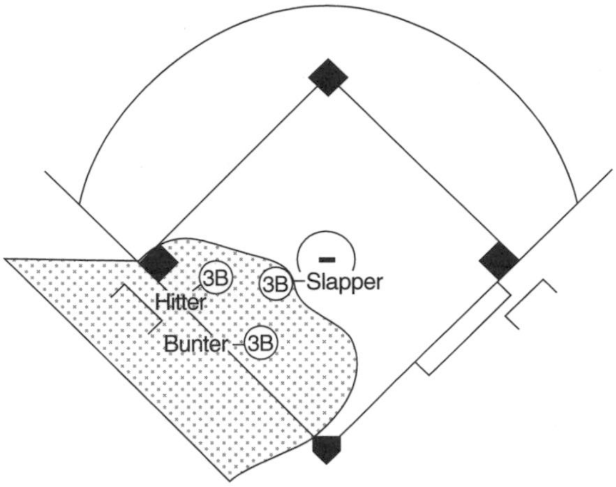

Figure 3.8 Third baseman's basic positioning and coverage area.

- **Bunter**—The third baseman plays as close as necessary to field the bunt and get the out, somewhere from half to two-thirds the distance to home depending on the player's quickness, ability to charge the ball, arm strength, and quickness of release.

- **Slapper**—The third baseman is in several steps closer than the position used when assuming a hit. She must move several steps toward the pitcher to help cut off slaps to the shortstop.

Special Plays

The third baseman is the first line of defense on the left side of the infield. She must be aggressive and on her toes. With a runner on third base, every effort must be made to keep the ball from going through and scoring a run. The third baseman must understand how to work with the shortstop to bolster the left-side defense.

Fielding Bunts.   Because the bunt is an important element of softball, the third baseman must be competent at fielding them. She should be the most aggressive player on bunts when the throw will go to second or first because her body is in the best alignment. For throws to third the third baseman should defer when possible to the first baseman. Because the third baseman will be fielding most of the bunts, she should work at developing quickness and fielding skills, fully described in chapter 7.

Working With the Shortstop.   The third baseman should be a ball hog, taking any balls she can get her hands on while being able to maintain balance and make a play. She should cut in front of the shortstop to get any balls she can field, moving straight across the diamond and being careful not to angle back toward the shortstop. It is critical that the third baseman cut off any slow rollers in the third base–shortstop hole because the shortstop will not have time to make the play. The third baseman should not dive for ground balls in the hole because she will not be able to recover in time to throw. She can leave that ball for the shortstop to play. She should know both her range and that of the shortstop and check her teammate's position on every pitch. She must know which balls are clearly hers and understand when she is in the best position to make the play. Any balls hit over the third baseman's head that require more than four or five steps of backpedaling belong to the shortstop, who has the better angle coming on a diagonal.

Figure 3.9 Third baseman pushes off hard with the right foot to make the force play and throw to first.

Figure 3.10 Third baseman looking the runner back.

Fielding Foul Balls. To play foul balls safely and successfully, the third baseman should check the distance to the fence and know how balls will rebound. She should be aware of dugout openings and dead-ball areas. With a runner on third base, it is critical that no ball enters a dead-ball area because the runner automatically scores. When fielding foul balls, the third baseman should imagine a line going at a 45-degree angle from third base to the foul-line fence and play any balls that will land in front of that line (see figure 3.8).

Force at Third. When fielding a ground ball near the base, tagging the base for the force at third and throwing to first should be a routine double play. The third baseman should clearly indicate to the shortstop that she has the bag. When tagging the base, the third baseman pushes off hard with the right foot to create momentum for the body turn (see figure 3.9). The feet and shoulders should turn fully to throwing position.

Runner at Third. With a runner at third the first priority when fielding a ground ball is to keep the runner from scoring. The third baseman looks at the runner to see how far she is off the base. If the runner has strayed too far, the third baseman can go after her to get the out. The shortstop should be in position at third to make the tag. The third baseman should not be surprised if the runner is going home. The runner may try to take advantage of the fact that the third baseman has her back to the runner. The third baseman looks for the catcher's target and establishes a throwing lane to avoid hitting the runner with the ball.

Unless the runner is automatically going, the third baseman, because of her proximity, can stop the runner with just a look. The third baseman turns only the head to look, being careful not to pull the shoulders back from throwing position (see figure 3.10). She quickly moves her feet to throw after she has decided where she will throw the ball. If the runner has stopped, the third baseman makes a hard, accurate throw to first so that if the runner goes on the throw, the first baseman will have a chance at doubling her off at home. A fake throw can also be effective at third base. A full description appears later in this chapter.

BASIC INFIELD PLAYS

Although infielders require specific skills to play their positions successfully, many general infield skills are important for all to understand and master. With good communication, the infield can make defensive adjustments that strengthen the defense and assure that all

Coaching Points for the Third Baseman

- Knock down or block hard-hit balls on the line. The left fielder will not have a play anyway, so keep the ball from going through for possible extra bases.
- Assume all bunts and shots on the line are fair. Play them out and let the umpire make the call.
- On bunts when you have no play, allow the ball to roll to see if it goes foul. Be quick to touch balls in foul territory that you want to the umpire to rule foul.
- When fielding a bunt on which you must hurry your throw, make sure your shoulders are level. If you don't have time to stand upright, throw from a semicrouch but even up your shoulders to keep the ball level. Allowing your throwing shoulder to drop will produce a high throw.
- With runners on base retreat quickly to cover your base when not fielding the ball. Because you are often drawn so far in, you cannot be lazy about getting back.
- On throws home always establish a throwing lane to avoid hitting the runner. Look for the catcher's target and then move your body as necessary to keep your throw out of the runner's path.

bases are covered. The infield works together to turn double plays, create force-outs, and stop the offense from scoring. Here are the important elements for these basic infield plays.

Playing the Bases

The traditionalists recommend straddling the bag when waiting for the throw. There are some real disadvantages to the traditional manner of playing the bases:

- The fielder is in direct line with the base runner, and if the runner doesn't slide or does so with cleats high, the fielder can easily be injured.
- Feet are planted parallel in a poor position for fielding. The fielder has limited mobility to make a play on a wild throw.
- Throwing errors are usually to the runner's side of the bag. If the baseman must step to get the ball, the foot will be directly in the path of the oncoming runner.
- If the ball and runner arrive at the same time, it's difficult to hang onto the ball. If the ball hits the runner, the defense is beaten.

Applying the following principles is a safer and more effective way to cover the base: The fielder stands on the side of the base the throw is coming from and out of the base path and takes a good fielding position with the foot that is closer to the bag slightly ahead of the other foot.

Third Base. On a throw from home the third baseman should assume a position on the home-plate side of the bag with the side of the left foot against the bag (see figure 3.11 on page 52). She gives the target at the front edge of the bag. The third baseman is out of the path of the runner. If the throw is to the inside of the diamond, she can use

Figure 3.11 Third baseman's receiving position for a throw from the catcher.

basic fielding skills to reach or block the ball. On a throw from the outfield, the third baseman places the side of her right foot against the bag.

Second Base. For a throw from the catcher, the shortstop takes a position on the inside of the diamond with the left foot slightly ahead of the right and against the front corner of the base (see figure 3.12a). The shortstop moves to the right-field side of the base when taking a throw from right field with the right foot touching the side of the base (see figure 3.12b). When taking a throw from left field, the second baseman stands on the left-field side of second with the left foot touching the base.

First Base. For a pickoff throw from the catcher, the first baseman or the second baseman would take a position on the second-base side of first with the left foot on the side and toward the back of the base. This is the best position for blocking the runner off the base, and it requires the runner to take the longest route to tag the base. By taking this position the second baseman does not have to run as far as she would if she straddled the base. Therefore, she can get there more quickly. For throws from the outfield, infielders take a position on the side of the base the throw is coming from, placing the foot closer to the base against the side of the base.

Traditionalists will argue that players who don't straddle the bag lose time applying the tag. If the throw is accurate, tag time is the same. If the throw is poor, the proposed method may save a leg and allow the player to catch the ball.

Tag Plays

The tag play is used to get a runner out by tagging her with the ball before she reaches the base. It is most commonly used to catch runners attempting to steal or when they have taken too big a leadoff at the base. The first priority is to catch the ball and then to apply the tag.

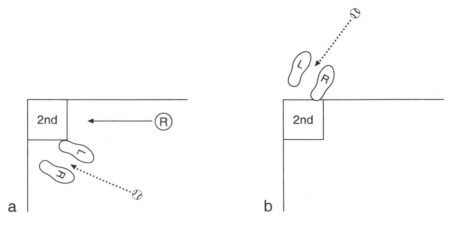

Figure 3.12 Shortstop's receiving position for (a) throws from the catcher and (b) throws from right field.

Infielders should get to the base as quickly as they can. The goal is to be waiting at the base for the throw. As the infielder nears the base, she shortens her steps and lowers her center of gravity, keeping her body under control. The infielder goes in low because that is where the ball should be thrown. It is also easier to adjust upward than downward if the ball is off target. The fielder should turn the upper body to face the incoming throw.

To prevent knee injuries, the player bends the knees as she applies the tag to help absorb any impact with the runner. After the tag is made, the fielder clears out of the base area and looks for any additional plays.

Infielders should not chase after or reach for a runner who misses the base. The best method is to keep the glove at the edge of the base nearest the runner and wait for her to return to the base. On a hook slide the infielder should keep the tag on the runner because the runner might overslide the base and lose contact.

Players should learn two ways to make the tag:

- **Two-handed tag**—The player catches the ball first. If the throw is on line, she does not reach for the ball but instead lets it come to her. If time permits, the fielder uses both hands to hold the glove on the ground at the front of the bag. She looks for the foot or hand of the runner reaching for the base and waits for her to hit the glove and tag herself out. The fielder must be sure to protect the bare hand with the glove and make the tag with the back of the glove so that the wrist can bend on impact (see figure 3.13). She should pull the glove back while making the tag, giving with the impact to absorb the shock and protect the ball. The two-handed tag is the most secure tag, the one that is less likely to cause a fielder to lose control of the ball. If the throw is off line, the fielder should go get the ball and then dive back to make the tag.

- **Sweep tag**—A late throw and close play requires a sweep tag. As the player catches the ball, she squeezes her fingers tightly to secure it. She bends her knees to get low to the ground and tags the runner with a rapid downward movement in front of the base. The fielder then gives with the impact and swings her arm back and up high in the air, showing the ball to the umpire.

Figure 3.13 Two-handed tag position.

Blocking the Base

The defensive player should take the base away from the runner whenever possible. If the ball will arrive ahead of the runner, the fielder blocks the runner's path to the base with her body, either stopping the runner or causing her to take the long way around the block. The fielder catches the ball and drops to one knee using the leg to block the base (see figure 3.14). If the player doesn't have time to drop the leg, she should at least lower the hips and become as big as possible. Obviously, when there is no chance for a play, the defensive player may not obstruct the runner. But in waiting for the play to develop, the defensive player should establish a position in the base path between the runner and the base. Then, if no chance of a play develops, the fielder steps out of the base path.

Figure 3.14 Blocking the base.

Force Plays

Force plays occur when a runner is forced to advance because the batter has become a base runner. To make the out, the defensive team can tag the runner or the base. A fielder should make the play herself if possible. The fewer throws a team makes, the less chance they have of making a mistake. A fielder making a play herself should wave off any teammate who may be moving to cover the base.

To receive a throw, the player gets to the base as quickly as possible. Throws coming from inside the base path are taken on the inside of the bag. Throws coming from outside the base path are taken on the outside of the bag. The receiver takes a position at the front of the base and places the side of the foot nearer the base against the front corner. She aligns her body so that her chest is facing the thrower and gives a target that recognizes the position of the runner so that the throw will not hit her. When the ball is accurately thrown, the receiver steps with the glove-side foot to the ball (see figure 3.15). The receiver must be careful not to reach too soon. She tags with the ball of the back foot, pushes off the inside edge of the base, and then steps in a straight line toward the next target. Whenever possible the receiver catches with two hands and squeezes the ball in the glove. The receiver should anticipate a bad throw and be ready to stretch if necessary. If the throw is wide, the receiver moves to catch the ball first and then kicks back with the opposite leg. If the receiver can't catch the ball, she at least stops it.

If the receiver can't get to the base in time, she becomes a moving target for the thrower. Again, alignment is with the chest facing the thrower as the ball is thrown. Ideally, the receiver catches the ball behind the base and then steps on the bag. Short steps and good balance will enable the player to react to balls that are off line. Timing and communication are the keys. The receiver should give a target, call the fielder's name, and request the location for the throw, inside or outside.

Figure 3.15 Receiving the throw for a force play at second base.

As soon as the force-out is made, the receiver vacates the base and looks for the next possible play. At second base the shortstop covers all throws from the infield except hit balls that require her to be in a backup position. Other bases will be covered by the infielder closest to the bag and in the best position to make the out.

Looking Runners Back

An important defensive goal is to prevent runners from advancing on ground balls, particularly on ground-ball outs. When fielding a ground ball with a runner at third, the first priority is always to keep the runner from scoring. Good communication from teammates will tell the fielder if the runners are automatically going. If they are, the fielder must look to see if she can get the lead runner. If the runners are not automatically going, then the fielder must "look the runner back" to keep the runner close to the base, to stop her forward momentum, and to keep her from easily advancing on a throw to first. The fielder looks at the lead runner to see how far she is off base. If the runner has strayed too far, the fielder can go after her to get the out. The fielder must always check the lead runner even though she may not be the runner closest to her. Playing on a runner behind the lead runner will give the latter an opportunity to advance on the play.

All infielders except the third baseman look the runner back by turning the head and upper body toward the lead runner. The infielder doesn't commit the feet to that throw, but she is ready to move the feet quickly into the proper throwing position for the throw she chooses to make.

Since the third baseman's fielding position puts her back to the runner, she must avoid being caught by surprise if a runner at third is going home. She looks for the catcher's target and establishes a throwing lane so that the ball does not hit the runner. If the runner is not automatically going, looking at her is all that is needed to get her to stop. The third baseman turns only the head to look, being careful not to pull the shoulders back from throwing position. She quickly moves her feet to throw and then makes a hard, accurate throw to first so that the first baseman will have a chance to double off the runner at home if she goes on the throw.

Fake Throws

The shortstop, third baseman, and pitcher can try a fake throw to pull the runner off the base and create an out. The goal is to get the runner leaning the wrong way, thus delaying her return to the base and providing more time to make the out. With the ball gripped firmly in the throwing hand, the fielder uses a compact windup as she fakes the throw to first base, being careful that the ball does not slip out of her hand. She may totally ignore the runner in faking the throw or may first look the runner back and then attempt the fake. By totally ignoring the runner the fielder is hoping to provide a false sense of security and encourage the runner to take a slightly bigger lead. The fielder then quickly brings the glove, the ball, and the throwing hand together to regrip for the actual throw. On sharply fielded balls, the fielder has time to attempt a fake, check the runner, and still make the play to first if the runner is not fooled. Getting the lead runner is certainly the preferred out.

Double Plays

When trying for a double play, the first priority is to field the ball and then, if possible, get the lead runner. Because of the short base paths, the defense has relatively little time to turn two, so this is a difficult task. The second baseman and shortstop must shade (cheat) by moving two to three steps closer to second base when they take their defensive positions. Several elements are required for success: the fielder must field the ball cleanly and make an accurate feed, and the pivot player must perform a quick release.

Feeder.   The feeder must not rush when fielding the ball. It has to be caught first. If the ball is bobbled, the team may have to forfeit going for two. If in doubt, the feeder goes for one sure out and the safest play, which is usually the out at first. When close to the bag, the feeder shows the pivot the ball and then throws shoulder high to the pivot's throwing shoulder. A dartlike throw is the most accurate but also requires the most time. Other throws that may be used are the underhand toss, the glove toss, and the backhand flip.

The fielder should tag the runner herself if she can get the out. If a double play is a real possibility, the fielder should not waste time chasing a runner who goes outside the base path; she should make the throw instead.

Pivot.   The second baseman makes the pivot on balls hit to short or third. The shortstop makes the pivot on balls hit to first, second, and the pitcher. An exception is a ball that pulls the pitcher to the extreme right, in which case the shortstop has to be the backup. Both the second baseman and shortstop should use the following technique when making the pivot:

- The player sprints to the base in line with the throw, showing her chest to the thrower.
- When time permits, the pivot slows almost to a stop behind the bag and waits for the throw. The pivot should expect a bad throw and be ready to react in any direction to make the catch.
- The pivot catches the ball first and then tags the base. By reaching with two hands the feet will quite naturally fall into place.
- The pivot does not cheat but makes a sure out. She touches the base when she has the ball, making sure the umpire can see the out!
- The pivot must be quick in getting rid of the ball, so she should work on a quick release.
- The rule is to always get one out:
  —Bad throw: The pivot catches the ball first and touches the base with the foot that can more easily reach the base.
  —Late throw: The pivot steps toward the throw and stretches to complete the force play, becoming a first baseman.
  —Unassisted double play: When fielding the ball within two to three steps of the base, the second baseman or shortstop makes the play herself, yelling "I've got it" to avoid a collision.

Footwork.   To keep it simple, the pivot player needs to become comfortable with only two basic sets of footwork. The choice of footwork will be determined by the location of the fielded ball (infield side or outfield side of the baseline), how close the thrower is to the base, and how quickly the pivot is able to get to the base. This will determine the type of throw that must be made and the footwork (push-off or drag) that should be used.

The *push-off* is most commonly used when the ball is coming from the inside of the base path. The push-off should put the body two feet from the bag and out of the runner's path. The pivot player steps directly toward first to shorten the throwing distance.

- **Shortstop push-off**—The left foot is against the edge facing third base. The shortstop must push off hard after the catch (see figure 3.16a) and pivot on the back foot, turning to get the shoulders parallel to the base line and in good throwing position (see figure 3.16b).

- **Second base push-off**—The ball of the left foot contacts the edge of the base nearer right field (see figure 3.17a). After the catch the second baseman pushes backward off the base, transferring the weight to the right foot (see figure 3.17b). She is now in a perfect position to step with the front (left) foot and throw.

The *drag* is used on long throws from outside the base path when the pivot has plenty of time to get to the base. The pivot player moves her body across the bag after catching the throw.

a

b

Figure 3.16
Shortstop's push-off. *(a)* Push hard off the left foot and *(b)* pivot on the right foot to turn 180 degrees to make the throw to first.

a

b

Figure 3.17
Second baseman's push-off. *(a)* Push hard off the left foot and *(b)* and transfer weight to the right foot to step and throw to first.

• **Shortstop drag**—The shortstop approaches with her chest toward the thrower and receives the ball as she takes a small step on the right foot before the bag (see figure 3.18a). The shortstop then steps completely across the bag with the left foot in the direction of the throw and drags the toe of the right foot across the middle of the bag (see figure 3.18b). Using the middle of the bag allows for a margin of error in either direction and helps the umpire see contact. The shortstop then steps with the right foot behind the left foot (see figure 3.18c), turns the shoulders parallel to the base line (see figure 3.18d), steps with the left foot toward the target, and throws. Step, drag, step, step. The player must be sure to do all four steps before throwing.

Figure 3.18
Shortstop's drag. *(a)* Take a small step on the right foot before the bag to receive the ball, *(b)* step completely across the bag with the left foot and drag the toe of the right foot across the middle of the bag, *(c)* step with the right foot behind the left foot, and *(d)* turn the shoulders parallel to the base line to step with the left foot and throw.

a

b

c

d

- **Second-base drag**—The footwork is reversed for the second baseman. She takes a small step on the left foot before the bag (see figure 3.19a), steps with the right foot across the bag and drags with the left foot (see figure 3.19b), and steps with left foot toward first base to make the throw (see figure 3.19c). This sequence requires only three steps: step, drag, step.

The pivot clears the base path but stays close to the bag and keeps her body compact. When stepping across the base the player keeps the heel of the stepping foot only two to three inches from the base. The pivot's step forward is directly toward first base for the shortest, quickest throw.

a

b

c

Figure 3.19 Second baseman's drag. *(a)* Take a small step on the left foot before the bag, *(b)* step with the right foot across the bag and drag with the left foot, and *(c)* step with the left foot toward first base to make the throw.

INFIELD PRACTICE DRILLS

When practicing with all infielders in their defensive positions, the key is to keep everyone active. Combination drills with throws to various bases keep everyone in the game. Drills should be fast paced so there is little standing around. Use a catcher and a hitter on both sides of home plate to double the amount of balls hit, but be sure to make it clear which base each fielder is throwing to.

When hitting to the infield have the catcher place the next ball in the hitter's extended hand. This allows the hitter to keep her eyes on the infield play and replaces a toss that too often ends up in the hitter's face. Create pressure through competition to make the drills more gamelike, and add runners to allow the defense to develop the timing and game speed that is required. Use a variety of ground ball drills and specific game situations to make sure all techniques are covered, and don't overlook drills that improve conditioning. The following combination drills add variety to your infield practice while accomplishing several goals.

Short Throw to First

Purpose: To practice pivot footwork while saving the pivot player's arm.

Procedure: A feeder has a bucket of balls from which to feed the pivot. One pivot or a single-file line of several players can perform the drill. The feeder throws to the pivot from a distance of about 15 feet, from either the shortstop or second-base side of the infield. (You can also include feeds from the pitcher's position to the shortstop, who makes the pivot.) The receiver is several steps from the base facing the feeder. She catches the ball, turns the pivot, and makes a short throw to the first baseman, who is set up on the base line midway between first and second. The emphasis is on making the pivot, so the pivot player can save her arm by throwing to the first baseman at half the normal distance. The pivot player returns to repeat the drill or goes to the end of the line.

Variation: Set up obstacles in the base path directly in front of second base to make the pivot more difficult and realistic. A football dummy or stuffed equipment bag can simulate a sliding runner.

Turning the Double Play

Purpose: To turn double plays as in a game.

Procedure: Infielders assume normal double-play defensive positions. The shortstop and second baseman shade several steps toward second. The hitter at home hits ground balls to all infielders so that they can practice proper angles, feeds, and pivots. Don't forget to include the pitcher and the catcher fielding and throwing to second base. Include all types of hits—slow grounders, high bouncers, and hard shots—to all parts of the infield.

Variations:

- Practice the pivot with a runner coming to second, first standing and then sliding.

- Use two runners, home to first and first to second, so that you can gauge the time element.

Rotating Infield

Purpose: To work on throws from the four basic infield positions and the first baseman's technique for tagging the base. This is an excellent tryout drill. It is also an effective conditioning drill when using no more than five infielders.

Procedure: Draw lines on the infield at the four positions where you want the players to field the ball (see figure 3.20). Five infielders line up behind line 1 at third base. All field a ball at that spot, throw to first, and then run to wait their turn behind line 2 at the shortstop position. Have the hitter hit to all fielders in line before going to the next spot and the new line. At each line, fielders throw to first and run immediately to the next spot, where they can rest. Position 3 is near second base. Here, the emphasis is on showing the ball and using a three-quarter or sidearm throw so that the first baseman can always see the

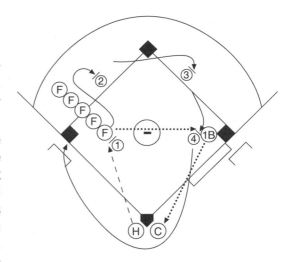

Figure 3.20 Rotating infield drill.

ball. Position 4 is a slow roller toward first base. The fielder charges, fields the ball well in front of the base, throws to first, and then runs behind the hitter to the third-base line to continue the drill. The first baseman does not field any balls, working instead on proper technique at the bag, always tagging the base for the out. She returns each ball to a catcher at home, who feeds the hitter. The first baseman should ignore all balls that she cannot catch so that she is ready for the next throw. The hitter hits the next ball as soon as she hears the previous ball smack the first baseman's glove. This drill should be done quickly.

Safety Reminders:

- The first baseman ignores all throws she cannot catch cleanly so that she can be ready for the next throw.

- Infielders must make sure the first baseman is ready to receive the ball. This is good practice in looking to see the target before throwing, a routine infielders should always follow in a game.

- Infielders must run to the next line so that they are not in the way of the hit or throw. From first base they run behind the hitter.

Merry-Go-Round

Purpose: To warm up or work on conditioning while fielding ground balls.

Procedure: Players form two fielding lines at opposite corners of the infield—one to the left of second base and one at home (see figure 3.21). Be careful that the players in line at second do not trip over the base. Two hitters hit or throw from the pitching-circle area, one to each line. Players field and run to the end of the opposite line. Hitters hit ground balls, fly balls, range balls, line drives, and scoops. Players return the ball to their hitter or place it in a bucket at the line they are running to. Hitters should have a bucket of extra balls to replace balls that fielders miss so the drill can be done at a steady pace.

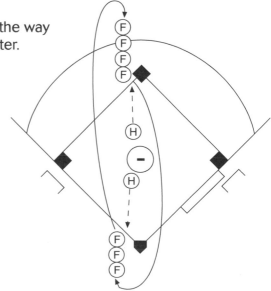

Figure 3.21 Merry-go-round drill.

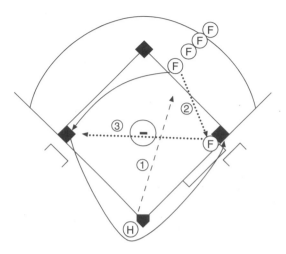

Figure 3.22 Four corners drill.

Four Corners

Purpose: To work on conditioning and on making accurate throws to first and third.

Procedure: A hitter hits to an infielder at second base, who is first in a line that players have formed there. One fielder is at first base. The fielder fields the ball, throws to first, and sprints to third base to receive a return throw from the player at first (see figure 3.22). The fielder must be at third in proper receiving position (left foot against home-plate side of third), where she catches the ball and applies a tag. The fielder then sprints home to give the ball to the hitter and runs behind the hitter on the way to first, getting there in time to catch the throw to first on the next hit ball. The fielder catches the ball at first base, throws back to the next fielder at third base, and goes to the end of the line at second base to wait for her next turn. Use no more than five players so that there is not a lot of standing around. Have an extra bucket of balls at home and first in case of errant throws.

Infield Loop

Purpose: To work on conditioning and fielding ground balls.

Procedure: Three fielders form a line at third, and a first baseman and catcher take their normal positions (see figure 3.23). A softball is placed on the mound. A hitter at home hits to the first fielder at the third-base defensive position. The player fields the ball and throws to first. She then runs to the ball on the mound and throws it to first. (Balls thrown to first are thrown immediately by the first baseman to the catcher at home.) The fielder runs around behind second base, fields another ball hit to the shortstop position, and throws that ball home. The hitter rolls a ball out to same fielder, who is charging toward home. She fields that ball and places it on the mound. The drill continues with the next fielder. Don't forget to have the catcher and first baseman do the drill.

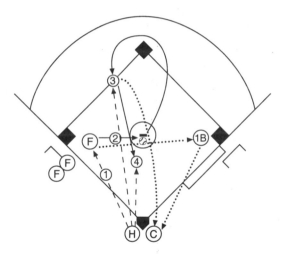

Figure 3.23 Infield loop drill.

4 × 4 Gut

Purpose: To add pressure to fielding and throwing to all the bases. Infielders practice covering the bases. The drill creates competition.

Procedure: Infielders take normal defensive positions with a hitter and catcher at home. The hitter hits four times to one player, who fields the balls and throws in order to home, first, second, and third. If an error occurs she must start over. The cycle is repeated three times.

4

Outfield

When a ball gets through the infield, it is just a hit. When a ball gets by the outfield, it is usually a run and often means a win for the other team. The outfield is the last line of defense. Outfielders are not often noticed until they make a mistake. Good outfielders make catches look easy. They are smooth, not flashy. Outfielders should have pride in a job well done and a philosophy that no catchable ball will ever drop in their area, that no hit will ever get by them, and that no runner will ever run on them.

Although some skills will vary by position, all three outfielders should share the following characteristics:

- Good speed and agility
- Strong overhand throw
- Sure-handed
- Ability to anticipate and get a jump on the ball
- Good judgment under pressure
- A love of catching fly balls
- Stay focused and alert

The center fielder should be the fastest of the outfielders because she has the most area to cover. She must get a good jump on the ball and be aggressive. The center fielder has priority on all balls. She should be a good diver because she can afford to gamble knowing that a teammate will back her up on every attempt. The center fielder needs to be a vocal leader because she needs to communicate to the other outfielders and the middle infielders. Your best outfielder usually plays center field.

The right fielder has the longest throw to third base, so the most important consideration is the strength of her throws. A left-handed thrower is in the best position to make throws from the right-field line, but the most important consideration is throwing ability. A right fielder who can charge ground balls well and release the ball quickly is a real asset because she can turn what looks like a hit to right into an out at first.

The left fielder has the left-field line to cover. A right-hander has a slightly easier throw on balls hit down the line, but here too the more important factor is throwing ability. The left fielder's longest throw is to home, so her arm can be the weakest of the three outfielders. The left fielder should have the ability to go back well because most batters are right-handed and their hard-hit balls will be in that direction.

THROWING

Outfielders need to develop a quick release, good velocity, and accuracy on their throws. The long throw often required of outfielders demands particular attention to the mechanics of the overhand throw and the long bounce throw. For extra strength on a throw, outfielders may need to use the crow hop. Review the section on long throws and the drills in chapter 2 (pages 24, 31–35). On the overhand throw outfielders should think "over the top" and exaggerate the follow-through by reaching forward and picking up grass. They should focus on a straight-line throw with good vertical backward spin to get the perfect bounce on the throw to the plate. The ball should come off the fingertips with the thumb pointing toward the ground. Outfielders should snap the wrist down and feel the fingers pulling on the seams.

Outfielders throw on a direct line in the air when close to the base or when throwing to an infielder for a relay. When the distance is too great for a quick, straight shot, the throw goes to the relay person or bounces 10 to 15 feet in front of the receiver. Throws to the relay person should be to the glove-side shoulder. Throws to the bases for a force should be chest high and knee high for a tag. Throws home from left field must be inside or outside the base path to avoid hitting the runner. On throws home the target is the plate no matter where the cutoff person is. The throw goes to the plate and through the chest of the cutoff.

When warming up, outfielders should include long-distance throwing to stretch and develop all the muscles involved in making longer throws. Players start about 30 feet apart and gradually back up to a distance of about 100 feet. During games, outfielders should keep their arms warm between innings by throwing among themselves (left to center to right and back) or by using an extra player from the bench to warm up the nearest outfielder. They throw sharply and accurately using correct technique.

Using the one-step throw allows outfielders to get rid of the ball quickly. By fielding with the throwing-side foot forward, the player needs to take just one step to throw. A right-handed thrower fields the ball with the right foot forward, then steps with the left and throws. The crow hop is added when the player needs more velocity on the ball or lacks arm strength. An outfielder may start with either foot forward, depending on the position of the feet when fielding the ball. A player will probably come to prefer either the left or the right foot forward and will automatically adjust the feet to be in that position.

• **Crow hop starting on the left leg**—A right-handed thrower fields the ball with the weight on the forward left leg (see figure 4.1a on page 66). Then, when turning sideways to throw, she brings the right foot to the heel of the left foot (see figure 4.1b). The thrower hops on the right foot, steps forward with the left foot in the direction of the throw, and transfers the weight forward onto the left foot as she throws (see figure 4.1c). The outfielder should develop a rhythm or smoothness in executing the crow hop.

• **Crow hop starting on the right leg**—A right-handed thrower fields the ball with the weight on the forward right leg (see figure 4.2a on page 66). After fielding the ball she turns sideways while hopping on the right foot (see figure 4.2b), steps with the left foot to the target, throws, and transfers the weight forward onto the left foot.

Coaching Points for the Outfielder's Throw

- On short throws use one step and throw.
- On medium to long throws use the crow hop.
- An overhand throw is essential to avoid straining the arm and to create good vertical spin.
- Exaggerate the follow-through by reaching for the grass.
- Make straight-line throws—no rainbows.
- On throws to home bounce the ball 15 feet in front of the catcher. Two bounces are better than no bounce.

CATCHING FLY BALLS

The basic ready fielding position is described in chapter 1. The key is to be in a balanced position ready to move quickly to the ball. As noted, outfielders in their ready position generally hold their gloves a little higher than infielders do (see figure 1.3 on

a   b   c

Figure 4.1   Crow hop starting on the left leg. *(a)* Field the ball with the left leg forward, *(b)* turn sideways to throw and bring the right foot to the heel of the left foot, and *(c)* step forward with the left foot in the direction of the throw.

a   b

Figure 4.2   Crow hop starting on the right leg. *(a)* Field the ball with the right leg forward and *(b)* turn sideways while hopping on the right foot before stepping with the left foot to throw.

page 4). Players should use proper catching techniques whenever possible but must remember that the goal is to catch everything. See the ball, catch the ball. On routine fly balls the catch should always be made with both hands slightly above the head and in front of the throwing shoulder. Players track the ball all the way into the glove.

Footwork

An outfielder's first movement when the ball is hit is back—a short drop step of two or three inches. This step back puts the body in motion and prevents the player from being caught back on her heels. The drop step is the key to having quick reactions. The player makes the drop step back and locates the ball. Then, after reading the ball, the fielder decides the angle she needs to take to catch the ball. Drop step, locate, go on an angle to the ball.

For balls hit in front of her, after the drop step the outfielder pushes off the back foot and goes directly to the ball. For balls to the sides, the jab step followed by the crossover step (see chapter 1, page 8) is used. For balls diagonally back, a quick pivot off the drop step to get in position and then an inside or outside roll is most effective.

On balls diagonally back and over her head, after the first drop step the outfielder turns to the side that she perceives the ball is coming. If the outfielder misjudges the ball or it drifts to the other side and is no longer in sight, an inside or outside roll is used to turn to the opposite side (see chapter 1, page 13).

Players should not think too much about footwork. Quick feet, balance, and good judgment are the keys to getting to the spot where the ball can be caught. Players should practice so that they are balanced and comfortable going after every type of ball.

As an outfielder runs with her back to home after a ball directly over her head, the ball will occasionally drift from one shoulder to the other. By simply turning her head to the opposite shoulder, she can locate the ball for the catch.

The outfielder should run on the balls of the feet with a smooth stride to prevent jarring her eyes and blurring her vision. She should glide to the ball using good running technique, pumping the arms back and forth while keeping them close by her side, and reach for the ball with the glove at the last second.

Angle to the Ball

To catch the ball, the outfielder must first reach the spot where it will come down. Great outfielders get there early and are waiting for the ball, making the catch look routine. If the ball is high enough and in front of her, the player can circle around it to get in the best catching and throwing position, but she must use a direct angle to hard-hit balls when the first concern is simply getting to it.

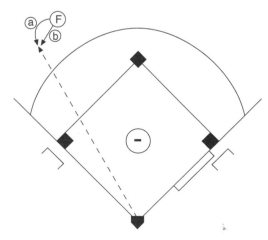

• **Circle around the ball**—On routine fly balls the ideal technique is to circle around the ball, line up with the receiver, and be waiting for the ball (see figure 4.3). This requires the outfielder to know the direction of the hit before the catch and to be where the ball would land in time to back off and gather momentum into the throw. She should sprint to a spot about 10 feet beyond where the ball would land. The player never drifts to the ball; instead, she hurries and is there waiting. She moves her body around the ball to face the direction of the throw before making contact with it. The outfielder should track the ball from the hitter's contact spot to the glove. She times the approach so that when she touches the

Figure 4.3 Circling around the ball (a) versus taking a direct angle to the ball (b).

ball all the momentum is moving forward and through the ball on line with the target. Players should use this technique for ground balls as well.

• **Direct angle to the ball**—A player often doesn't have the time to circle and be waiting for the ball. Quickness to the ball is the goal, and moving to the ball in a straight line on a direct angle is always the fastest way to cover any distance (see figure 4.3). The player sprints directly to the spot where she will field the ball and then turns her body abruptly to face the ball as she fields it.

Diving for Balls

Outfielders can usually take the chance of diving for short fly balls in front of them. Because of the trajectory, the ball won't go far even if it is not catchable. On the other hand it is risky for left or right fielders to dive for a line drive that is between them and the foul line because there is no backup. Outfielders can dive for balls that are falling between them if they are sure the other outfielder can get to the backup position should the ball get through.

Coaching Points for Catching Fly Balls

- Always catch with two hands. The ideal position is above the head and in front of the throwing shoulder.
- The first movement of your body is a short drop step back.
- Locate the ball and determine the angle you should take.
- When time permits, circle around the ball and take your momentum forward through the ball on line with the target.
- When you need to be quick, use a direct angle to the ball. Sprint to the spot for the catch and then turn to the target to throw.
- Always attempt to keep your eyes on the ball.
- Be comfortable with both the inside and outside rolls. Use quick feet to maintain balance.
- Run on the balls of your feet using good running technique. Don't extend your glove until the last moment.

CATCHING GROUND BALLS

To field ground balls, the outfielder should keep the ball in front of the body. She positions the feet slightly closer together than an infielder would when fielding ground balls. Ground balls can be categorized as controllable (rolling smoothly and slower) or uncontrollable (bouncing wildly). The game situation dictates how each should be played:

1. No reason to take a chance of misplaying the ball.
2. There is an advantage in taking a slight chance that the ball will get through.
3. Do it or go home a loser.

Blocking

When there is no possible play for a putout and no reason to take a chance, the outfielder blocks the ball. This technique should always be used on a sure hit with no runners on base, with uncontrollable balls, and on very rough ground when there is no backup should the ball get by. The goal is to make a wall behind the ball to eliminate the possibility that it will get by. The fielder runs directly to the ball, assumes a set position in line with the path of the ball, and waits for it to come the last 8 to 10 feet. She turns sideways to the ball in a stride position and drops on the back knee. The knee should be against the heel of the front foot with the shin of the back leg lying parallel to the ground (see figure 4.4). The shoelaces of the back foot are flat on the ground so that the leg forms a barrier to the ball. The outfielder twists the upper body so that the chest remains facing the ball. She places the glove on the ground in front of her body to catch the ball.

Some players may feel comfortable using either leg, depending on the direction they are running. Players can choose to use the same leg on every play, however, because they have enough time to turn themselves in the proper position.

Figure 4.4 Blocking the ball in the outfield.

One-Hand Scoop

Outfielders use the one-hand scoop when a play to the infield is an option, for example, a throw to a base on a force play. This technique is safest on controllable balls or when a backup is in position. The outfielder charges hard at the ball and in the direction of the throw. To do this, she may have to come around the ball slightly. The outfielder keeps the ball in front of the body and is square to it when fielding. She stretches the glove in front of her body, keeping the glove low to the ground and concentrating on forward momentum. The fielder tracks the ball all the way to the glove. The glove action is a snap up or a slight give to control the ball. If giving or gathering the ball, the player makes sure the glove is well out in front of the body so that even with the backward give, the glove remains in front of the body. Some players have a tendency to draw the glove too far back and run past the ball.

Should the play be made in front of the body or to the side? By fielding the ball in front of the body, the player can still block a ball she can't handle. Fielding to the side is a little more advanced and more comfortable for some, but doing so increases the odds that a ball will get by. Review the section on running through the ball in chapter 1. Because outfielders are scooping to go after a runner, they should practice short throws to the bases from the scoop, throwing or flipping in one step.

Do or Die

In some situations the game is over if the play is not made. So regardless of the type of ball (a hard shot, uncontrollable bounces, the ball bouncing close to the feet, or a shot to the player's side), the outfielder must try to make the catch. She may have to short hop it or reach to the side without attempting to block it as she would in different circumstances when playing it safe. She must charge directly to the ball, keeping her body under control. The fielder scoops up the ball using the technique described earlier for a one-hand scoop but without attention to fielding it safely. The main difference is the speed of the approach to the ball. Although the player is gambling with her glove work, she must maintain balance to have a chance at making the play. The player should estimate the time she has to make the play so that she does not commit an error by rushing more than necessary. On sinking line drives the fielder will have to short hop the ball and hope to catch it.

Coaching Points for Catching Ground Balls

- Your goal is to always keep the ball in front of your body.
- Know the game situation. Can you afford to take a chance?
- Always block uncontrollable balls unless it is a do-or-die game situation.
- Scoop controllable balls when there is a possible infield play.
- Dive for short fly balls in front of you.
- Don't dive for hard-hit balls if there is no backup.
- Always be aware of your backup before you commit.

BASIC POSITIONING AND ADJUSTMENTS

Outfielders must consider several factors in positioning themselves. Additional information on adjusting to the game situation and the importance of communicating adjustments are covered in "Defensive Positioning" in chapter 7. Outfielders must consider these items:

- Their abilities. How well does each outfielder go up, back, sideways? What is the strength of their arms?

- Speed, strengths, and weaknesses of adjacent players. Outfielders should use the strengths of their teammates and help with their weaknesses.

- The ability of the infielders in front of them to go back.

- The type of pitcher, pitch, and pitch location. The kind of pitch and the speed with which it is thrown has an expected outcome. Outfielders should adjust in for a drop-ball pitcher and back for a predominately rise-ball pitcher. If the pitcher is slow, the outfield looks for the batter to pull the ball. When playing behind a pitcher with speed, the outfielder expects late swings and more balls to the opposite field. Outfielders should know the count. If the pitcher is ahead, they pull in. If the pitcher is behind, they shade to the power alley and back up a few steps.

- Type of hitter. Outfielders should move back a few steps for the power hitters and pull way in for the slappers. Which way is the batter trying to hit the ball? With an open stance to pull the ball? Or with a closed stance to hit to the opposite field? Shifts may be made according to the hitter's tendencies and by knowing how the pitcher is going to pitch to the hitter. Outfielders must be careful not to leave significant gaps that can hurt the team should the pitcher miss her spot or hang a pitch. Shifts should be only a few steps in the direction the batter is expected to hit the ball. The defense should play an unknown batter in regular position.

- Number of outs, inning, and score. Do the outfielders play aggressively or safe? When the team is ahead late in the game, they play a few steps deeper to prevent extra-base hits and don't gamble on line drives or hard-hit ground balls. With the winning run on third base and less than two out, they play in close enough that on a fly ball they can comfortably throw out the runner. A deep fly ball ends the game, so they don't have to worry about a ball over their heads.

- Distance and height of the fence. The outfield can use a high fence as an extra player and play in several steps. A deep fence or no fence means that they have to play back so that nothing gets by for extra bases.

By knowing the pitch to be thrown, outfielders have valuable information about what to expect. Having the infield signal when the pitcher is throwing a change can help the outfield adjust. When a pickoff is called, outfielders need to know so that they can be prepared to back up the throw. By continuously talking and reviewing the game situation, the number of outs, and the speed of any runners, players will be less likely to make mental errors. Outfielders are in position to spot a steal attempt and should help alert the infield. Talking helps keep everyone's head in the game and results in a cohesive, coordinated team effort.

OUTFIELD RESPONSIBILITIES

Outfielders never just stand around—on every play there is something to do. From backing up infielders to covering bases or rundowns, outfielders have many responsibilities. Catching a fly ball may appear easy but catching the "betweeners" requires a lot of teamwork. With runners on base the priority is getting the ball quickly to the infield and knowing where to throw. Outfielders also need to learn to play the fence and to use the rules to their advantage. They must understand their position well.

Runners on Base

Deciding where to throw the ball is the most difficult decision outfielders must make. The choice must often be made in a high-pressure situation. Before each pitch the outfielders should review the situation and anticipate the play they may have to make. How fast are the runners? What are the capabilities of the batter? Is the opposing coach aggressive or conservative? Knowing what to expect can help the outfield respond more quickly. Knowledge gives confidence, and confidence improves execution.

As soon as the outfielder catches the ball, she must get it to the infield. She cannot stand and hold the ball. The outfielder makes the play on the lead runner when possible. When she is unlikely to throw out a runner, she tries to keep the back runner from advancing.

When the runner is obviously not going, the outfielder can run the ball in or throw to the relay infielder. Closing the gap by running toward the infield helps eliminate errors on the throw. But the outfielder must first make sure that the runner is not going anywhere.

If there is no play, the outfielder can try to make one. When a ball is hit to the outfield with the bases loaded and two outs, all runners must get safely to the next base for the run to count. The slowest runner is usually the runner going to second because that runner has a tendency to slow and watch the play at home. A quick throw to second can end the inning. In any bases-loaded situation, the outfielder should look for someone to throw out if she can't get the lead runner.

Betweeners

Balls hit between players must be caught. Fear of a collision, however, often causes a player to back off the play and leave it for another. When both back off, the ball drops without a play being made. Players need to understand which fielder has priority and communicate clearly about who will make the catch.

The outfielder always has priority over an infielder because the outfielder is in a better position to make the play. The outfielders are moving in to make the play, so the ball and all possible plays are in front of them. Infielders should go back hard after the ball until an outfielder calls for it. The ball should be called for early so the infielder can get out of the outfielder's way. If the infielder is to make the play, the outfielder acts as a backup. The outfielders must avoid coming so close that their footsteps or shadows scare the infielders off the ball.

The center fielder is usually the strongest outfielder and generally has priority over the other outfielders. The coach should clarify this after evaluating individual abilities. Players should understand and accept strengths and weaknesses, and practice giving way when appropriate. For example, when a ball is hit past two outfielders, the one with the stronger arm should make the throw. Position will also determine who can best make the play. On a ball hit between center and right, a right-handed right fielder is in the best position to throw to third.

Outfielders should not back off the ball too early. Each fielder should assume that she alone is making the play. Players must pursue the ball hard until one of them calls for it. On many fly balls two outfielders could make the catch, so it is critical that the ball be called for early and decisively with an understanding of who has priority. Players should call for a fly ball when it is at its highest point. The other outfielder then backs up the play and, if possible, checks the runner and tells the fielder where to throw.

Backing Up

Errors will occur and balls will get by fielders, but a good backup will limit the damage. Outfielders should hustle to back up every hit ball and throw. From the backup position a player can also help direct the throw. Backup responsibilities do not end until all possibilities of further action are exhausted (see table 4.1 on page 74 for a summary of the backup responsibilities of each outfielder).

Outfielders must hustle to back up the adjacent outfielder going for the ball. The backup player should be 10 to 12 feet behind the fielder in a position to react to a ball that gets through (see figure 4.5). Only then can the outfielder making the play try for the ball confidently and aggressively. Knowing that someone is behind her gives her the freedom to dive for balls.

On balls to the infield, the appropriate outfielder should move directly to the ball with the assumption that the ball

Figure 4.5 Outfield backup position.

will get by the infielder. All fielders should take several steps to the ball until it is clear which player is in the best position to be the primary backup.

If the ball is not hit in a particular outfielder's direction, she has responsibility to back up a base. The outfielder lines up with the anticipated throw and 10 to 12 feet behind the base. The center fielder is the primary backup for second base. The left fielder covers third base and backs up second base on throws from the right side when the center fielder is not able to be there. The right fielder always backs up first on every throw from the infield. When the ball is hit toward the second baseman, the right fielder must first play the ball. If the infielder fields it, the right fielder hustles to back up the throw. On all other infield ground balls, the right fielder must instantly sprint to backup position behind first base.

Outfielders must also be ready to adjust for secondary throws. A good example occurs when the center fielder is backing up second base on a sacrifice-bunt attempt. With a runner on first,

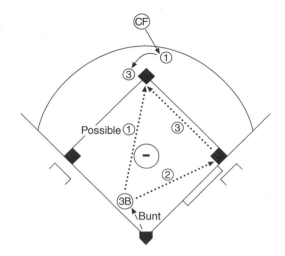

Figure 4.6 Center fielder's backup adjustments.

the infielder fielding the bunt first looks to second to make the throw. The center fielder must line up expecting that throw. If the infielder changes her mind and throws instead to first, the center fielder must quickly adjust her position toward left field to back up a possible pickoff attempt from first (see figure 4.6). During defensive practice, players should occasionally overthrow bases to make sure backups are in correct position to make the catch.

Covering Bases

In some instances outfielders need to cover a base. They should know the proper footwork to cover the base and know how to apply a tag (see chapter 3, pages 52–53). On a bunt the left fielder should be prepared to cover third base if the shortstop has gone to second and the third baseman is fielding the bunt. On a bunt with a runner on second, the center fielder covers second because the shortstop is covering third. See table 4.1 for a summary of the base-coverage responsibilities of each outfielder.

Rundowns

When runners are caught in a rundown, the outfielders are often part of the defensive rotation. Review the techniques involved (see chapter 7, page 141) on team defense and see table 4.1 on page 74 for a summary of the rundown responsibilities of each outfielder.

Playing the Fence

Outfielders must have no fear of playing the fence. Right and left fielders must contend not only with the outfield fence but also with a sideline fence. Outfielders must know how the ball rebounds off the fence and how the fence will absorb body contact. If it is a breakaway fence, they should practice going through it while making a catch. High fly balls often permit the outfielder the luxury of first finding the fence and then focusing on the ball. Counting and remembering the number of running steps to the fence from the normal playing position can help the player know where the fence is when making a play. When making a catch near the fence, the bent-leg slide is a safe option. For more details see fence play in chapter 1, page 14.

Table 4.1
Outfield Defensive Responsibilities for Backups, Base Coverage, and Rundowns

Left fielder

Backs up: Balls hit to nonglove side of shortstop, third baseman, and center field; throws to second base from the right side.

Covers: Third base any time shortstop must go to second and when third baseman cannot get back.

Rundowns: Behind third baseman.

Center fielder

Backs up: Balls hit to glove side of shortstop, nonglove side of second baseman, pitcher, left and right field; throws to second including pickoff plays from catcher at second.

Covers: Second base when second baseman or shortstop are committed elsewhere, for example, bunt with runner at second.

Rundowns: Behind second baseman.

Special plays: May cover second on surprise pickoff play from catcher.

Right fielder

Backs up: Balls hit to first base, glove side of second baseman, and center field; all throws to first base; throws to second base from left field.

Covers: First base when first and second basemen are committed elsewhere.

Rundowns: Behind first baseman.

KNOW THE RULES

Players must clearly understand the rules that govern dead-ball situations and the effects of the catch-and-carry rule. With runners on base outfielders should not catch and carry the ball out of bounds unless they can afford to give runners a free base. When there is not a fence around the field, lines placed at least 25 feet beyond and parallel to the foul lines are used to indicate what is in-bounds and what is out-of-bounds. A catch-and-carry means that a player catches the ball in bounds to get the batter out but then carries the ball into out-of-bounds (dead-ball) territory by stepping beyond the line. Play is stopped, and if the catch didn't make the third out of the inning all runners automatically advance an extra base (so a runner on third would score). Catching a ball and falling over the fence produces an out as long as the fielder holds on to the ball, but catching the ball and then falling into dead-ball territory gives the runners a free base. Outfielders should not play a ball that is trapped (caught in a fence) unless doing so is to the team's advantage. Fielders should put up their hands to indicate the ball is trapped or has gone through a hole in the fence. Runners will get the base they are going to and one more when the umpire calls that the ball is trapped. By playing the ball and keeping it live the runner may go for as many bases as she can. If the award of two bases keeps the runner from scoring, the fielders should not play a trapped ball and make it live but should instead take the umpire's ruling. Similarly, if the ball is headed out-of-bounds, fielders should choose to let it go and limit the runners' advance to two bases.

Outfielders must know when to catch foul balls. With a runner on third they should not catch a deep foul ball unless the team can afford to give up a run when the base runner tags up. (With a big lead the out is sometimes more important than the run.) On foul balls close to the line, the base player can see the line better and should tell the outfielder whether to catch the ball or let it go. If in doubt as to whether the ball is fair or foul, players should assume it is fair.

OUTFIELD DRILLS

Outfielders must love to catch fly balls and should have the opportunity to do so every day. Footwork and confidence can be developed using toss drills at a short distance. With a partner, players can roll grounders and toss fly balls to work on the basic skills. Every day, players should use the footwork drills for catching fly balls covered in chapter 1 on page 18. Machines can throw balls of all types (bloopers, line drives, deep flys, and grounders), so outfielders can work at regular distance on the skills needed. Batting practice provides the opportunity to practice playing balls off the bat. Outfielders should play their regular positions and use proper technique. No opportunity to improve should be wasted. Because 90 percent of all outfield balls are in front of the outfielders, practice should emphasize skills relevant to those balls. Coaches and players must be aware of the danger of overusing the arm. Outfielders can save their arms by returning balls to buckets instead of throwing long distance on every play.

Killers

Purpose: To practice getting behind the ball while fielding and to improve conditioning.

Procedure: Partners stand about 30 feet apart. One partner tosses a ball to various spots in front of the fielder, who runs to get behind the ball, makes the catch, and makes a good return throw to the tosser. The tosser throws balls for one minute before the players rotate.

Around the Ball

Purpose: To practice circling around the ball when catching fly balls.

Procedure: Outfielders form a single-file line. A catcher sets up to the left of a hitter. The fungo hitter hits high, soft fly balls to the left side of the outfielder, high enough to allow the fielder time to get in position. The outfielder comes around the ball to line up for a throw to the catcher (see figure 4.7). Repeat the drill in the opposite direction with the catcher setting up to the right of the hitter.

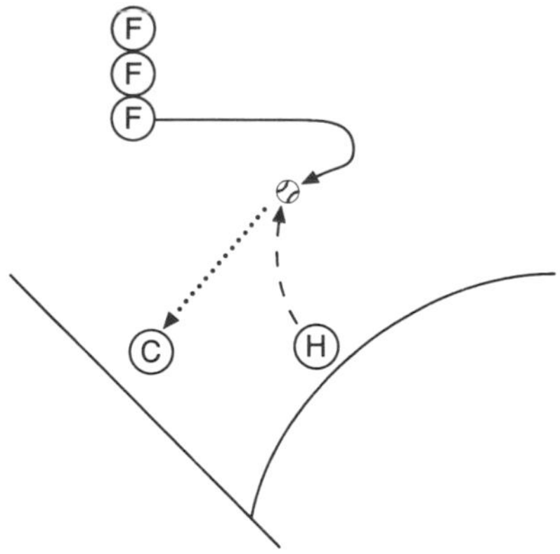

Figure 4.7 Around the ball drill.

Shoot the Gap

Purpose: To practice getting behind a hit ball in the ideal fielding position.

Procedure: Fielders are in line behind the left foul line with a hitter and catcher at home plate. Each fielder starts on the foul line, and the ball is hit in the gap between left field and center field. The fielder makes an intense effort to field the ball while facing the catcher. Have a group competition, awarding one point for fielding the ball, one point for a good throw, and one point for fielding the ball facing the catcher. Go to the opposite foul line and repeat from that side.

Fence Drill

Purpose: To learn to play the fence.

Procedure: This drill uses outfielders, a relay, and a catcher. The outfielders form a line in left, right, or center field. A tosser about 15 feet from the fence throws the ball so that it lands against the fence. From a fielding position about 20 feet in front of the fence, an outfielder goes quickly to the fence, plants her foot against it, picks up the ball, listens for the relay's voice, and throws to her. Emphasize the bent front leg for the throw and hitting the relay.

Variation: To save the relay's arm, save time, and eliminate the need for a catcher, the relay can fake throw home (still using proper technique) and put the ball in a bucket.

Covering Drill

Purpose: To have adjacent outfielders practice communicating, taking an angle to the ball, and backing up each other.

Procedure: Two lines of outfielders about 40 feet apart face a hitter with a catcher. Balls are hit between the two fielders. One outfielder calls for the ball and takes the direct (short) angle to the ball. The other outfielder takes a deep (long) angle and backs up her teammate, ready to field the ball. Players can put balls in buckets to save time and arms. Players rotate to the end of the opposite line.

Down the Line, Up the Alley

Purpose: To practice fielding balls and taking angles for balls down the line and in the alleys.

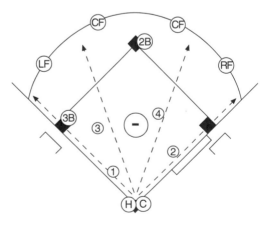

Procedure: This drill requires four outfielders, receivers at second base and third base, a hitter, and a catcher (see figure 4.8). Because the center fielder is always involved on balls to the gap, it is best to use two—one in left center and one in right center. The left and right fielders are in normal position. The ball is fungoed alternately to the two pairs of outfielders in the alley and down the line. The first ball is hit down the left-field line, the second to the right-field line, the third to the left-field alley, and the fourth to the right-field alley. Outfielders work on short-angle and deep-angle coverage and hitting the relay or bases. Have each fielder throw to both second and third base. Use extra outfielders or pitchers to cover the bases if the infielders are busy elsewhere. Have players return balls to the catcher or use a bucket at each base.

Figure 4.8 Down the line, up the alley drill.

Blooper Drill

Purpose: To communicate and establish coverage on balls hit between the infield and outfield.

Procedure: A catcher, middle infielders, and outfielders take their normal fielding positions. Use a ball machine or fungo bat to hit bloopers between the infielders and outfielders. Emphasize the infield going back hard until called off. If necessary, outfielders should dive for bloopers to make the catch. Players return the ball to the catcher at home, who feeds the hitter or machine.

Outfield Around

Purpose: To practice fielding all types of hits and throwing to bases from all outfield positions.

Procedure: Use receivers at first and third, a hitter and catcher at home, and at least four outfielders because the drill requires a lot of running.

Round #1
1. Players form a line in right field. Each player fields a ground ball, scoops and throws to first, and sprints to center field.
2. The player catches a deep fly ball in left-center field and throws to third. She then sprints to left field.
3. She catches a fly ball hit down the left-field line and throws home. She sprints to right field, going behind home plate (see figure 4.9).

Round #2
1. From right field the outfielder comes around a ground ball and throws to third.
2. In center field she scoops a ground ball and throws home.
3. She catches a fly to the deep left-field alley and throws to third (see figure 4.9).

Round #3
1. The outfielder catches a fly ball to right field and throws home.
2. She catches a short fly to the right-field alley and throws to third.
3. In left field she fields a ground ball, runs toward second to hold the batter–base runner, and then sets and throws home (see figure 4.9).

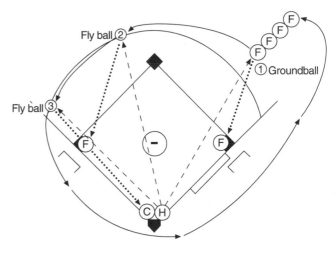

Round #1

(continued)

Figure 4.9 Outfield around drill.

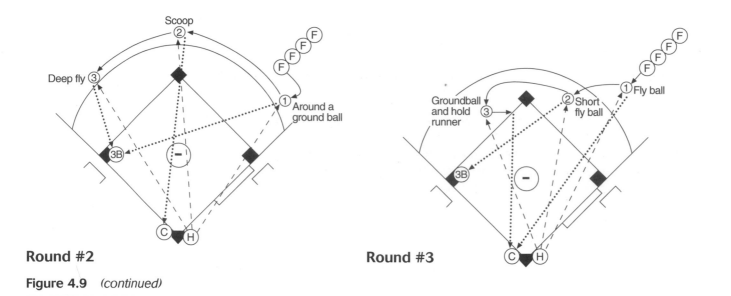

Round #2

Round #3

Figure 4.9 *(continued)*

Decision Drill

Purpose: To improve outfield decision making about whether to go for the lead runner or the batter.

Procedure: Use a full defense minus the pitcher with runners at home and first going on the hit. A runner at home starts on the right side of the plate out of the hitter's way and goes on contact to make the play realistic. She runs to first and joins the line there. The hitter hits various types of balls to the outfield. The fielder must decide whether to go for the lead runner or throw behind her and stop the second runner. Move runners to different starting positions and vary the types of balls played.

Scoring from Second to Home and Home to Second

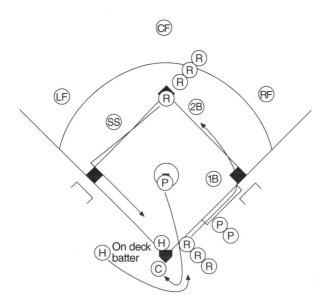

Figure 4.10 Scoring from second to home and home to second drill.

Purpose: To improve outfielder decision making on whether to go for the lead runner or the batter–base runner. The on-deck batter practices coaching the runner coming home, and pitchers practice backing up home.

Procedure: From home plate the hitter hits balls to all parts of the outfield. The runner attempts to score, and the batter tries to reach second (see figure 4.10). The runner at home starts on the right side of the plate out of the hitter's way and goes on contact to make the play realistic. The runner at second assumes a leadoff position and then reacts to the hit. The outfielder must choose to throw home or to the second baseman or shortstop covering second. The first baseman assumes the cutoff position. On the hit the pitcher immediately takes proper backup position at home (see chapter 5). The on-deck batter moves into position behind home plate, facing the runner and giving hand signals to the runner to stand or slide to one side of the plate or the other. Runners can actually slide or can stay upright and swing wide to the right to avoid any contact.

Players rotate. The runner going home moves to the on-deck batter circle (ready to coach the next runner at home) and then joins the runners at home. Pitchers rotate to the pitcher's mound from the line behind the first-base line.

Variation: Add the shortstop to practice relays on balls through or over the outfield.

Holding Runner to a Single

Purpose: To improve the left fielder's ability to hold the batter–base runner to a single.

Procedure: Several outfielders form a line in left field. A second baseman and catcher are at their normal positions. The outfielder assumes a normal defensive position. The hitter fungo hits down the left-field line. The runner makes an aggressive turn toward second, putting pressure on the left fielder to field the ball cleanly and hold the runner at first.

Variation: Add right fielders to practice proper backup of second base.

Weave Drill

Purpose: To improve conditioning while catching fly balls.

Procedure: Four players start in a line in left field (see figure 4.11). A tosser throws a ball to the first player, who fields and throws the ball back to the tosser and then runs toward center field to catch another ball thrown by the same person. The fielder returns that ball to another tosser at second base, who repeats the sequence as the fielder continues to run toward right field. A third thrower at first base repeats the sequence. Fielders wait in right field and then repeat the drill going the other way. This is a good drill for all players.

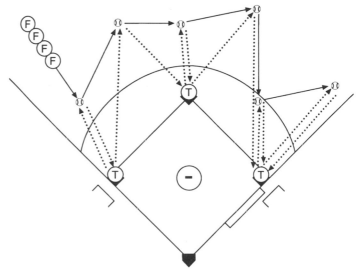

Figure 4.11   Weave drill.

Four in One

Purpose: To work on scoops, short hops, bloopers, and relays. This drill teaches aggressiveness and is a good conditioning drill when the line is not too long.

Procedure: Players stand in a single-file line about 20 feet from a tosser. They all complete each drill before moving to the next.

1. The first player runs toward the tosser and scoops a rolling ground ball. The fielder tosses the ball back and returns on the run to the end of the line. All in line complete drill #1 before the tosser starts the next drill (#2).

2. For drill #2 each player, in turn, fields a short hop, tosses the ball back, and returns to the end of the line.

3. In drill #3 each player fields a blooper, diving if necessary. The tosser simply pops (tosses) the ball up before the charging fielder. The fielder tosses the ball back and returns to the end of the line.

4. In the last drill players work on the relay throw. The first ball is a grounder that the fielder tosses back to the tosser. The fielder then turns to chase a ball thrown over her head. She gets the ball and hits the relay, who is the next person in line. The relay has moved out from the line and is waving her arms and calling for the ball. The relay makes the relay throw, then turns and runs toward the tosser to field a ground ball and continue the drill.

5

Pitching

In softball it is said that pitching is 90 percent of the game. Whether she is a beginner hoping to throw strikes or an overpowering ace who faces batters hoping to get a hit, the pitcher controls the game. Certain fundamental concepts and elements are the foundations for success for all pitchers, regardless of age, size, or individual quirks. But every pitcher is different. Therefore, pitchers must experiment with grips, mechanics, and style to find what works for them. There is also a difference between a thrower and a pitcher. What takes place above the shoulders will ultimately determine the label earned by the player.

Successful pitchers share several physical characteristics. Tall pitchers have longer arms, and those long levers can produce greater speed. Heavier pitchers can throw harder if they use their greater mass to advantage. Larger hands make it easier to apply different grips. Although these attributes are advantageous, some extremely successful pitchers are small in stature. Other desired attributes include arm strength, strong legs, endurance, flexibility, and coordination.

Besides physical attributes, successful pitchers also possess certain psychological traits and skills. On every pitch pitchers are always the focal point. They need poise, confidence, and discipline to handle the attention and the many situations that occur. Not everything goes as a pitcher wants it to. They must deal with umpires that don't give them the call, pitches that miss their target, and balls that are hit hard. Handling these challenges requires emotional control, discipline, and patience. Good recovery skills are necessary because pitchers must be ready to give their best on every pitch, sometimes immediately following a home run or a bad call. With the opportunity to control so much of the game, it is an advantage for pitchers to have an aggressive personality and a strong, competitive spirit. College pitchers should practice pitching every day, and young pitchers must practice regularly. Maintaining such a schedule requires a desire to excel, along with determination and dedication. As the center of attention pitchers who have leadership skills can do much to bring their teammates together as a team.

PITCHING STYLES

The two major pitching styles in softball are the windmill and the slingshot. Both have been used successfully at all levels. About 90 percent of pitchers today use the windmill delivery. Pitchers should try both styles and use the one that is most successful and comfortable for them. Please note that the following descriptions are for a right-handed pitcher.

Windmill

With the windmill technique the arm makes a full circle before the pitcher releases the ball. This full revolution permits the arm to gather speed and act as a whip to deliver the ball at great velocity. Using the windmill, top pitchers can throw the ball at 65 to 68 miles per hour. This delivery is glamorous because the full arm revolution is unique to softball pitchers. Because most pitchers use this delivery, the techniques described in the rest of the chapter assume a windmill delivery.

Slingshot

The slingshot is simply half of a windmill. The pitcher takes the ball back underhand from the glove and swings to a spot above the head before reversing the arm motion and pitching the ball. After the ball reaches the top of the backswing, all elements of the delivery are the same as those of the windmill. An advantage for the slingshot pitcher is that the hips open almost automatically toward third on the backswing of the arm. To increase the size of the backswing (the lever) for maximum arm and ball speed, the pitcher rotates the thumb upward and the palm away from the body as the arm extends back. Leading with the thumb and with a slight bend in the elbow, the pitcher can then get the ball to a position well above the head on the backswing.

THROWING THE FASTBALL

To learn the basic mechanics of throwing, the pitcher concentrates first on throwing a simple fastball, the foundation for all other pitches. Some pitcher's fastballs will naturally have some movement, which is a bonus. When a pitch doesn't move, it doesn't fool the batter and it can be hit very hard. For this reason some coaches of advanced pitchers ask their pitchers never to throw a straight fastball. For many pitchers, however, the fastball is an important pitch. Thrown with good location it can be an effective pitch on its own. Many pitchers rely on the fastball when they need a strike. Pitchers should develop mechanics, speed, and accuracy with the fastball before they throw other pitches.

Grip

The grip of the ball is across the seams using the fewest fingers possible needed to control the ball. The pitcher can release the ball more quickly when using fewer fingers, resulting in greater speed. The more skin that touches the ball, the slower the speed of the pitch. Players with larger hands can use three fingers to grip the ball (see figure 5.1). Pitchers with smaller hands will use a four-finger grip.

Figure 5.1 Three-finger fastball grip.

The grip should be firm but not tight, with good space between the ball and the hand. A grip that is too tight locks the wrist and prevents a quick snap. The ball is not buried in the hand but is held by the fingers at the first knuckle. Holding the ball out in the hand creates the longest possible lever. The thumb and the middle finger are the power-producing digits. The thumb should be placed on a seam directly across the ball from the middle finger. This arrangement balances the line of force on the ball. The index finger is curled slightly and placed closer to the middle finger than to the thumb. If the pitcher has to use a fourth finger, it too should be comfortably spread when placed on the ball. The position of the fingers must not tighten or lock the wrist. The grip must permit the wrist to snap easily. To work on correct finger release, practice these drills:

1. The pitcher holds a ball in the pitching arm out in front at shoulder height. She keeps the elbow straight and tosses the ball to herself using only a wrist snap and a fingertip pull against the seams to toss the ball up.

2. Partners 10 feet apart toss the ball underhand, letting it roll off the ends of the fingers.

Stance

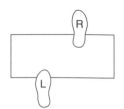

Two feet on rubber

One foot on rubber

Figure 5.2 Foot position on the pitching rubber.

College, professional, and Olympic rules require the pitcher to start with both feet on the rubber. Some other levels require only one foot to be on the rubber. Pitchers must know which rules apply. Starting with both feet on the rubber is more difficult, but it is the position that will be required as the pitcher advances.

The goal is to generate as much power as possible while maintaining balance. When using two feet on the rubber, the pitcher spreads the feet out from front to back by placing the heel of the front foot (pivot foot) on the front of the rubber and the toe of the back foot (stride foot) on the back edge (see figure 5.2). The pivot foot is always on the pitching-arm side. The feet are placed no wider than shoulder-width.

When the rules require only one foot on the rubber, the throwing-side foot is again the one placed on the front of the rubber (see figure 5.2). The back foot is placed one step behind the rubber in a spot that provides good balance. From that stance the pitcher should be able to shift her weight forward easily and push off comfortably for the stride forward. Again, the feet are placed no wider than shoulder-width.

Pitchers can alter the angle of their stance on the rubber in the same way that we change the setup on a pitching machine. To hit the outside corner, we angle the pitching machine slightly outside. For the inside corner, we angle the machine in that direction. The angle and placement of the front foot will allow the pitcher to hit the corners in the same way. To throw to the corners, the pitcher turns the front toe about a half inch in or out from the straight position she would use to throw down the middle of the plate. The batter will never notice the slight change of angle that will allow the pitcher to hit the corners.

Presenting the Ball

The rules use a fancy term, presenting the ball, to describe how the pitcher must stand on the rubber to start the whole pitching motion. The body is upright and relaxed, and the pitcher should feel comfortable. The shoulders are level and square with the rubber. The ball is in the glove, and the hands are separated. The arms should hang long and relaxed at the pitcher's side, with the shoulders down. (Shoulders up mean the pitcher is tense.) The pitcher takes a breath to relax the shoulders further, to let go of the past, and to focus on the next pitch. The rules require the signal to be taken with the hands apart. Weight is kept over the back foot to allow proper weight shift and a momentum shift at the beginning of the motion. The pitcher then brings the hands together. She does not hold this position too long because her body will tend to tighten up, which will affect speed and control. She reaches into the glove and grips the ball, making sure to keep the grip well hidden from the third-base coach.

The First Move

When presenting the ball, weight is on the back foot. The pitcher begins the motion by rocking forward from heel to toe over both feet. The upper body leans forward with weight shifting from the back foot to the front foot (see figure 5.3). As the motion begins, body lean puts the pitcher's head and chest beyond her front foot. The hand and glove are together at the navel, and they push down and out as far as possible to create maximum arc and arm swing. The path of the hands is down the zipper of a jacket and centered with the body. When the arms are extended, the pitching hand comes out of the glove and the arm comes directly up to the ear. The body begins to straighten. The glove is pointed at the catcher. The pitcher lifts the ball out of the glove with the palm of the throwing hand down and the arm relaxed. The arm movement, or take-away, is slower at the beginning and builds up speed on the downswing to create the whipping action. The pitcher thinks about being relaxed on the way up and accelerating on the way down. She must be careful not to rush. The knee of the stride leg is flexed and moving forward (see figure 5.4). The sequence is arm up, head up, and foot out. The pivot leg bears the weight with the knee slightly flexed and the foot turned slightly outward.

In a variation of the first arm movement, the pitching hand swings back outside of the glove. The glove stays over the ball as long as possible to hide the ball on the arm swing. From that point on everything else is the same. Swinging the arm back creates a larger arm circle, which can increase speed. Bringing the arm straight back can also help keep the arm and shoulders in proper alignment. A disadvantage is that the ball is visible and an alert coach or batter may pick up the grip and the pitch.

Top of the Backswing

The hips and shoulders are open at the top of the backswing, with the belly button facing third base. As the ball reaches for the sky, the back foot pivots. The simplest way to ensure that the hips open is to turn the pivot foot on the rubber about 45 degrees away from the body. That outward turn of the pivot foot accompanied by a strong pivot and a solid push off the rubber with the same foot helps open the hips. The stride foot should land on a straight line running from the pitcher's nose directly to the catcher.

Figure 5.3 Rock forward from heel to toe over both feet to start the pitching motion.

Figure 5.4 The knee of the stride leg is flexed and moving forward on the take-away.

The striding toes should point between one o'clock and three o'clock. The pitcher must be aggressive with the stride foot. She reaches out with the stride foot and feels the power from kicking the stride foot forward toward the plate (see figure 5.5). She thinks about moving the stride foot out, not just up. The force of the stride carries the body away from the rubber and creates power by helping to transfer body weight toward the batter.

The critical elements during the stride are being balanced when releasing the ball and having consistent foot placement. A pitcher may have her own style and deviate from the line toward home plate. Even so, placement must be consistent. If the stride is not on the target line, make sure that the step is not across the body, a movement that would force the pitcher to throw across her body. The aggressive reach of the forward leg and the ability of the pitcher to maintain balance on her stride will determine the length of the stride. The upper body must stay upright, or tall, during the stride; the need to keep the body upright will also affect the length of the stride.

On the backswing the biceps muscle of the pitching arm is close to or brushes the right ear. The pitching arm is extended (long), but not hyperextended. The pitcher must be careful not to lock the elbow. Not extending the arm is called short-arming, and it decreases the arc, greatly limiting speed. The pitcher must keep the arm loose with the wrist in a cocked position ready to whip the ball. At the top of the backswing, the palm has rotated outward to face third base (see figure 5.6). The arms form a 90-degree angle with the pitching arm straight up and the glove pointing at the catcher.

Figure 5.5 An aggressive stride.

Figure 5.6 Top of the backswing.

Middle of the Downswing

As the pitching arm reaches the middle of the downswing, the hips and shoulders are starting to close. The right shoulder is lower than the left, and the shoulders are back (see figure 5.7). The pitching arm is slightly bent with the elbow coming into the pitcher's right side. The wrist is cocked with the fingers pointing up and the palm pointing away from the body. The body is upright. The stride leg is flexed to absorb the shock of forward movement. The back foot drags off the rubber on the side of the toe at about a 45-degree angle, and the pitcher ends on one leg. We call this the flamingo position. (Dragging the toe keeps the feet legal. You are not replanting.) The arms work in opposition as the glove arm and pitching arm move down together.

Release

On the release the striding foot is firmly planted with the knee still flexed. The upper body remains upright with the head even or slightly ahead of the right knee and between the feet. The hips and shoulders are almost closed with the forearm of the pitching arm close to or brushing the right side. The wrist is snapping fast, and the fingers apply resistance on the ball at release. The wrist goes from hyperextension to flexion. The pitcher thinks about dragging the fingers through. She should have the feeling that the ball is being pulled throughout the delivery, with the ball trailing the forearm and wrist up to the time of the wrist snap. This motion builds centrifugal force. The glove arm pulls down hard to the side of the front hip as the pitching hand comes forward.

The ball will go where the pitching hand is pointing at the time of release. The pitcher can imagine a dot in the middle of her palm; where the dot is pointing when she releases the ball is where the ball is going to end up. She releases the ball when the wrist snaps at the hip (see figure 5.8). The wrist goes from full extension to full flexion as it passes the hip. Beginning pitchers often snap at the elbow instead of the wrist, greatly sacrificing speed and control.

Leg Drive

There are two theories on use of the legs to drive off the rubber and follow through. Because the ball has already left the hand, the legs at this point have no effect on the pitch. The pitcher uses the legs to generate power by increasing the speed of the arm before releasing the ball. Therefore, the pitcher should choose the style that allows her to maintain her balance and develop maximum arm speed on the downswing.

- **Drag the back foot**—The toe of the nonstriding foot simply drags forward so that the knees of the pitcher come

Figure 5.7 Middle of the downswing.

Figure 5.8 Release point.

together. It is easier to keep the shoulders in line with the target using this technique.

- **Push off the rubber**—Once the arm passes the hip and the ball is released, the back leg comes through hard, propelling the right side through. As the back leg comes through, the front (stride) leg pushes up like a spring uncoiling. This helps drive the back hip through. The pitcher may actually jump up off the front leg. As the right side drives through, the back will arch, the hips will thrust forward, and the shoulders will come back. The pitcher then finishes tall. A disadvantage of this method is the tendency to close the shoulders and hips too early (before the ball is released), which shifts the body off the target line and reduces accuracy.

Follow-Through

To create maximum speed when releasing the ball, the hand must go even faster during the follow-through than it did at release. This is the only way the hand can attain maximum speed. The hand moves well out in front of the body. The pitcher can think of shaking hands with the catcher. The hand also finishes high. That can mean that the elbow is up near the forehead or that the biceps finish near the cheek (see figure 5.9). If the arm is truly relaxed and acting like a whip, it will fly up to the end of its range of motion and then fall back down. Movement should be natural and comfortable. The pitching hand must be on line to the target, staying within the line of force and striving to complete the perfect circle. The glove arm stays close to the body so that the shoulders are not pulled off line. The glove pulls down hard and hits the outside of the front hip.

Figure 5.9 Follow-through position.

The pitcher's first responsibility is to pitch the ball. Following the release as she pushes off the rubber, she uses her forward momentum to bring the pivot foot forward and almost parallel with the stride foot to achieve a well-balanced fielding position. The glove is waist high with the fingers pointing up and the pocket open toward the hitter. The pitcher should not hurry to reach this position; she must complete her follow-through. She waits until the pitch is well on its way before assuming the fielding position.

SPEED VS. ACCURACY

Pitchers need both speed and control. Pitchers must learn the speed at which they can control their pitching motion. If the delivery is not consistent, their pitches will not be accurate. True, the goal is to throw the ball hard. By concentrating first on developing maximum speed, beginning pitchers develop the feeling, mechanics, tempo, and timing required to throw the ball hard. Control is specific to the velocity of the ball. The correct release point is speed specific and is determined by the velocity of each thrown ball. Therefore, decreasing speed will not necessarily improve accuracy. In a game the idea that slowing down or lobbing the ball to home will result in strikes is just not true! Only a consistent delivery and hours of practice produce accuracy. Because the goal is to throw as fast as possible, pitchers should develop a consistent motion while throwing as fast as they can. Speed first and then accuracy. Pitchers should throw hard against a wall or fence without worrying about where the ball goes. Eventually, they will develop accuracy at that speed and can start to throw to a catcher.

All pitchers want to increase their speed. Speed comes from a smooth, relaxed delivery and from the centrifugal force created by a long whiplike action of the arm. The pitcher swings and whips the arm; she doesn't just move it. Speed can be increased by the push off the mound and the snap of the wrist. A pitcher's strength also contributes. Changing grips and finger pressure can sometimes increase speed.

Pitchers should only throw the fastball as they work on developing consistent mechanics. Use the following drills to help your pitchers develop speed first. When the pitcher can throw hard with consistent mechanics, then focus on accuracy. Remember, until a pitcher is consistent in these areas she shouldn't begin to throw other pitches.

Coaching Points for Fastball Pitching Mechanics

- Make sure your grip is comfortable and firm yet doesn't lock the wrist. You need a relaxed wrist for a good, quick snap. Work on gripping the ball firmly while not tightening the wrist.
- Don't stop or pause during the arm circle. Don't stop the momentum you are building. Use one continuous motion.
- Don't guide the ball. Release the ball at your hip with a strong wrist snap.
- Use two checkpoints to keep your arm properly aligned. Your biceps brush your ear at the top of the backswing, and your pitching hand brushes your hip at release.
- Don't step with the stride foot pointed toward home plate. Your hips will then not be able to open, and your belly button will not point to third base. You must land with the foot somewhere between the one o'clock and three o'clock positions.
- Don't short-arm the ball. The longer the lever, the greater the potential for producing force, just as a rock swinging on the end of a long string moves faster than one swinging on a short string. Keep your arm straight throughout the arm swing with a slightly flexed and relaxed elbow.
- Don't crow hop off the rubber because doing so results in an illegal pitch. To get more impetus on the ball, some pitchers replant the pivot foot by pushing hard off the rubber and actually jump to a second push-off spot. Others simply step forward with the pivot foot and walk off the pitcher's rubber before they pivot. Keep your pivot toe on the rubber as you push off it and drag the toe of your pivot leg on the follow-through so that you will not be called for being off the rubber.
- Don't hurry to assume a fielding position. Turning too early pulls your shoulders off line. You must keep your hips open until you release the ball and it is well on its way.

THROWING OTHER PITCHES

Only when pitchers develop a consistent motion and know exactly where their hands are every time they release the ball can they successfully begin to throw other pitches. Pitchers should concentrate on developing one pitch at a time and learn it well. Many young pitchers want to learn several pitches, and they end up having mastery over none. Only so much time is available for practice.

Top pitchers seek to have about four good pitches, including an off-speed pitch. They select pitches that cover the various areas of the plate and then set out to master each one. A good plan would be to have a fastball, a drop, a rise, and a change-up. The easiest pitch to learn is the drop. The curve and the rise have many similarities, with the rise being the most difficult pitch to learn. A pitcher should add a change only after they develop a good fastball.

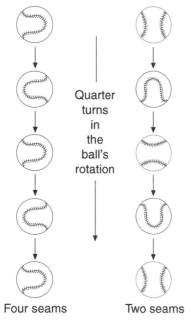

Four seams   Two seams

Quarter turns in the ball's rotation

Figure 5.10 Four-seam versus two-seam rotation.

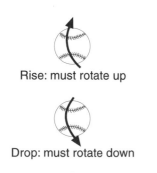

Rise: must rotate up

Drop: must rotate down

Curve: must rotate sideways

Figure 5.11 Rise, drop, and curveball spins.

Ball Movement

A pitch that moves as it approaches the plate—up, down, in, or out—is more difficult to hit than a straight ball. Spin and speed make the ball move. The faster the spin, the greater the movement. The faster the wrist snap, the greater the spin and the faster the speed. For example, a change-up uses no wrist snap and as a result has no speed. As a softball moves through the air, it moves in the direction of the least pressure. Four seams rotating against the wind and biting the air will create more movement than two seams will (see figure 5.10). For a four-seam rotation the pitcher grips the ball across the seams with the thumb on one seam and the fingers on the opposite seam. When the pitcher looks at the ball to assume the grip, she should see a C (see figure 5.1 on page 83). She should try to get the four seams turning at right angles to the direction of the break. A two-seam rotation is preferred when throwing a change-up. The pitcher grips the ball with the fingers going with the seams. The thumb is still under the ball on a seam for ball control. Altitude and weather affect ball movement. Humid or heavy air slows the movement and speed of the ball, and lighter air does the opposite.

The spin of the ball determines the direction it will move. The ball will break in the direction it is rotating (see figure 5.11). The spin on a drop ball is down and away from the pitcher. The spin on a rise ball is up and back toward the pitcher. A curveball spin is sideways. From a right-handed pitcher the curve moves away from a right-handed batter. A left-hander's curveball breaks in on a right-handed batter's hands and is a tough pitch to hit.

The grip is what the pitcher uses to impart spin to the ball to make it rotate a particular way. Hand size, finger length, and arm strength vary widely among pitchers, so each must experiment to find the grip and pressure points that produce the desired spin. The grip must be comfortable so that it does not produce tension in the wrist that could limit the wrist snap. The grip, wrist action, and follow-through are the keys to throwing "stuff." Quality pitches break sharply just before they reach the plate.

Steps for Learning Pitches

Pitchers should use the following progression when learning a pitch:

1. Find a comfortable grip and experiment to find a grip and finger pressure that creates the greatest combination of spin, speed, and control. The pitcher, not the coach, must choose the grip.
2. Assume the stride and pitching position and spin the ball into the glove using only the wrist.
3. Throw easily to a catcher 15 to 20 feet away, concentrating on proper spin and release. Start without a full windup and stride. When successful add a complete motion. If the pitcher has trouble seeing the spin, put a stripe on the ball or color the seams. The catcher can provide feedback about the spin.
4. Pitch at normal distance.

THE DROP

The drop is the most reliable pitch, the easiest pitch to learn, and the most effective pitch because it is the most difficult to hit solidly. The drop results in many ground balls. The drop should never be thrown more than four inches above the knee. The best location is between the knee and the shoe tops. The drop ball breaks best when thrown low, and it becomes difficult to hit as it breaks out of the batter's line of vision. The batter sees only the top of the ball and is likely to hit it on the ground. If the pitcher misses with this pitch, she should be sure to miss down. With runners on, of course, the catcher must be able to block balls in the dirt.

The two common drops are the peel drop and the turnover drop.

Peel Drop

Most pitchers find the peel drop easier to learn than the turnover drop. The basic mechanics are similar to the mechanics for the fastball, so learning the peel drop is a natural progression. The difference is the emphasis on the spin and the lower follow-though. The spin is a true vertical spin that can produce a sharp or heavy drop.

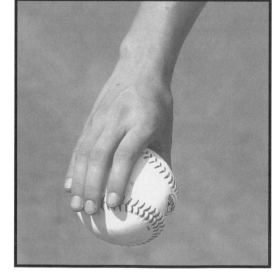

- **Grip**—The pads of the fingers are across the seams for a four-seam rotation (see figure 5.12). The ball is held more loosely in the hand than it is for a rise (see figure 5.17 on page 94).

- **Spin**—The spin is down and away from the pitcher and toward the catcher in a six o'clock–twelve o'clock rotation.

- **Mechanics**—The thumb is the first digit released from the ball. The ball rolls straight off the ends of the fingers with the palm facing the plate (see figure 5.13 on page 92). At release the wrist should snap straight forward and up. The pitcher pulls up on the seams and feels the friction of the seams leaving the finger pads and imparting a downward rotation from six o'clock to twelve o'clock. If the spin is not vertical, the pitcher has not maintained a direct line of force to the target and has not kept her hand directly behind the ball.

Figure 5.12 Peel drop grip.

Figure 5.13 Peel drop release.

Figure 5.14 Turnover drop grip.

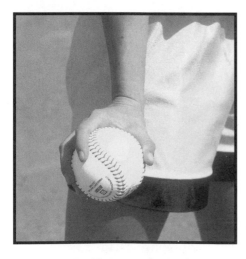

Figure 5.15 Turnover drop release.

- **Follow-through**—The fingers should snap straight up and come to rest on the shoulder about armpit high. All four fingers should be touching the shoulder, indicating that the wrist did not rotate off line. This follow-through is slightly lower than the follow-through for other pitches. If the ball is too low, the pitcher should increase the follow-through to bring the ball up slightly.

Turnover Drop

The turnover drop is not as sharp as the peel drop, and its speed is not as great. Some pitchers consider it a distinct pitch, an off-speed variation of their peel drop. The turnover drop is the more difficult pitch to learn because it involves snapping the wrist over the ball and timing becomes a factor. But if the pitcher's hand naturally turns over at release, this is the pitch for her. Good curveball pitchers often prefer this drop because the wrist snap is similar to what they use for the curveball.

- **Grip**—The grip has the index finger pushing against a seam. A common grip is to grip the backward C of the ball with the thumb on one seam and the index and middle fingers on the outside edge of the opposite seam where they can push against it (see figure 5.14). Variations include a split-finger grip with the first finger against the pushing side of one seam and the middle finger against the pushing side of another seam. For this grip the pitcher will have to place the two pushing fingers against the two seams where they are closest together (the most narrow point) on the ball. She must find a position that creates a four-seam rotation.

- **Spin**—The spin is down and away from the pitcher and toward the catcher. The turnover drop will not have a true vertical rotation like the peel drop. The spin will be down with a counterclockwise sideways rotation as well. A drop curve and slower speed will result.

- **Mechanics**—As the ball approaches the bottom of the downswing, the pitcher initiates the wrist snap by lifting or shrugging the pitching shoulder, trying to touch the right ear. At the top of the shrug, the hand, wrist, elbow, and shoulder come over the ball and help push it down into the ground. With the shrug the wrist begins to turn in automatically, similar to what happens in turning a doorknob to the left. The wrist snaps on top of the ball, and the fingers pull up and over the ball. The action resembles dribbling a basketball. At release the fingers holding the ball should be on top, and the thumb should be underneath pointing at the ground (see figure 5.15). The thumb comes off first, and the pitcher should then feel the ball coming off the inside of the fingers. The forearm should be close to or brushing the side at release. A common problem is for the elbow to extend away from the side.

To help the pitcher see and feel the correct wrist snap for the turnover drop, have her hold the ball with the palm up in front of the body. With the elbow in close to the side, she snaps the wrist over and throws the ball to the ground. The elbow must not fly out from the pitcher's side. This drill shows how the hand comes over the ball.

• **Follow-through**—The pitcher finishes the wrist snap with the hand and thumb pointed down. The hand finishes lower than the release point, between the legs mid-thigh or lower (see figure 5.16). The pitcher focuses on keeping the follow-through close to the body. Some pitchers follow through with the back hip and leg coming over the ball and the back foot landing close to the striding foot.

THE RISE

The most difficult pitch to throw correctly is the rise because it requires complex wrist action at release. A good rise ball jumps as it approaches the batter. The pitcher should throw to the batter's armpits or above. She cannot afford to miss low. She should use it when she wants a fly ball or when facing a batter who goes after high pitches. Because the ball is up and in the power zone for most big hitters, it is a dangerous pitch that can lead to home runs. Slappers can also do damage because the ball is on the same plane as the eyes and bat. But a high pitch is tempting for most batters and can lead to many strikeouts. Some pitchers have been able to dominate using only this pitch.

Figure 5.16 Turnover drop follow-through.

• **Grips**—Four basic grips are used for the rise ball.
 —Flat: The index and middle fingers are flat on the ball. The fingers can be together or split. If they are together, they should be on the inside of the same seam (see figure 5.17a on page 94).
 —Finger curl: The index finger is curled with the inside of the index finger on the ball (see figure 5.17b).
 —Fingertip: The fingertip of the index finger is on the ball (see figure 5.17c). The pitcher must keep her fingernails short!
 —Knuckle: The knuckle of the index finger is on the ball (see figure 5.17d).

In all grips the outside of the middle finger should be placed where it can push against a seam. The thumb is always placed on an opposite seam. The ability to use a bent index finger or knuckle depends on the size of the hand and fingers. The pitcher must always strive for a four-seam rotation. Note that the ball rolls off the sides or bottom surface of the fingers for the rise and the curve.

• **Spin**—The spin is up and toward the pitcher, and the ball is spinning backward. To help the pitcher feel the backward spin, try these drills:
 1. With a comfortable rise grip, the pitcher holds the ball out in front of the body. She twists her wrist backward (a doorknob turn to the right) and makes the ball spin as she tosses to herself.
 2. The pitcher stands sideways with her glove side to a catcher three to five steps away. The pitcher holds the ball on the palm of her pitching hand with no specific grip. She swings her arm backward and forward in a scooping motion, releasing the ball from underneath with the palm up.

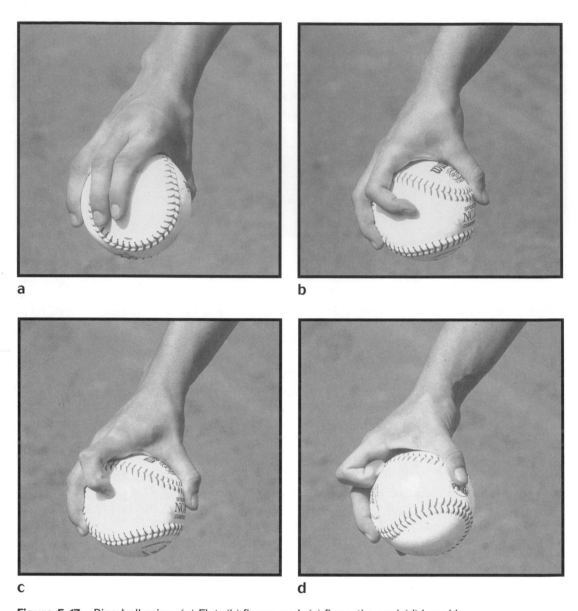

Figure 5.17 Rise-ball grips. *(a)* Flat, *(b)* finger curl, *(c)* fingertip, and *(d)* knuckle.

• **Mechanics**—The pitcher lengthens the stride and keeps a stiff front leg. Body lean is slightly back, and the right shoulder is lower, angled toward the ground (see figure 5.18). This posture helps the pitcher lower the release point and get under the ball. On the downswing the wrist and arm turn so that when the arm reaches the back leg, the back of the hand and forearm are against the leg. The knuckles of the pitching hand should be no higher than the back knee. Note that the pitcher's arm is between her body and the ball.

The elbow is in and the arm is turned back as the heel of the hand leads to the release point. The wrist is cocked coming into the release area. At release the hand is cupped under the ball with the little finger pointing toward home and the palm of the hand pointing toward third base (see figure 5.19). The pitching hand is facing away from the side of the body. The pitcher snaps the wrist forward with the hand cutting underneath the ball to impart the backspin. The action is like turning a doorknob to the right.

Figure 5.18 Rise-ball downswing.

Figure 5.19 Rise-ball release.

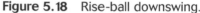

The pitcher must get under the ball with a long arm. The body leans back at the point of release. The pitching shoulder should stay back so that the body faces third base throughout the pitch. The back knee bends more at release, enabling the pitcher to get under the ball better. At release the pitcher bends into the pitch, which lowers the shoulder and helps her get under the ball. The elbow is relatively straight at release, and any bend occurs only on the follow-through.

To help the pitcher get the feel of this motion, have her stand against a wall with her pitching hand raised overhead and palm flat on the wall. She makes a complete arm circle, keeping the palm flat against the wall. A complete circle duplicates the arm motion for a rise. She also rotates the hips through to feel the arm and hips working together.

• **Follow-through**—The arm reaches out and continues up and over the head. The elbow should be in closer to the body than the wrist, with the hand turned completely over. The palm is out and up with the thumb pointed down.

THE CURVE

As the name implies, the curveball curves sideways, moving in the direction of its spin. From a right-handed pitcher the curve will move away from a right-handed batter and break in to a left-handed hitter.

The curve can be used effectively in all parts of the strike zone. It can be thrown inside to a right-handed batter to break over the plate or over the outside corner, or it can be thrown over the plate to break outside beyond the reach of a right-handed batter.

The safest location is low and outside. The pitcher must be careful with a target low and inside; if she misses inside the pitch will hit the batter. Most hitters are weakest at hitting outside pitches because they try to pull every pitch. When a pitcher has good control of both her inside pitches and her curve, she can move the batter on and off the plate. Pitchers should be able to throw the curve to both right-handed and left-handed batters. Throwing the curve at different speeds increases its effectiveness.

- **Grip**—The grip for the curve is the same as that used for the rise. Some pitchers will spread their fingers a little more. Holding the ball deeper in the hand and cocking the wrist more at release will result in a slower curve. The curve is easier to master than the rise because the motion is more basic. The curve is sometimes referred to as an underdeveloped rise ball.

- **Spin**—The spin is directly sideways. The ball rolls off the sides of the fingers to create proper sideways rotation. The ball does not come off the fingertips! The action is similar to turning a doorknob to the right. This spin may occur naturally for some pitchers. Some coaches don't like the curve because it stays on one plane as it moves sideways, thus being easier to see and hit. Pitchers can add an up or down spin to the curve to change the plane. By understanding spins and rotation the pitcher can make the ball do many things. To help the pitcher improve spins, try these drills:

1. The pitcher holds her hand out in front of the body with the palm up and hand flat. She brings her fingers in toward the center of the body by moving her hand sideways. This is the proper wrist position for the curve. She adds a ball and a comfortable curve grip. She then spins the ball to herself using a strong sideways snap of the wrist and a twisting action with the fingers.

2. To develop the spin, the pitcher can pitch a hockey puck into a wall. She grips the puck around the edges with the flat side down. The focus is on keeping the elbow to the side, keeping the palm up, and developing the proper wrist snap.

- **Mechanics**—The shoulders are level, the body is upright, and the stride is slightly shorter than the stride used with the rise. (The pitcher does not want to get under the ball.) The arm is turned back as it is for the rise, and the hand position is the same with the hand under the ball and the little finger toward the catcher. The difference is in the wrist snap. The wrist snaps around the hip (toward first base) and occurs a little sooner. The pitcher must be careful to snap the ball, not carry it! The middle finger really pulls the ball. The action is like a karate chop in front of the waist with the palm up, and the spin is created in the same way that one creates spin when throwing a Frisbee (see figure 5.20). For a tighter spin, the pitcher snaps the thumb to the target. The palm must stay up throughout the pitch. The elbow bends before release. The forearm brushes against the side as the right hip is driven forward. The right hip closes more on this pitch, and the toe of the right foot drags to provide body resistance. The pitching shoulder also closes to the catcher and is higher than it is with the rise. The pitcher brings the right shoulder to the left.

- **Follow-through**—The arm comes across the body at the waist, going from one hip to the other. The pitching elbow moves slightly away from the body just after release (see figure 5.21).

Figure 5.20 Curveball release.

CHANGE-UP

The purpose of the change-up is to deceive the batter. The change-up throws off the batter's timing and increases the effectiveness of other pitches. The change-up doesn't have to be fancy to be effective; it only has to fool the batter. Therefore, the pitching motion for the change-up must look like that of any other pitch. A change-up should be 15 to 30 miles per hour slower than the pitcher's fastest pitch.

The ideal location for the change-up is knee high on the outside corner. Because the speed has fooled the batter, her hands should have already passed the ideal contact spot for the outside pitch. On the other hand, a hitter can commit early and still have a chance of hitting an inside change. The pitcher's ability to throw the change for a strike will also determine when she can throw it. Generally, she should not use the change with two strikes when the batter is protecting the plate or against a weak hitter who cannot get around on faster pitches. The change-up should not be used in a sacrifice or squeeze situation.

The change is a relatively simple pitch to learn. Unfortunately, because of the emphasis on speed many pitchers do not work to develop a good change-of-speed pitch. The two types of change-ups are the stiff wrist and the back-of-the-hand.

Figure 5.21 Curveball follow-through.

Stiff Wrist

The easiest release to use for the change is usually the stiff wrist, but the choice should depend on which release is easier and more comfortable for the pitcher. A problem with the stiff-wrist release is a tendency to stop the hand completely with no follow-through. The hitter can easily pick up this action. In addition, it is difficult to avoid snapping the wrist because doing so is important for all other pitches. This technique is just the opposite of what the pitcher has worked so hard to develop. Now she palms the ball, locks the wrist, and pushes the ball.

• **Grip**—The more skin on the ball, the slower the speed. Putting the ball deep in the hand against the palm locks or stiffens the wrist, greatly reducing the speed. Palming the ball with the fingers going with the seams (see figure 5.22a on page 98) causes any rotation to be a two-seam rotation. When gripping across the seams, pitchers have a tendency to snap the ball and pull on the seams, thus increasing the speed. Going with the seams will help break this habit. For control purposes, the pitcher should place the thumb on a seam if possible.

The pitcher can try one, two, or four knuckles, or the fingertips, on the ball. When using the fingertips on the ball, the fingers should be bent with the nails digging into the seams or just in front of the seams (see figure 5.22b). If the knuckle grip is being used, grip the ball firmly with the thumb and little finger while placing the first bend (flat fingernail protion) against the ball's surface (see figure 5.22c). The grip must be secure enough that the pitcher can use her regular fastball motion without fear of losing her grip of the ball. The size of a pitcher's hands will eliminate the use of some grips.

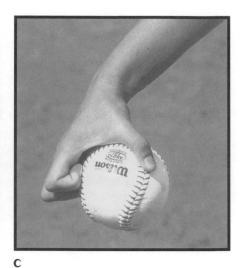

a b c

Figure 5.22 Stiff-wrist change-up grips. *(a)* Flat, *(b)* fingertips, and *(c)* knuckles.

- **Spin**—The ball may or may not spin. The lack of speed, not ball movement, is what makes the pitch effective, so spin is not a concern.

- **Mechanics**—Differences in mechanics between the change and a pitcher's other pitches should be few and never visible to the batter. The pitcher locks or stiffens her wrist at the release point by spreading her fingers as wide as possible and pushing the ball with her palm (see figure 5.23). She does not use the fingers to push the ball because speed will result. Normal hand speed must be maintained into the release point. If the hand slows, the pitcher will tip the pitch and lose needed distance. The release is in front of the back hip. The pitcher must focus on staying under the ball and reaching out to hand the ball to the catcher. For some, stopping the wrist at the side by bumping the hip is effective.

- **Follow-through**—The pitcher should keep the follow-through low so that the pitch stays down in the strike zone. She turns her hand down at release as if shaking the catcher's hand. She may want to experiment with bumping the hip to stop the arm and limit the follow-through.

Back-of-the-Hand

The back-of-the-hand is the more difficult change to throw. Few pitchers use it successfully. But some of the best change-ups you will ever see are thrown this way. It takes much practice to learn the right release point and to be consistent. A difficulty is that the pitcher may drop the ball when trying to keep the arm moving at full speed.

- **Grip**—The grip is not a factor in this pitch, so the pitcher should use one that is comfortable. Most use the fastball grip or an across-the-seams grip.

Figure 5.23 Stiff-wrist change-up release.

- **Spin**—The ball may spin excessively or simply float with little spin. Spin is not a concern because the lack of speed is what deceives the batter.

- **Mechanics**—As the pitcher begins her downswing and well before the release point, she turns her hand over so that the back of the hand faces the catcher (see figure 5.24a). The back of the hand leads into the release point. She snaps the wrist to release the ball (see figure 5.24b).

- **Follow-through**—At release the thumb is angled down slightly, and the follow-through is across the waist (see figure 5.25). This hand action at release will keep the ball angled down. If the thumb is pointing at the hip on release, the ball has a tendency to arc up before it goes down. Hanging a change can be costly.

a

b

Figure 5.24 Back-of-the-hand change-up release. *(a)* Turn the hand over before the release point and *(b)* snap the wrist to release the ball.

Figure 5.25 Back-of-the-hand change-up follow-through.

Coaching Points for Throwing Other Pitches

The Drop

- Take a slightly shorter stride to raise your release point. Doing this makes you taller and gives the ball a greater distance to drop.
- Lean slightly forward at release with your head and shoulders over your front foot. Emphasize landing on the ball of your foot.
- Throwing the ball at about 90 percent of maximum speed allows the ball to drop more.

The Rise

- To increase the "hop" of the rise, experiment with spreading your fingers more on the ball and squeezing the ball out of the fingers at release. Doing this increases the resistance on the ball, thus creating more spin.
- A sideways spin will flatten out this pitch.
- Don't try to make the ball go up. Allow the spin to take it up.
- If the ball is curving instead of rising, make one or more of these adjustments:
  - Make sure your elbow is not flying away from your body at release.
  - Your right shoulder may be too high coming into the release area.
  - Your wrist snap is sideways. Have your wrist and fingers rotate back toward your body after release.
  - Increase the spin by changing grip and finger pressure. Relax your fingers and wrist more.
- If the ball is rising too much, make one or more of these adjustments:
  - Shorten your stride.
  - Make sure your release point is not too far in front of your body. Don't hang on so long.
  - Reduce the amount of follow-through.
  - Relax your grip, particularly the thumb pressure.
  - Lower your shoulder to get under the ball instead of bending at the back and getting behind the ball.

The Curve

- Be careful not to exaggerate your lean to the glove side. Too much lean will lead to loss of control and often result in a drop ball as you come over the ball. Let your wrist and shoulder create the spin.
- If the ball is sailing you may be throwing too fast. Think spin instead of speed. Also, check that you are not stepping forward with the right foot at release, which would carry your shoulder forward. Instead, drag your back foot to create body resistance.
- Is the ball rising instead of curving? Your right shoulder may be folding against your right side at release. Allow your elbow to move away from your body and use a higher right shoulder.
- To maximize the curve, visualize a series of dots from the mound to the outside corner of the plate. Pitch along those dots.

- Experiment with striding across the body to see if you can improve your wrist snap and your ability to keep the ball in the strike zone. With the catcher in receiving position behind the plate, aim your stride foot at the catcher's left foot instead of her right foot to evaluate the effect of the stride on your curve.

The Change-Up

- Deception is the key to success. Have teammates and coaches look for any changes in your delivery that telegraph the change-up. Use a videotape to compare deliveries.
- Keep the ball low in the strike zone. Turn your thumb down at release and keep the follow-through low.
- Don't always throw a change-up in a given situation. Vary your pitch selection.
- Use the change-up to set up other pitches. Follow a change-up that is low and out with a fast drop low and in.
- Do not throw a change to a batter who doesn't stride. The premature stride is what pulls batters off balance.
- Great change-up pitchers don't throw the change near the strike zone where it can be hit. They get the strike by fooling the batter and getting her to swing at the motion, not the pitch. The ball may bounce in front of the plate, but the batter has already started to swing.

HOW MUCH AND HOW TO PRACTICE

The amount of time pitchers devote to practice will depend on their age, goals, and commitment. College pitchers throw at least five days a week and up to 400 pitches a day. The length of practice is usually based on time (one hour a day) or the number of pitches. Each pitcher should find the system that works for her. Pitchers should not quit before they are tired nor go too far beyond fatigue. They must push themselves, but when fatigue sets in fundamentals start to break down. Only perfect practice makes perfect.

To make the most of practice, pitchers should have a plan and purpose for each day. Practice should prepare them to do their best in the game, so practice should be gamelike. Pitchers should throw to real catchers whenever possible and use a home plate. Pitchers should vary the number of pitches of the same type that they throw consecutively, and they should alternate speeds. Practice should include game situations and throwing to live batters. For practice to carry over to the game, they must pitch in practice just as they pitch in a game.

Pitchers should make endurance a priority. Pitchers can never run enough. They should strengthen the legs because they are what give out in a game. A weight program will increase overall body strength and improve power. At the end of every pitching practice, pitchers should put ice on their arm to prevent swelling and soreness.

WARMING UP

A total-body warm-up is as important for a pitcher as it is for any player. Pitchers should increase their body temperature by jogging and then use a good stretching program, stretching all major muscle groups and joints. Pitchers should begin warming up the arm by throwing easily overhand, then pitching slowly at a short distance, working on tempo and timing. Pitchers concentrate on ball spin and work on one pitch at a time until each is working to their satisfaction. They should begin with their primary pitch and work down the middle of the plate before moving to the corners. Pitchers work on visualizing the path of a successful pitch, warming up mentally as well as physically.

Pitchers should not struggle with a pitch that is not working. They should go back to the basics, beginning with the spin and release, and make the necessary adjustments. They should throw all of their pitches hard, pinpointing targets, and working with the catcher. This is the time to discuss the game plan: which pitches are working well, which do not feel as comfortable, and so forth. The pitchers should time their warm-up to be fully prepared by game time.

GAME CONTROL

Pitchers must approach every pitch the same way. The steps they take to the mound, the way they put the foot on the rubber, the place they hold the ball, the focus of the eyes—every physical movement should be the same regardless of the count, the score, or the situation. Having a familiar routine to go to relieves pressure and allows them to focus on the task. The routine creates confidence and improves consistency. A consistent routine also sends a message to teammates and the batter that the pitcher is in complete control!

Many pitchers tip off their pitches by showing too much of the ball or by using different movements for different pitches. By practicing in front of a mirror or studying videotapes of their deliveries, pitchers can make sure that they give nothing away.

Pitchers may telegraph pitches by

- not hiding the ball or grips from the base coach or batter,
- showing more white on the ball, particularly overhead or on the backswing,
- turning the glove or wrist differently,
- presenting the ball higher or changing the arm angle on certain pitches, or
- making a different sound, especially on changes or rises.

The coach or catcher may call the pitch. When someone else makes the call, pressure on the pitcher is lessened. The pitcher may be given the right to overrule the calls. Chapter 6 includes a section on calling pitches and covers many factors that go into choosing a certain pitch. If the pitcher does not make the final decision, she should have confidence in any call that is made. Pitchers can better understand the decision-making process by reading the relevant section in chapter 6 and studying the pitch-selection charts for the batter and the situation.

Pitchers should be committed to each pitch they are throwing. They must believe in the success of each one. If a pitcher doubts her ability to throw a called pitch effectively, she should not throw it! Some coaches therefore believe that the pitcher (not the catcher or coach) must call the pitch to be thrown. Once the pitcher has decided on the pitch, she visualizes the pitch hitting its target. She makes a mental picture of the path of the ball, using a series of dots to mark the path to the target. This exercise will increase control, ball movement, and confidence.

Getting ahead on the first pitch is an important goal. Many batters take the first pitch. If it is a strike, the chance that the batter will walk is greatly diminished.

Pitchers should evaluate their pitches honestly. They should know their best pitch for each location, their poorest pitches, their strikeout pitch, and the pitch they'll throw when they need a strike. Pitches should be thrown to the corners of the plate, never through the center.

Pitchers know that they will give up some hits, but they should remember that the outs they get will far outnumber the hits they allow. A great hitter will succeed only 4 times in 10. The defense will get her out 60 percent of the time. Knowing that the batter will fail most of the time and that eight players are behind her to help when the batter does hit the ball, what is the big worry?

Much of the game is out of the pitcher's control. Their only job is to throw the ball to the target. They have no power over what happens after that. When they realize this, the job of throwing each pitch becomes much easier. What pitchers can control is how they respond to what is going on around them.

Pitchers should avoid showing emotion on the mound. By letting the batter know that they've lost control, pitchers give the batter the advantage. Umpires are people too and don't like to be shown up in a game. Seldom will pitchers get a call if they have reacted negatively to the last one. Instead, pitchers should use that energy to focus on a plan of attack and the next pitch. They should evaluate their performance and adjust as needed, go to their routine, and step up to give their best.

To be a team player, pitchers support their teammates the way they want to be supported. They acknowledge great plays made behind them. If they pitch a no-hitter, they give credit to the catcher. When a teammate makes an error, they exhibit no more displeasure than they want to receive when they unintentionally give up a walk. When a fielder has a bad day and really needs support, the pitcher should be the first to offer encouragement. She is the center of attention and should use her position to be a leader.

PITCHER AS A DEFENSIVE PLAYER

Once the pitch is delivered, pitchers must prepare to function as another infielder. They quickly assume a well-balanced position with the glove out in front of the body, the fingers up, and the pocket open toward the batter. A pitcher's defensive ability (fielding and throwing) will determine her defensive assignments. If the pitcher is an excellent fielder, the coach may want her to play every ball that she can easily reach. If she is less skilled than the first and third basemen, she may be limited to backing them up and fielding only balls hit directly to her. The pitcher should know where the infielders are playing and be careful not to deflect balls that are clearly another fielder's responsibility. Making an out on a deflected ball is extremely difficult.

Pitchers must often field slow rollers and push bunts toward second base. Because the pitcher is running toward first, an underhand throw is the safest, the easiest to see, and the most accurate. The pitcher should field the ball with two hands when possible to make sure she catches it. For maximum reach she may need to reach with only the glove and then quickly bring the hands together to get a grip for throwing. She should lock the elbow and wrist and straight-arm the ball to the first baseman. The pitcher uses the same technique on suicide bunts for the throw home, concentrating on keeping the toss low for the tag.

Pop-Ups

The general rule is that the pitcher catches any ball within the pitcher's circle or any popped-up bunts that aren't airborne long enough for the corners to reach. On pop-ups to the other players, the pitcher can provide valuable assistance about the direction of the ball (up, back, first, third) and warn of obstacles and fences. The pitcher may need to cover the base of the fielder catching the ball.

Backing Up

The pitcher must back up all throws to the catcher from the outfield. When the play will be on the lead runner going to third, she should back up third base. If it is not clear where the play will be, the pitcher first runs across the foul line midway between third and home and then looks for the play before deciding where to go. The normal backup position is 15 feet behind the receiver. Occasionally a base is left uncovered. This can happen when two players are going after a fly ball. The pitcher must look for any vacated base and quickly move to cover it. She should also be prepared to back up or participate in rundowns.

On a wild pitch or passed ball with a runner on third, the pitcher must cover home. As the catcher chases the ball, the pitcher continuously calls the catcher's name and waves her arms until the ball is released. The pitcher assumes a foot position at home that protects her legs from being taken out on a slide and gives the runner a corner to go to (see figure 5.26). She bends the knees, lowers the hips, and establishes a balanced position to apply the tag.

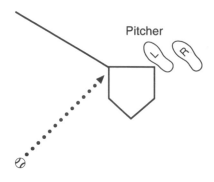

Figure 5.26 Pitcher's foot position when covering home.

Checking Runners

The pitcher must be aware of all runners on base and consider them always a threat to advance. As soon as she receives the ball in the circle, the pitcher checks the position of the runners, lead runner first. The pitcher should understand the look-back rule and use it to her advantage. When the pitcher has the ball in the circle and has caused the runner to stop after rounding a base, the runner must immediately advance or return to the base. The runner cannot delay, fake, or reverse direction. Once the runner returns to the base, she cannot leave again as long as the pitcher holds the ball. Proper understanding and use of the rule stops runners from advancing and takes the pressure off the defense.

FASTBALL DRILLS

Pitchers must first develop a consistent delivery. These drills isolate and emphasize the basic mechanics that are the foundation for developing speed and accuracy.

Arm-Speed Development

Purpose: To learn the feeling of arm speed and to develop acceleration through the arm circle.

Procedure: The pitcher works alone on her arm circle. The drill has two parts.

1. The pitcher stands in a sideways pitching position with the stride leg forward and the pitching arm above the head at the top of the circle. She moves the arm around in a perfect circle as fast as she can to get the feel of high arm speed. She keeps the arm totally relaxed, as loose as a noodle.

2. The pitcher then focuses on building acceleration through the circle. Still sideways, she begins with the pitching arm at waist level. The pitcher focuses on lifting the arm in a relaxed manner and increasing the speed of the arm by

accelerating on the downswing with a whiplike action. The arm is extended (elbow relaxed) to create the biggest arc and lever possible. The longer the lever, the more force it can produce.

Wall Pitching

Purpose: To develop speed without worrying about accuracy.

Procedure: The pitcher stands 10 to 15 feet from a wall and throws hard, focusing on mechanics and the feeling of throwing the ball hard. The repeated impact will soften a ball before long, so the pitcher should use the same ball. Don't use a rubber ball that lacks seams because the pitcher must be able to grip the ball properly. An advantage of this kind of practice is that pitchers can do it on their own at any time.

Speed Pitching

Purpose: To develop speed while throwing to a catcher.

Procedure: The pitcher works with a catcher, concentrating on exploding off the mound and attempting to throw each pitch a little harder.

Distance Pitching

Purpose: To develop strength of throws.

Procedure: After warming up to be sure the arm is loose, the pitcher throws to a catcher at a distance greater than that used in a game, throwing 10 to 15 feet farther than normal. The focus is on speed, not control, for a specified number of pitches. The distance should not be so great that it changes the basic mechanics.

Wrist Snap Behind Back

Purpose: To develop the wrist snap by isolating the wrist, which prevents the pitcher from using the elbow to snap the ball.

Procedure: The pitcher stands sideways 5 to 10 feet from the catcher or a wall. The glove side faces the target, and the ball is behind the back. The pitcher flips the ball by snapping the wrist.

Wrist Snap Under Knee

Purpose: To practice the wrist snap by isolating the wrist.

Procedure: Partners stand about 10 feet apart. Pitchers can throw to pitchers. If right-handed the pitcher kneels on the left knee with the right leg bent and the right foot flat on the ground. The pitching arm is placed against the leg with the ball and hand under the knee. The pitcher flips the ball in the air to her partner by snapping the wrist.

No Stride

Purpose: To promote proper ball release and speed.

Procedure: The pitcher delivers a ball to a partner without using a forward stride. The partner can be another pitcher, so this is a good warm-up drill. The stride foot is even with the pivot foot. The pitcher pitches the ball using good hip rotation, a strong snap of the wrist, and a good follow-through, focusing on proper hip and arm mechanics. Pitchers should be aware of the danger of not rotating the hips and then throwing only with the arm.

Wall Drill

Purpose: To develop proper rotation of the arm.

Procedure: The pitcher throws imaginary pitches using a wall to keep the arm straight in a perfect circle. She stands perpendicular to a wall with the pitching arm close to the wall and about four inches away. The pitcher uses the full pitching motion (including the stride and the opening of the hips), keeping the arm straight and in tight so that it does not contact the wall. The pitcher walks and moves down the wall throwing imaginary pitches.

Baseball Mound Pitching

Purpose: To develop proper body lean and weight transfer.

Procedure: The pitcher pitches to a catcher off a baseball mound using the baseball rubber and a catcher at the regular softball distance. The angle of the mound forces a longer stride and helps the pitcher feel the importance of body lean and weight transfer.

Four-Corner Control

Purpose: To develop control and accuracy.

Procedure: The pitcher throws to the extreme four corners of the strike zone. When she achieves accuracy at one spot, she moves the target to the next corner. A catcher or a target on the wall can be used. To adjust for the in and out targets, the pitcher must adjust her body angle from her normal stance. She turns the toe on the rubber about a half inch in or out from the position she used to throw to the middle of the plate.

OTHER PITCHING DRILLS

Use these drills to develop and feel the finer points of these specific pitches. Emphasizing the visual patterns for each pitch also helps develop the proper release point and followthrough. "Low Net Throws" and "Basket Throws" are for the drop, "Football Toss" and "Long Toss" are for the rise, and "Bucket Toss" and "Fast and Slow" are for the change-up.

Low Net Throws

Purpose: To focus on proper release and keeping drops low.

Procedure: From a distance of about 10 feet, the pitcher throws into the bottom of a catch net, exaggerating her release of the drop.

Basket Throws

Purpose: To focus on making the ball drop by using a visual target.

Procedure: The pitcher throws from regular distance and attempts to pitch the ball into a laundry basket at home plate. This drill helps imprint the image the pitcher should see before every drop pitch. The pitch can be thrown to a bucket, but the ball will not ricochet as much off the softer basket.

Football Toss

Purpose: To develop correct rise-ball release.

Procedure: The pitcher throws a junior-sized football underhand to a partner. Grip it along the seam with all the fingers and with the thumb on the opposite side. The ball should spiral. If it wobbles in flight, the palm has turned toward the catcher at release.

Long Toss

Purpose: To practice getting under the ball for rise-ball release. The drill also develops body and arm strength.

Procedure: The pitcher pitches to a catcher from second base or farther, lobbing the ball up as if she is throwing it over a telephone pole. This action forces the pitcher to get under the ball. To develop strength, the pitcher keeps backing up (from second base, to center field, to the fence) to see how far she can throw it.

Bucket Toss

Purpose: To practice keeping the change-up pitch low.

Procedure: The pitcher pitches the ball into a bucket two to three feet in front of home plate. She avoids having a big loop in the pitch.

Fast and Slow

Purpose: To practice changing speeds.

Procedure: Working with her catcher, the pitcher alternates fast and off-speed pitches. The goal is to keep the delivery the same.

GAMELIKE PITCHER DRILLS

Pitchers must do more than just throw the ball. Work with your pitchers on their fielding techniques to strengthen your infield, and include conditioning so they have strong legs they'll need to go the distance in a game. Pitching under pressure is much more difficult than throwing in the bullpen, so coaches should use competitive drills to create gamelike pressure during pitching practice.

Pitchers Field and Cover First

Purpose: To practice fielding all types of balls after delivering a pitch. This is an excellent conditioning drill as well.

Procedure: The drill works best with at least three pitchers, a catcher, and a hitter. If you don't have three pitchers, another player may play first and pitchers rotate only on the mound. Pitchers form a single-file line at the mound, and one pitcher is at first to catch the throw. The pitcher pitches the ball to the catcher, and the hitter hits a ground ball back to the pitcher for fielding practice. The pitcher fields, throws to first, and then rotates to first to receive the throw from the next pitcher. After catching at first, the receiver rotates to the end of the fielding line. Vary the type of balls hit, hitting to each side of the pitcher and bunting and slapping as well. Include a sequence of having pitchers look imaginary runners back before making the throw.

Pitchers Cover Home

Purpose: To practice footwork for covering home on wild pitches.

Procedure: Pitchers rotate on the mound, and catchers rotate at home. The pitcher throws a wild pitch to the catcher in receiving position and runs home to cover the plate for the return throw. The pitcher's feet must be well out of the way of the sliding runner. The pitcher should call the catcher's name and wave her arms until the throw is on its way.

Play a Game

Purpose: To experience gamelike pressure during pitching practice.

Procedure: The pitcher pitches a specific number of innings with the catcher calling balls and strikes. If you have a batter standing at the plate, she should assume different positions in the box and stand in as both a left-handed batter and a right-handed batter.

Three Points

Purpose: To create competition and pressure for the pitcher when pitching to a catcher's targets.

Procedure: The catcher gives a target, and for advanced players she may call a pitch. If the pitcher hits the target, she gets one point. If she misses, she loses a point. When the pitcher reaches three points, the game is over. Add difficulty by requiring every fourth pitch to be a change-up.

6

The Catcher

The catcher, as the only player who faces the entire field of play, has a unique opportunity to direct the defensive play of the team. A catcher can also help the pitching staff immeasurably by knowing the pitcher's abilities that day, by studying the batters, and by using that knowledge to exploit the batters' weaknesses. The emotional state of the pitcher can greatly affect her performance; a good catcher works with each pitcher's personality to bring out her best while helping her stay in control. The catcher and the pitcher must work as a team if they are to be successful.

Successful catchers will demonstrate the following skills and characteristics:

- Agility with quick feet
- Strong arm and soft hands
- Quick reaction time and hustle
- Exceptionally strong knees and legs
- Size (bigger and taller) for blocking the plate and catching high and wide pitches
- Leader of both defense and pitching staff
- Student of the game

Tradition says that a catcher should be a right-handed thrower so that a right-handed batter will not interfere with throws to second. Of course, left-handed batters will interfere in the same way on their side of the plate. Today we see an increasing number of good left-handed catchers. A left-handed catcher has a couple of advantages: her body is in perfect position to field bunts and throw to first, and a runner at first cannot see her throwing arm during pickoff attempts. A good catcher is a good catcher no matter which arm she throws with.

EQUIPMENT

Catchers use a first baseman's glove with a web or a softball catcher's glove. Common injuries include bruising of the index finger and "fast-pitch thumb," in which the ligaments become jammed. Catchers must use a large pocket that provides some protection. The mask must fit snugly, be lightweight, and include some kind of throat protection. Full helmets are required at most levels. The chest protector should not sag or slide around and should protect the shoulders and collarbone as well as the chest. Shin guards, with flaps to cover both the top of the foot and the bottom of the thigh, should fit tightly so that they do not turn.

BASIC RECEIVING STANCE

Catchers squat about 150 times in a game. They can save their knees by going down with both heels on the ground as far as they can and then going to the toes.

The basic receiving position must be comfortable and well balanced, and it should allow the catcher to rise and move quickly. The feet are a little wider than the shoulders, with weight on the inside of the feet and on the balls of the feet (see figure 6.1). The feet are in a half-step stagger with the glove-arm leg in front and the back foot even with the instep of the front foot. This position promotes a faster body turn as the catcher opens to throw. The knees are slightly angled in, and the heels lightly touch the ground. The butt is low as if sitting on a small stool. With runners on the catcher must raise the hips and butt, pressing the heels flat on the ground. Keeping the heels down has them in a position to push off immediately. The elbows are in front of and outside the knees. The catcher takes a position in the box as close to the batter's back leg as possible without interfering with the swing. This position is usually within two to three feet of the batter's back leg. The bare hand must be protected by placing it behind the back or behind the leg. The best position from which to make a quick throw is to have the hand behind the thumb of the glove, but that position leaves the hand more exposed to injury. Most catchers use the leg position without sacrificing too much speed. The fingers should always be closed in a loose fist with the thumb inside.

GIVING THE TARGET

The catcher can help the pitcher be more accurate by showing her where to throw the ball. The glove should be as large as possible and held stationary until the ball has been released. By moving her body behind the glove, the catcher offers a bigger target. When moving her body the catcher must be careful not to move too early and tip the batter.

Figure 6.1 Basic receiving position.

The catcher must know how much the ball breaks for each pitcher. If a pitcher is missing consistently, the receiver adjusts the target in the direction opposite the error. The catcher should know what the pitcher looks at when throwing. If the pitcher aims at the glove and the ball breaks from there, the catcher places the target on the corners. If the pitcher throws so that the ball breaks and lands in the glove, the catcher places the target just outside the strike zone.

CATCHING THE BALL

When receiving pitches the catcher has the glove arm slightly bent and the glove extended in front of the body. The shoulders are relaxed with the elbows down. She does not reach for the ball. She lets the ball come to her and then gives with the catch. The catcher should attempt to catch all pitches with the fingers pointed up. Only on extremely low balls should the glove turn down. A pitch caught in that way rarely earns a strike call from the umpire.

More advanced catchers can point the fingers (the top of the glove) at the pitcher with the palm down after giving the target. This downward flip puts a break in the wrist and keeps it relaxed. As the ball is caught, the wrist gives with the pitch and the glove backs up. This saves the hand and arm while helping to secure the ball.

The catcher focuses on the flight of the ball from the moment it is released until the batter hits it or she secures it in the glove. The catcher must not shut her eyes. She can force a blink just before the pitcher releases the ball so that the eyes can stay open during the flight of the pitch.

The catcher must stay low until the umpire makes the call, being sure not to move and obstruct the umpire's view. For balls that are just out of the strike zone, the catcher shifts her body, but not her feet, to catch the ball. When the ball is farther out, she steps in the direction of the ball and shuffles her feet to make the catch.

Framing

Framing the ball is the technique of catching the outside of the ball as if the glove were a frame around a picture. By showing the umpire this view, the catcher can better sell the pitch as a strike. She catches the sides of the ball for inside and outside pitches and the top of the ball for high and low pitches (see figure 6.2a–d). When possible, low pitches are caught with the palm down. When she catches a low pitch with the palm facing up, the catcher has effectively widened the picture, causing the ball to look lower than it is. On the catch she rotates the wrist slightly toward the plate and holds the position until the umpire makes the call. The catcher should not use this technique when the pitch is obviously a ball because the umpire will think she is begging or testing his or her intelligence. To practice framing, have a partner stand in front of the squatting catcher and move a ball on a stick to simulate low, high, inside, and outside pitches. The catcher moves the glove to frame each pitch.

Figure 6.2 Framing (a) low, (b) high, (c) inside, and (d) outside pitches.

Blocking Balls

Low balls that can't be caught should always be blocked. Even with the bases empty the catcher should be in the habit of blocking all balls in the dirt. This effort gives the pitcher confidence in throwing drops and keeps the catcher sharp.

The catcher must try to keep the body in front of the ball and the ball in front of the body, using the chest protector to block the ball. On low balls directly to her, she replaces her feet with her knees (see figure 6.3). She kicks out as quickly as possible, as if ropes were tied to her ankles and pulled out from under her. The receiver gets low to the ground, falling on the shin guards. The body should be in the shape of a C over the ball and angled to the plate. The arms are relaxed with both hands on the ground. The catcher shrugs the shoulders forward and with the chin down looks the ball into the chest protector. The glove is used to protect the trap door, the gap between the legs, as well as the lower body. The glove is open, but the goal is to block and stop the ball, not to catch it. The bare hand is close by, ready to grip the ball for any throw or tag. With a runner at third the catcher must think of blocking and smothering the ball. With a runner at first she should try to block it, catch, and throw.

On a ball to the side the catcher must make every effort to get behind it. The hands initiate movement to the ball. The catcher follows the hands by jumping in the direction of the ball and landing on the knees (see figure 6.4). The emphasis is on driving the outside knee out and down. The body must be angled with the belly button toward the plate so that balls rebound forward instead of bouncing away sideways. The glove goes down to block any gap under the legs. Every catcher has a weak side and can compensate by turning the body a little more in that direction.

The catcher can also step in the direction of the ball with the nearer foot and drop down on the back knee (see figure 6.5). She pushes off with the back foot, supporting her weight with the stepping leg. The glove is pointed down, and the body is over the ball and angled to the plate.

Passed Balls and Wild Pitches

To prepare for the possibility of a passed ball or wild pitch, the catcher should throw balls at the backstop before each game to see how and if they rebound. If a ball gets by in the game, the catcher can then go straight to the ball. The catcher runs hard after every ball and grabs it with both hands. She gets her chest over the ball as she picks it up and plants the throwing-side foot. She then transfers her weight to that foot and makes a hard pivot toward the plate. To locate the player covering home, the catcher listens for her voice and looks for her waving arms. To make the throw to the plate, the catcher stays low, steps with the glove-side leg, and makes a sharp underhand throw. The shouts of the player covering home will often indicate how quickly she needs the ball. When the catcher doesn't have time to look, she simply throws at her teammate's voice.

Figure 6.3 Blocking a low ball to the front.

Figure 6.4 Blocking a ball to the side on both knees.

Figure 6.5 Blocking a ball to the side on one knee.

Foul Tips and Foul Balls

The key to catching foul tips is to be close to the batter. The catcher reaches for the ball and doesn't pull the glove back when catching it. She should remember that on caught foul tips the ball is live and in play. With inside pitches to a right-handed batter, the ball will usually be fouled off to the catcher's left. Outside pitches will be fouled to the catcher's right.

As soon as the catcher realizes that the ball has been fouled off in the air, she should stand and turn toward it. The pitcher or the corners should be helping by calling the direction of the ball, saying something like "Up 3" or "Up 1." If the ball is over the catcher's right shoulder, she turns to the right. A ball over the left shoulder calls for a pivot to the left. Foul balls behind the plate have a tendency to drift toward the infield. Whenever possible, therefore, infielders should make the play.

If the mask does not hinder vision, it is safer and easier to leave it on. (Wearing a helmet makes the mask more difficult to remove.) If the mask obstructs the catcher's vision or she feels more comfortable catching with the mask off, she can remove it after determining the direction of the ball. The catcher must not drop the mask until the ball is located. Then, as she goes after the ball, she tosses the mask in the opposite direction, far enough away that she will not step on it.

Catching the ball with the glove above the shoulders provides some time to recover should the ball be bobbled. Basket catches are harder to master but sometimes are the best choice when the ball is spinning in an unpredictable descent. Balls that the catcher plays with her back to the infield usually drift back to her.

Figure 6.6 Position for an intentional walk.

Intentional Walks

When the pitcher throws far outside to walk the batter intentionally, the catcher stands upright facing the pitcher with the feet at the extreme edge of the catcher's box. For a right-handed batter the catcher reaches out with the right arm parallel to the ground and uses a fist or glove as a target (see figure 6.6). For a left-handed batter the catcher reaches out the other way. After the pitcher releases the ball, the catcher quickly moves behind it to be certain of making the catch.

Pitchers who have difficulty throwing accurately to the extended glove can instead throw to the outside shoulder of the catcher as she stands at the edge of the box. The catcher's body provides a bigger target, and the catcher is in a better position, behind the ball, to catch it.

The defense must protect against a pitch thrown so close to the batter that it could be hit. Because the ball will be pitched outside, the corner player on the same side of the diamond as the outside pitch must stay back in case the batter reaches out and goes with the pitch. For a right-handed batter, then, the first baseman plays back in regular position. The third baseman moves way in to cover home in case of a wild pitch.

THROWING TO BASES

A catcher needs a strong arm, a quick release, and quick feet to throw out runners. Each of these aspects can be improved with practice and by using proper techniques. Good catchers stop runners who try to advance. They also give the defense more time to make outs by preventing runners from getting big leadoffs.

Footwork

To get the feet into throwing position, the catcher uses either the pivot or two-step footwork. A real advantage of the two step is that the added momentum from taking two steps puts more speed on the ball, which is beneficial for players with weaker arms. The two step also works well with outside pitches and pickoff plays with a right-handed batter. The catcher can step and catch the ball in front of the throwing shoulder at the same time, a movement that provides a quick release and a stronger throw. The two step is more difficult and slower to use with inside pitches because the catch is in front of the left shoulder and the ball must be brought to the throwing shoulder as the step is made. With a left-handed batter this step brings the catcher close to the batter, who may interfere with the throw. (For a left-handed catcher, of course, the foregoing situation works the opposite way.) Use of the pivot in these instances helps the catcher keep away from the batter and opens up the throwing lane. The pivot requires a strong arm, quickness, and strong legs to spin or jump to this position. A good catcher is able to use either style, depending on where the ball is caught.

• **Pivot**—As the catcher starts to stand and pulls the ball back in preparation for the throw, the weight shifts to the back foot and the body turns in that direction. The player spins on the ball of the foot until the front shoulder points at the target. When the ball and the weight are over the back pivot foot, the glove arm extends forward and the striding foot steps in the direction of the target. Another option is a jump shift, which is simply a quarter-turn jump and throw.

• **Two step**—As the catcher receives the ball, she simultaneously rises and takes a short step forward with the throwing-side foot to the ball. The stepping foot should be angled outward at about a 45-degree angle, with the inside anklebone pointing at the target. All the weight is on that foot. The catcher then takes another step directly to the target. The added momentum from taking two steps can help increase the speed of the ball. The catcher turns comfortably sideways with the feet outside the shoulders. She should check the length of the stride. On a long stride the throw goes up. On a short step the throw goes down. If the shoulders are not turned sideways (and the front foot is turned less than 45 degrees), the throw will drift to the shortstop side of second.

The Throw

Throwing mechanics for the catcher are the same as those for outfielders. The catcher receives the ball with both hands and quickly separates the ball from the glove. She does not bring the throwing hand across the body to get the ball. Instead, the catcher turns the body and brings the glove to the throwing hand. She then brings the ball back past the ear, making sure the ball does not drop below the elbow. The action is like shooting an arrow with a bow. Keeping the hands and arms in tight will increase quickness. On the backswing the fingers and palm rotate away from the thrower. This hand rotation is critical because it puts extra snap on the ball.

The catcher's throw differs from the outfielder's throw only in its more compact windup. (For throwing mechanics refer to chapter 2.) In the forward motion the elbow is above the shoulder throughout the entire throw. The catcher should think about getting both the elbows and the hands up high. The higher the throwing arm, the easier it is to pull down on the seams to produce the desired vertical spin. The catcher pulls the glove arm down inside the body to stay on the target line. Although the arms work in opposition, the action is unlike swimming, in which the arms are outside the body. That motion will pull the catcher's shoulders off line. The catcher uses the stomach muscles to pull down on the torso and increase power.

A shoulder-high pitch to the throwing shoulder promotes a quick release because it brings the catcher up to throwing position. A pitchout (waist-high outside fastball) allows the catcher to move away from the batter and concentrate entirely on the throw. For a quicker release to third, a left-handed catcher should exaggerate the stagger in the stance. The same is true for a right-handed catcher throwing to first. The exaggerated stagger turns the shoulders closer to throwing position for quick throws to the corner bases.

A batter's position in the box may appear to put her in the catcher's throwing path. The catcher should not waste precious time moving around the batter; she maintains her position and throws by or over the batter's head. She will not need to think about this because her hand and release point will automatically adjust to create a throwing lane and avoid hitting the batter. If there is no way the throw will get by the batter, then, depending on the batter's position in the box, the catcher either steps in front of the batter to make the throw or uses a drop step and throws behind her. Time is critical, so the catcher should always try to move directly to the target.

Pickoff throws to first or third should go to the fair side of the base. Throws to second base go slightly to the inside of the base. The catcher should not aim for a perfect throw at the sliding runner's foot; a knee-high throw gives the fielder a chance to make the catch and then the tag. On a passed ball the first baseman takes a position on the outside of the base and gives a target with her outside hand. On a bunt the catcher throws from inside the diamond to an inside target. With a runner going to first, the throw must never go across the base path. See chapter 3 for more details on how infielders should position themselves to cover each base.

On a low pitch a strong catcher may choose to throw from the knees or with one knee down. Get the hands and ball up high and concentrates on pulling down with the stomach muscles. Strength and confidence are developed by starting at a short distance and building up to regulation distance.

Fielding Bunts

In bunt situations the catcher puts the back foot farther back than usual in the squat to get a better running start and raises the hips as she does in a steal situation. On a bunt to the right the catcher doesn't chase it but gets in front of the ball to field it. She explodes low and beats the ball. She picks up the ball with both hands in the middle of the body and between the legs. The feet are already in position to make the throw to first. Taking an extra step before throwing is fine. On a bunt to the left side the catcher uses a reverse step (turning toward the glove) and then makes the throw. She throws overhand when time permits. When the catcher needs to make a quicker throw, she throws semi-sidearm from a semicrouch position. Additional details on bunt coverage are in the section on bunt defense in chapter 7 (see page 131). If the catcher can see well with the mask on, it is not necessary to get rid of it.

OTHER DEFENSIVE RESPONSIBILITIES

Catchers do much more than catch the pitch. In addition to playing bunts just in front of home plate, it is the catcher's responsibility to hold runners tight or to pick off any base runners trying to advance. Catchers need to take charge of baserunners and do all in their power to keep them from reaching home, from making force plays at home to blocking the plate. Other defensive situations involving the catcher are relays, cut-offs, pickoffs, and rundowns. These are discussed in detail in chapter 7.

Holding Runners

With runners on base the catcher must always be expecting a steal and cannot be in a full, deep squat. As soon as she catches the ball, the catcher must check the position of the runners from a position in front of the plate. By taking that position the catcher shortens the throw and eliminates the possibility of slipping on the plate. The best way to stop a runner or chase her back is with the eyes. By looking and being prepared to throw, the catcher may discourage thoughts of stealing. If no throw is necessary, she returns the ball sharply to the pitcher. The catcher uses the same motion for every throw, whether to the pitcher or to a base. The throw to the pitcher goes to her left shoulder as a practice throw to second base.

The catcher picks people off by making them fall asleep. When a runner drops her head, the catcher gets her! The catcher always checks the lead runner first. She never throws behind a runner at second base unless the runner is moving back to the base and there is a legitimate chance of getting the out. At third the catcher must be careful because a mistake there means a run. Some coaches have a rule that a catcher never attempts a pickoff at third. For full details on pickoffs, including drills and use of the pitchout, see the section on pickoffs in chapter 7 on page 135.

Covering Home Plate

With the bases loaded the catcher can focus on catching the ball, tagging the base, and turning the double play to first. This is a relatively easy play because the approaching runner is not a big factor. The most difficult play for a catcher is when the runner is coming home and the catcher must catch the ball, block the plate, and make the tag. Fear of a collision can cause the catcher to take her eyes off the ball to see where the runner is. Hard contact can make it difficult to hold on to the ball. Even all the equipment is not a real comfort. Proper positioning and lots of practice under gamelike conditions can help the catcher prepare for this critical play in which a mistake means a run.

Force Plays.   When there is a chance for a double play, the catcher waits just behind the plate with the chest facing the thrower to provide a good target. The catcher catches the ball behind the plate and then steps directly on the plate with the right foot or steps across the plate with the left foot and drags the right foot across it. As the foot drags across the plate, a right-handed catcher jump pivots (crow hops) toward first base to make the play. The throw to third does not require a full pivot, but the catcher must be sure to get the shoulders properly aligned as she steps toward third on the throw. When practicing the force play at home, the drill should use runners from home so that the catcher has a realistic measure of the time and quickness she needs to complete a double play.

Blocking the Plate. As the catcher waits to receive the ball, she should take a position up the third-base line two to three feet from home and in fair territory. The left foot is in line with the left corner of the plate, and the left leg and knee directly face the runner. If the runner slides into the leg, the knee will flex with a normal range of movement, reducing the risk of a knee injury. The feet are comfortably spread with the knees bent, and the catcher is ready to move if the ball is thrown off line. Although the lower body is square to the runner, the upper body is turned to catch the ball. Body position is relatively low, putting the catcher in a better position to catch a bounced ball or drop down to block the ball if necessary. While making this play the catcher is also in position to block the runner from the plate.

The catcher must focus on the ball and catch it before a play can be made. Doing this is difficult because there is a tendency to look for the incoming runner and worry about a collision.

The catcher should not reach for the ball but should let it come to her. When the throw is off line, she must go get the ball and then dive back to apply the tag.

The catcher catches with both hands to secure the ball and then turns to face the runner. The body and glove are lowered to block the runner's path to the plate (see figure 6.7). The left leg remains facing the runner, and the right knee is bent and on the ground. The catcher holds the ball in the throwing hand inside the glove and places the glove on the ground in front of the left foot. The body is in a low C position facing the runner. Body weight is transferred forward as the tag is applied. The tag is made with the back of the mitt at the lowest part of the incoming runner's leg or, if she is diving, on the hand. The catcher doesn't reach to make the tag; she lets the runner tag herself. As the tag is made, the glove and arms give with the impact to keep the ball from being jarred loose. Immediately after the tag the catcher takes both hands high in the air to prevent the runner from attempting to knock the ball loose and to be ready for any further play.

If the runner attempts to go back door (to run beyond the plate and return from behind), the catcher does not chase her. She waits for the runner to come back to the plate, as she must, and applies the tag there.

Figure 6.7 Blocking the plate.

On plays in which the runner is hung out to dry and obviously going to be out, the catcher makes the tag and tries to avoid a collision. She should remain on her feet, move up the line, and make the tag. If a runner attempts to collide with her, the catcher should use a drop step to avoid the collision and pivot away while making the tag.

Backing Up

With no runners on or when the infield may be attempting to complete a second-to-first double play, the catcher should back up first base on ground balls to the infield or to right field. As soon as the ball is hit, the catcher runs parallel to the foul line in foul territory. She establishes a position in a straight line with the throw and stays 10 to 15 feet behind the player receiving the ball at first. The catcher does not back up first when a runner is at second or third. She never leaves the plate when there are runners who may advance to home.

WORKING WITH THE UMPIRE

The attitude of the battery and their actions toward the umpire can affect the umpire's performance. The pitcher and catcher should not become emotional because no umpire likes to be embarrassed. Although intimidation may work with some umpires, consistent calls do not result. Catchers, not pitchers, should ask the questions. Catchers should be calm, tactful, polite, and rational and ask while looking straight ahead. If they turn, the crowd will notice and the umpire may feel he or she is being shown up. If the umpire is repeatedly not calling a certain pitch, catchers can ask if they are blocking the view and how the pitcher is missing the plate. Catchers should rarely complain and only when they know that questioning a call will keep the umpire sharp and not threaten him or her. Catchers should know the umpire's zone and, if it is consistent, adjust their target appropriately. They must not be stubborn and lose strikes because they refuse to adjust. I know a Hall-of-Fame catcher who applied perfume throughout the game—it can't hurt!

GIVING SIGNALS

When giving signals the catcher assumes a squat position with weight on the balls of the feet, the heels up, and the knees narrow. Right-handed catchers have the glove on the left knee with the pocket facing the other knee to hide the signals from the third-base coach or runner (see figure 6.8). The bare hand is against the crotch, and the fingers are spread. Left-handed catchers need to turn slightly away from third base to use the left knee to hide the signals. Signals should be deep, concise, consistent, and definite. Pitchers gain confidence from signals that are given quickly and firmly. Catchers must be sure that movement does not give away the signals. The muscles in the

forearm may indicate which fingers are being moved. Body movement may tip off the batter. On a change-up the catcher often jumps forward; on a rise the head often moves up. Each finger represents a pitch. Additional signals may be given with a closed fist, a wiggle of the fingers, or a combination of signals. The catcher may also pat the left or right leg to indicate an inside or outside location. A pitcher may shake off a signal if she does not agree with the pitch called. When the pitcher shakes off the catcher too often, it usually means that there are problems that need to be worked out.

With a runner on second the catcher may need to use a series of signals. She should use at least three signals and predesignate which set will be live. If visibility is a problem, she can tape the ends of the fingers with athletic tape to help the pitcher see them better.

The catcher will also give signals to the defense for pickoffs and pitchouts. Because these plays require teamwork, the defensive players involved need to know that the play is on. They should give a return signal to confirm that they are ready. With this advance knowledge they can make the necessary defensive adjustments. They can break on the pitch if they know that a

Figure 6.8 Giving the signal.

pitchout is on and the batter will not be hitting the ball. The signals may be oral (using a player's last name or the team name when calling out encouragement) or physical signs, usually given when the catcher is standing before going to the squat. Sometimes the signal will be that the play will occur on the second pitch.

When catchers are practicing giving signals, the coach can have a player walk around to identify the angles from which the signals can be read. Catchers must know where their teammates can see the signals and where the offense might pick them up.

CALLING PITCHES

Good catchers have the ability to observe the batter, interpret those observations, and understand how to use different pitches. They effectively use the pitcher's strengths to limit the batter's success. Although pitchers control the game, the smart and educated catcher controls the pitcher and gives her the chance to succeed.

Coaches and catchers should approach every game with a plan. Coaches should do research before the game on the batters, team tendencies, and conditions that may affect the outcome. In warm-ups, coaches and catchers should find out what the pitcher is capable of that day. Between innings they should study the next three batters with the scorer and pitcher, reviewing what they did last time to develop a plan for the next inning.

Many factors must be considered in deciding what pitch to call. These include the pitcher's capabilities, what pitches are working that day, the batter's capabilities, and the game situation. Field conditions are important as well. Does a fence makes the rise ball vulnerable to home runs? Is the infield soft or hard? Will ground balls get through quickly or will they die? Is the ground wet, making ground balls difficult to field? Must the team adjust for the wind?

A good plan begins by recognizing and identifying three strike zones: the hitter's zone, the pitcher's zone, and the umpire's zone (see figure 6.9). The hitter's zone is where she can make the best contact and where she likes to swing. It is smaller than the pitcher's zone, located more in the middle of the plate and midway between the knees and the armpits. The pitcher's zone is the largest as she hopes to get strike calls and swinging misses with balls slightly outside the legal strike zone. The umpire's zone should be what is defined by the rulebook, but it will depend on the umpire's judgment and what she or he really calls. Catchers should understand the best location for each pitch within the three zones and use and adjust to the zones as necessary.

- When ahead in the count the catcher calls for pitches to the pitcher's strike zone, just outside the batter's zone. The goal is to make the batter swing at the pitch.
- When behind in the count the catcher calls for pitches to the umpire's strike zone while trying to avoid the batter's strength.

The catcher can apply several general rules when calling pitches:

- In tight situations she should rely on the pitcher's best pitch, not on the batter's weakness. If the pitcher gets beat, let it be with her best pitch. The pitcher should challenge the hitter.
- The catcher should keep the pitcher ahead on the count. On a 2-2 count she doesn't ask the pitcher

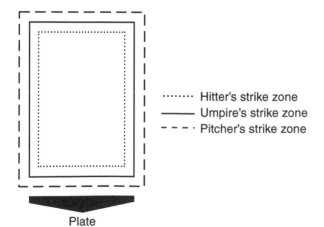

········ Hitter's strike zone
——— Umpire's strike zone
- - - · Pitcher's strike zone

Plate

Figure 6.9 The three strike zones.

to throw a pitch that she wouldn't call for on a 3-2 count. They need the strike now!

- If the first two batters went down on the first pitch, the catcher should know that the next batter is probably taking and should go right after her with a sure strike.
- The catcher can use one pitch to set up another and increase its effectiveness. She can move the batter off the plate with an inside pitch and then use the outside corner.
- The catcher should be careful not to get in a pattern that the opponents can recognize and thus anticipate the pitch.
- After two strikes or with two out, the catcher must not let up.
- She should understand the probable outcome of each pitch. Drops will produce ground balls, and rises will likely result in balls in the air. Outside pitches to a right-hander will go to the right side, and inside pitches are usually pulled to the left. The probable outcomes are opposite for lefties.
- Every batter, regardless of her place in the order, deserves respect.
- As hitters develop and add power, catchers must urge their pitchers to keep the ball low, use the corners, and mix speeds.

In calling for a certain pitch, catchers and coaches can only use their best judgment based on the information available. They must believe in the call, knowing it is the best choice they can make. If the result is unfavorable, they should not second-guess the decision. Doing so will drive them crazy and cause them to doubt the next decision. Simply take whatever can be learned from the result and save it for future reference. What pitches should the catcher call? Table 6.1 on page 122 summarizes what can be learned from the batter and how to use that information to advantage in selecting the pitch and location. Table 6.2 on page 123 summarizes the game situations that must always be considered. Both coaches and catchers can use these charts to develop a plan that works for the pitcher and the team.

Coaching Points for the Catcher

- Hustle on every ball, including passed balls, covering at first, all foul balls, and between innings. Your alert, aggressive play can set the tone.
- Return the ball sharply to the pitcher. Don't lob it, but be sure she is ready.
- Learn to work with your pitcher. It is your job to bring out her best. You must learn how best to work together. You and the pitcher control most of the game.
- Block every ball even when the bases are empty. Doing so is good practice, develops your confidence, and gives the pitcher confidence that she can throw the same pitch when runners are on.
- Work with the umpire. Keep your emotions under control. Never let others see you arguing or questioning a call. Ask questions to get the results you want.
- Be a team leader. All your teammates are looking to you. Use this to your team's advantage.
- Study your opponents at every available opportunity. Figure out how you can beat the batter and the team. One observation and one piece of information may make the difference.

Table 6.1
Pitching Chart

The Batter	Factors and characteristics	Weakness	Pitch and location
Psychological	Anxious approach to plate	Lacks confidence	Change-up
	Swings at first pitch	Overaggressive	Waste pitch off the plate
	Made fielding error	Pressing	Waste pitch, change-up
Position in box	Up in box	Fastballs—high	Fastest pitch on corners
			Rise—high
			Change-up—low and outside
	Back in box	Balls with stuff, drops	Drop, breaking ball
	Crowds plate	Inside pitches	Fastball, curve—inside
	Off plate	Outside	Fastball, change-up, curve, drop—outside
Characteristics	Stands tall, is tall	Low	Drop—inside
	Crouches	High	Rise, high fastball—inside or outside
Hands	Chokes	Outside	Drop—outside
	Held high	Low	Drop, low fastball—inside or outside
	Held low	High inside	Rise, high fastball—inside
	Away from body	Inside	Drop, rise—inside
Stance	Closed	Inside	Drop—inside
	Open	Outside	Low pitches—outside
Stride	Away from plate	Outside	Same as open stance
	Toward plate	Inside	Same as closed stance
	Overstrides	High	Rise—inside or outside
			Curve or change-up—low and outside
	No stride	Balanced	No change-ups
Weight shift	Lunges, front-foot hitter	Off speed, high	Rise—inside or outside
			Change or curve—outside
Swing	Late	Lacks bat speed	Fastball—inside, no change-ups
	Hitch, uppercut	High	Rise—inside or outside
	Chop	Low	Drop—inside or outside
	Big		Change-up
Type of hitter	Slapper	Low outside, high inside	High fastball, rise—in at head
			Drop, low change-up—outside
	Bunter	Low pitches if tall	Low inside or high inside or outside
	Pull	Outside	Outside pitches, change-up
	Opposite-field hitter	Inside	Any inside pitch
	Weak	Fast pitches	No change-ups or off-speed pitches

Table 6.2
Pitching Chart for Game Situations

Situation	Desired result	Pitch and location (right-handed batter)
Bunt	Pop-up or poor bunt	Rise—inside or outside Drop—low and inside
Steal	Ball up and outside for catcher	Fastball—outside or pitchout
Runner on second	Ground ball to left side	Best low pitch—inside
Runner on third, less than two out	Strikeout or ground ball to left side No fly balls	Best low pitch—inside Strikeout pitch—low
Double-play possibility	Ground ball	Low pitch
Bases loaded, none or one out	Ground ball to left side	Low inside
Intentional walk	Called ball easy for catcher to handle	Medium fastball, well outside, chest high
Pitchout	Pitch batter cannot hit	Fastball outside, waist high

CATCHER DRILLS

Catchers need regular practice to develop their skills. Have your catchers practice in full gear so they learn to use their bodies appropriately and to make drills as gamelike as possible. Catchers must regularly practice blocking balls, catching foul balls, and making throws to all bases, as well as working with the infield on turning double plays and fielding bunts. Of course, a catcher can't practice everything every day, but those skills that the catcher is weakest in should be practiced daily until she can confidently execute that skill.

Cathers have multiple responsibilities. The following drills help target specific skills.

Catchers need to practice blocking every low ball that can't be caught. Practice this skill daily using the first three drills and also instruct your catchers to block every low ball during pitching practice. Make sure the balls in these drills are thrown like a pitched ball for gamelike practice. Use soft safety balls or tennis balls when first beginning blocking drills. Catchers must be in full gear.

The catcher's abilities to find the foul ball and to get to it quickly are addressed in the second three drills. Work on improving agility and always have catchers practice in full gear. Practice both removing the mask and catching balls with the mask on. Catchers should dive when necessary and be willing to get dirty when practicing these drills!

Catchers must get their feet in proper position to make accurate throws. On pickoffs the catcher must quickly get her feet around. Use the drills "Two-Step Catch," "Quick Pivot," and "Quick Feet" to develop the quick feet needed to make a variety of throws.

Throws from the catcher need to be quick and accurate. Time how fast the ball gets to the target as a measure of each catcher's improvement. Use the last five drills to help catchers develop speed and accuracy and to learn to create throwing lanes.

No Hands

Purpose: To learn how to use the body to block the ball.

Procedure: Balls are thrown from about 30 feet away. The catcher places her hands behind her back. With shoulders rounded and head down, she drops directly to her knees to block balls. The goal is to keep the ball in front of the body and near the plate. The catcher should also work on blocking balls that are a foot or two off the plate.

Boxing Glove

Purpose: To practice blocking the ball instead of trying to catch it.

Procedure: The catcher wears boxing gloves or special flat fielding gloves so that she doesn't try to catch the ball but blocks it instead. Balls are pitched in the dirt, and the catcher uses only this equipment and her body to block the ball. The goal is to keep the ball in front of home plate.

Wild Pitches

Purpose: To practice making throws to a player covering home after recovering passed balls or wild pitches.

Procedure: The catcher assumes a squat position. Another catcher or pitcher faces home plate and throws wild pitches that the catcher lets go by. The thrower then covers home to receive the return throw from the catcher. The drill can also be started by dropping the ball against the backstop.

Catcher Agility

Purpose: To improve agility and the ability to catch foul balls.

Procedure: The catcher lies flat on her stomach. A partner tosses simulated foul balls behind her, calling "Ball" as the ball is tossed. The catcher scrambles to make the catch.

Foul-Ball Toss

Purpose: To practice catching foul balls.

Procedure: From the normal receiving position behind the plate, the catcher fields foul balls thrown to all areas. The tosser faces the catcher and makes an underhand toss. A pitching machine can also toss the ball. The ATEC Rookie or Hummer pitching machine has a foul ball setting that can even impart backspin.

Foul-Ball Communication

Purpose: To practice communicating and working together to catch foul balls.

Procedure: Use a catcher, pitcher, third baseman, and first baseman in their regular defensive positions. Foul balls are tossed in all directions in foul territory. Players assist each other in calling the direction of the ball, calling for the ball, and making the catch.

Two-Step Catch

Purpose: To learn to catch with the throwing foot forward as the foundation for the two-step release.

Procedure: The catcher plays catch with a partner. She receives each throw with the right foot forward (if right-handed) and then steps with the opposite foot to make a two-step throw.

Quick Pivot

Purpose: To develop a quick pivot.

Procedure: From the squat position the catcher pivots to the throwing position as quickly as possible on the command "Throw." She uses the jump pivot as well.

Variation: A coach holds the ball in front of the catcher and then drops it. The catcher tries to pivot before the ball touches the ground. Create a contest by progressively lowering the height from which the ball is dropped.

Quick Feet

Purpose: To improve quickness.

Procedure: A pitcher throws from a distance of about 20 feet, pitching the ball inside or outside to a catcher in receiving position. The catcher's hips are up to improve quickness for throwing out the runner. After catching the ball, the catcher quickly moves her feet and assumes the throwing position with both arms up, then freezes in that position to check for proper alignment.

Timed Throws

Purpose: To evaluate quickness of release and speed of the throw.

Procedure: The catcher catches a pitched ball in full gear so that the drill is gamelike. The coach starts a stopwatch when the ball enters the glove and stops it when the ball is released or when the ball reaches the shortstop's glove at second base. Good times for the ball to go from glove to glove for college catchers are between 1.65 and 1.75 seconds. High school catchers should make the throw in less than 2 seconds.

Catcher to Bases

Purpose: To practice throwing to bases.

Procedure: An infielder covers each base. The pitcher delivers the ball, and the catcher throws to the player covering the base. Have a batter stand in the box and adjust her position so that the catcher learns to create a throwing lane. Use runners so that the catcher can judge the quickness of her throw. If you do not want players to slide, have them swing wide (away from the infield) as they approach the base.

Random-Ball Conditioning

Purpose: To practice throws to bases and improve conditioning.

Procedure: Randomly place six to eight balls in front of home. From the squat position the catcher explodes and throws to a receiver at the base, hustles back into catching position, and continues until all of the balls have been thrown. Repeat the drill with the catcher throwing to a different base.

Knee Throwing

Purpose: To practice throwing from the knees and to strengthen the arm.

Procedure: Two catchers kneel about 30 feet apart on one or both knees. They throw back and forth, using an overhand throw and pulling with the stomach muscles. They gradually increase the distance until throws are regulation distance to all the bases.

Catcher Fielding Bunts

Purpose: To practice fielding bunts and throwing to a base.

Procedure: The catcher is in squat position. A thrower standing behind her rolls out bunts for the catcher to field and throw to a receiver at the base. The catcher should explode from the box and get ahead of the ball.

7

Team Defense

Softball is a team game. Together the team is stronger than the individual parts. All players have responsibilities on every pitch and every play. No one should be standing around; the only spectators are in the stands. Previous chapters have dealt with the infield, outfield, and battery as separate units. This chapter covers specific areas in which everyone must work together to achieve success as a team.

DEFENSIVE POSITIONING

The team's overall defensive plan and strategies are designed by the coach and used as a starting point. Chapters 3 and 4 describe basic positioning for the infield and outfield. From the basic defensive setup, individual adjustments (see table 7.1) are made for each pitch based on many factors:

- Batter—Power, speed, and tendencies.
- Base runners—Number, position, speed, and offensive philosophy of the opponent.
- Pitcher—Speed, control, count, and pitch location.
- Opposing pitcher and team—The probability that a team will score more runs than their opponents will determine how aggressively they play each base runner.
- Abilities of the defensive players—Those of each player and the players around her.
- Game situation—Score, number of outs, and inning. Does the defense play aggressively or safe?
- Environment—Field, outfield fence, wind, temperature, wet or dry.

Players should go with the percentages. Statistics and scouting will tell players the positioning that offers the best chance of success. The game is a matter of inches and surprises. Players should play for the best odds, but when it doesn't work they should not second-guess their decisions. They made the best decisions they could with the information they had. That is the best they can do.

An adjustment of one or two steps may be all that is needed to be in the right place to make the play. But players must be careful not to leave significant gaps that can hurt the team should the pitcher miss her spot or hang a pitch. Shifts should be only a few steps in the direction the batter is expected to hit the ball. The team should play an unknown batter in regular defensive position. Any changes and adjustments must be communicated to adjacent teammates to eliminate gaps and clarify the areas each player is responsible for covering. Players can't work together if they don't know what their teammates are doing. They must constantly talk and communicate. If the outfield is back, they must warn the infield that they need to cover more territory. Two minds are better than one. Players should share information so that the wisest decision can be made:

- The center fielder adjusts the outfield because she is in the best position to communicate with the other two.
- The shortstop is usually the team leader on the infield. Her ability—she is usually the best infielder—and central position work to her advantage.
- The catcher has the entire defense in front of her, so she can most easily see the defensive setup and direct adjustments.

All players are involved in the specific plays covered in the rest of this chapter. Each player should understand her responsibilities and those of her teammates. She should work on the individual techniques involved and apply them to the teamwork required.

Table 7.1
Defensive Positioning Summary

Situation	Outfielders	Middle infielders	Corners
Batter			
Power hitter	Back 3 steps and 2 steps toward pull side	Back 2 steps	Back 2 steps
Bunter	In 5 steps	In 2 steps, second baseman 3 steps toward first base, shortstop 3 steps toward the base she covers	In as far as necessary to get the out
Slapper	All in 3 steps, left fielder 3 steps toward foul line	On base line, second baseman in bunt position	First baseman in 3 steps and shade toward pitcher, third baseman in 2 steps and 3 steps toward pitcher
Fast runner	Normal	In 2 steps	Normal unless looking for a bunt
Base runners			
Double play	Normal	Shade 2 to 3 steps toward second base	Normal
Runner on third and less than two out	In 2 steps	On base line	In 1 step
Winning run on third and less than two out	In to spot where player can throw out runner after catching a fly ball	In front of base line	In 1 step
Ahead by comfortable margin and fifth inning or later	Back 3 steps	Behind base path	Normal
Runners on, close game	In 3 steps	On base line	In 2 steps
Runners on first and third	In 2 steps	On base line	In 2 steps in case of a bunt
Runner on first and two out	Back 3 steps	Shortstop shades toward second base expecting a steal	Normal
Pitcher			
Slow speed	Back 3 steps and 2 steps toward pull side	Behind base line and 1 step toward pull side	Back 1 step
Fast speed and overpowering	Move 3 steps toward opposite field	Move 2 steps toward opposite field	Normal
Ahead in count	In 2 steps	Normal	Normal
Behind in count	Back 2 steps	Normal	Normal

(continued)

129

Table 7.1 (continued)

Situation	Outfielders	Middle infielders	Corners
Full count	Back 3 steps and 2 steps toward pull side	Back 1 step	Back 1 step
Drop	In 2 steps	Normal	Normal
Rise	Back 2 or 3 steps	Normal	Normal
Change	Back 3 steps and 2 steps toward pull side	Behind base line and 1 step toward pull side	Back 1 step
Curve	Back 2 steps and 2 steps toward batter's opposite field	Shade 1 step toward batter's opposite field	Normal
The Elements			
No fence	Back 3 to 5 steps	Normal	Normal
High fence	In 3 steps	Normal	Normal
Wind blowing in	In 3 steps	In 1 step	Normal
Wind blowing out	Back 3 steps	Back 1 step	Normal
Hard infield	Normal	Back 2 steps	Back 1 or 2 steps
Soft infield	Normal	In 2 steps	In 2 steps

From backing up, to bunt and slap defenses, pickoffs and rundowns, relays and cutoffs, and the first-and-third play, it will take nine players to achieve team success.

BACKING UP

Inexperienced players sometimes think they have nothing to do on some plays. But the responsibility of backing up falls on everyone on every play. Any player not going after the ball or covering a base should move into a position to back up the hit or a throw. Players should always assume that a hit ball is going to be missed and will have to be fielded by the backup. The player moves to the ball first. She goes directly behind the fielder making the play, being careful not to interfere with her or distract her in any way. If the ball gets by the first defender, the backup must hurry to make the play. If the first defender fields the ball successfully, the player adjusts to back up the throw. She should be in a direct line from the thrower to the intended receiver, 15 to 20 feet behind the receiver. For example, the pitcher should be close to the fence when backing up third or home so that she can quickly retrieve the ball off the fence. On a hit ball the player may move first to one position and then another, all the while hoping not to touch the ball.

Fielders have the following backup responsibilities:

Catcher: Backs up first on an infield hit unless a runner is on second or third base
Pitcher: Backs up throws to third or home
Outfield: Backs up the fielder on the ball; the extra outfielder backs up the base for the anticipated throw

Right fielder:	Backs up first on all infield plays
Center fielder:	Covers second base when no infielder can (for example, bunt with runner on second)
Left fielder:	Covers third base when no infielder can (for example, on a bunt to the third baseman with a runner on first)
Shortstop or second baseman:	With runners on base, back up every return throw from the catcher
First baseman:	Backs up the catcher on first and third plays if the runner is going; backs up the second baseman on throws from left and center field

BUNT DEFENSE

The abilities of the defensive players must be the primary consideration of the coach in deciding how to defend the bunt and who will make the play. The speed of the bunter–base runners and their ability to execute the short game (with all its options) will also be a factor.

The third and first basemen usually field most of the bunts. If the pitcher is a strong fielder, however, the coach may ask her to field many of the bunts, including those down the first-base line. The first baseman can then stay back to play first, and the second baseman can play in regular position. The coach should select a plan that best uses the abilities of the players. The person in the best position to field and throw should call for the bunt. Consideration should also be given to who has the strongest and most accurate arm when deciding who has priority. Communication is the key. "I've got it" or "Mine" helps clear the area and eliminate confusion.

With a runner on first, the first and third basemen take positions close enough to the bunter that they can consistently get the out. This often means that the corners are at least halfway down the line. The pitcher's responsibility is to back up the corners should the bunt get by them. The pitcher fields only bunts hit directly to her. On all other bunts she delays charging ahead and instead fans out to a backup position behind the player fielding the bunt.

When the third baseman fields the ball with a base runner on first, the catcher should follow her momentum to third base to cover the bag and prevent the runner from advancing from first to third. The third baseman calls "Mine," and the catcher follows with "I have third." The left fielder assumes a backup position.

The defensive assignments when anticipating a bunt with a runner on first base are as follows (see figure 7.1 on page 132):

Second baseman:	Moves several steps toward first base
	Covers first base
Shortstop:	Covers second base
Third baseman:	Covers the area between third base and the mound
	If not involved in the play, retreats to cover third base
First baseman:	Covers the area between first and the mound
Pitcher:	Delays and fans, except on balls hit directly to her
Catcher:	Fields all bunts close to the plate
	When the third baseman fields the bunt, covers third base
Left fielder:	Backs up third base
	Plays third base if an infielder does not get there in time
Center fielder:	Backs up second base for a throw from home
	If the throw goes to first base, shifts backup position to cover a possible second throw from first base
Right fielder:	Backs up first base

With a runner on second or third or with several runners on, the shortstop must cover third. The second baseman still covers first. The first and third basemen play up in their normal bunt positions. Second base is thus left open unless the first baseman is playing back. The center fielder covers this open base, and all defensive players must understand that they never throw to second because there is no backup in case of a bad throw (ideally, the center fielder will bluff the runner into staying). With a runner at or running to third, players should not be throwing behind her anyway.

The defensive assignments with runners on second or third or with multiple runners are as follows (see figure 7.2):

Second baseman:	Moves several steps toward first base to cut down the distance
	Covers first base
Shortstop:	Moves several steps closer to third
	Covers third base
Third baseman:	Covers the area between third and the mound
First baseman:	Covers the area between first and the mound
Pitcher:	Delays and fans, except on balls hit directly to her
Catcher:	Fields all bunts close to the plate
	Does not leave home plate
Left fielder:	Backs up third base
Center fielder:	Covers second base
Right fielder:	Backs up first base

When anticipating a bunt, the corners must be in close enough to have a good chance of getting an out. With runners on base the goal for advanced players is to get the lead runner. But if they can't get the lead runner, they must definitely get the batter. The goal is always to get an out on a sacrifice bunt. Whether it is wise to go after the lead runner will be determined by the speed of the runner, the speed and placement of the bunt, and how quickly the fielder gets to the ball. Even when these factors are in her favor, the defensive player must field the ball cleanly to get the lead runner. If she mishandles the ball even slightly and has any doubt about getting the lead runner, she must throw to first. Only advanced teams should go for the lead runner. For many teams, throwing to first base should be the only option.

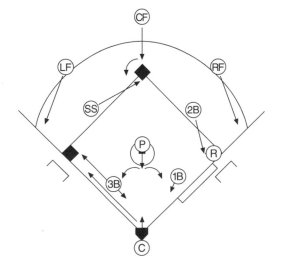

Figure 7.1 Bunt defense with runner on first base.

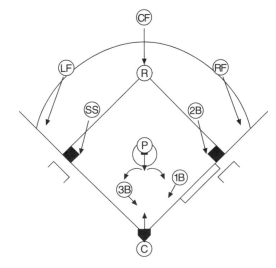

Figure 7.2 Bunt defense with a runner at second or third.

Fielders should watch the batter for tips that she is bunting. They should key in on the top hand; as soon as it starts to slide up the bat, they yell "Bunt." The bunter's feet or position in the box may also give away her intentions. The first baseman must be particularly observant with right-handed batters; likewise the third baseman for left-handed batters.

When the batter shows that she is bunting, the corners should begin to creep (move) in. As the bunt is put down, the fielders charge. They must be careful to charge the bunt, not the bunter. If they charge the batter, the ball may get by them.

Fielders should play all bunts as if they are fair and let the umpire make the call. If they cannot field the ball and get the out, they should let the bunt roll to see if it goes foul. The instant it reaches foul territory a fielder should touch it with the glove or foot so that it is ruled a foul ball, not taking the chance that it will roll back into fair territory.

The player fields a bunt by positioning her body so that the feet are already in line to throw. An approach from the side, instead of straight on, allows the feet to be in throwing position. The fielder surrounds the ball and sets her feet to the base she wants to throw to (see figure 7.3). When possible the ball should be fielded off the back foot. She fields with two hands to get a secure and firm grip. Advanced players should field with the feet aligned to throw to the lead base. If no play is possible there, the player still has time to adjust the feet for a throw to first base.

When the fielder must turn her body to make the throw, she always turns toward the glove to get the feet and shoulders in throwing position. This means that a right-handed first baseman fielding a bunt down the first-base line will turn her back to third when making a throw to second base. (The exception is when a right-handed first baseman throws to third base, as explained below.)

The first baseman's footwork will be different from that used by the third baseman or pitcher. Footwork will also vary depending on whether she is a left-handed or right-handed thrower. A left-handed first baseman will field bunts with the left foot ahead and weight on the throwing foot (see figure 7.4). The ball is fielded on the inside of the left foot. The first baseman then pushes off the left foot and steps directly to the target.

Figure 7.3 Third baseman fielding the bunt for a throw to second base.

Figure 7.4 Left-handed first baseman fielding the bunt for a throw to second base.

Coaching Points for the Bunt Defense

- When fielding bunts in practice, play all bunts as fair to save time and to develop the habit of playing all balls out, as you should in a game.
- Field the ball with two hands to get a firm grip.
- Dive for any bunts that are popped up. This will be a big out!
- When hurrying a throw you may not have time to straighten all the way up but make sure to level your shoulders to keep the ball on a straight line to the target. If the back shoulder is lower than the front shoulder, your throw will be high.
- With multiple runners, advanced players should approach each bunt with the feet in position to get the lead runner. If the player fields the ball cleanly, she looks to see if she can get the lead runner. If the player has any difficulty handling the ball, she should automatically go to first.
- When two players can field the ball, the player in the best throwing position should make the play. For example, for a play at third the first baseman should field the bunt rather than the third baseman. For a play at second the third baseman should make the play over a right-handed first baseman.

The action is the same for throwing to any base. A right-handed first baseman throwing to first or second base fields the ball with the right foot ahead. She pushes off and pivots on the right foot as she turns and steps toward the base. Her back will be to the infield as she turns toward the glove. She must not spin and throw at the same time. A right-hander throwing to third base does not pivot around because it is too difficult to find third base quickly. She fields the ball with the left foot ahead and pivots on the back foot. The turn is toward the right shoulder with the eyes always toward third.

On bunts down the first-base line, the first baseman should tag the runner when possible. This play has less chance of error and puts the defense in a better position to make additional plays. If the first baseman can make the runner stop and back up, a dead ball results, which means that all runners must return to their bases. This is the ideal situation—the defense gets the out without making a throw and the runners stay put.

SUICIDE SQUEEZE

A suicide squeeze is one of the most exciting plays in softball. With a runner on third the batter hides the intent to bunt until the last moment and then bunts the ball. Meanwhile, the runner breaks for home on the pitch and is coming home regardless of where the pitch is or whether the bunt is down.

The defense should look for tips that the suicide is on. Often the opponent's dugout will become quiet, and more players will stand to watch the play. More signals may be given and more time taken, along with extra looks between the coach and the batter. The defensive team should also know the opposing coach's tendencies. They should look for the suicide squeeze any time a runner is on third with less than two out. If they suspect a suicide squeeze, the catcher should call for a pitchout so that the batter cannot reach the ball and the runner is hung out to dry. The catcher will have the ball and can tag the runner or pick her off.

As soon as the squeeze is attempted, everyone should be yelling "Bunt." Seeing the runner break for home, all should be calling "Four" or "Home." The corners charge the ball. The fielder making the play has her body low, fields with two hands, and uses the underhand toss to get the ball to the catcher quickly. The wrist stays stiff as she swings the arm and tosses the ball. The ball is released quickly on a fast but low trajectory, knee high and slightly up the line. This may be a desperation play. It is sometimes necessary to catch the ball against the backside of the glove, not using the pocket, to save time.

SLAP DEFENSE

The fast slapper puts a lot of pressure on the defense to field the ball quickly and make the throw. The slapper also tries to bounce the ball to the shortstop, who has the longest throw. To help reduce the time needed to complete the play, the shortstop moves in closer to the batter, assuming a position at least as close as the base path. The third baseman pulls off the line to help the shortstop by cutting off slow hits and bouncing balls between them (see figure 7.5). The second baseman shades several steps toward first as she does for a bunt. The first baseman shades toward the second-base alley to cut off balls hit slowly toward the second baseman. The outfield moves in to be in position to field soft bloopers and shades several steps toward left field. The left fielder moves even closer to the left-field line in case the ball is slapped past the third baseman, who has opened up the line by moving in to help the shortstop.

Another option is to have the first baseman take a position midway between the pitcher and first base to cut off the right-side alley. The second baseman plays behind the line but near first base to eliminate the foot race with the runner to the base. This defense is vulnerable to a drag bunt.

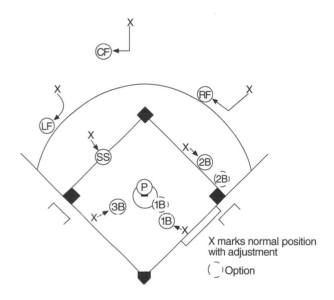

Figure 7.5 Slap defense.

PICKOFFS

When a runner takes a big lead, the defense can attempt to get her out using the pickoff. An alert catcher will always be looking for the opportunity to catch a runner off base. Not all picks are prearranged. That is why it is critical with runners on base that infielders always cover their bases in position to take a throw for a possible out. When the defensive player goes to the base, the runner must react, usually by going back to the base. When the runner is far enough off base and slow in returning, the catcher may attempt to pick her off. This is not a called pickoff but simply the reaction of an alert catcher. The play is set up by a defensive player who hustles back to cover the base and beats the runner there. When time permits, the baseman should give a target with the glove.

To attempt a called pickoff, the catcher or coach will signal for a pitchout. The catcher must give the signal to the pitcher and the defensive player taking the throw. The player who will receive the throw must give a return signal to the catcher and make sure that the backup knows the pickoff is on. It is critical that the backup be in proper position in case of a bad throw. The catcher may signal the defense even before she assumes the squat position, perhaps with a casual hand signal that is visible to everyone. The signal may also be given as one of the pitching signals, but this method requires all involved to be looking for the catcher's signals on every pitch.

The signals must be clear for the defense and not obvious to the offense. Here are some additional ideas for signaling the pickoff:

- The catcher may wipe the forehead, chest, or leg; pull on the mask; or throw some dirt. The signal can be given before assuming the squat position or in the squat.
- The fielder who will receive the ball must give an acknowledgment with a return signal. Examples are a tap of the glove or body or picking up dirt.
- The backup must also receive a signal and give a return signal. Verbal signals are often the easiest. For example, players can communicate using last names: "Hey, Smith, nobody scores!"
- The catcher should not proceed with the play if she does not receive a return signal. She should not waste the pitch and cannot assume that someone will be covering.

The pitchout is used not only to see the opposition's intentions but also to get the out by picking off the runner.

- If the runner is attempting to steal, the pitchout will give the catcher more time and put her in better throwing position.
- If the hit-and-run is on, the defense might throw out the runner without giving the batter an opportunity to hit the ball.
- If the bunt is on, the runner will often take a bigger lead. The defense should attempt to get the runner for the out.
- If the suicide is on, a pitchout will prevent the runner from scoring.

A pitchout is not always called when trying for the pickoff. In that case, the pitch should be one that the catcher can handle easily—outside, preferably high, and not a drop ball. The battery must be wary of throwing change-ups with aggressive runners on base.

Pickoff at First

To execute the pickoff at first, most often the second baseman will come in behind the runner, hoping to catch her by surprise. By moving back three to four steps into right field, the second baseman is out of the runner's line of vision. The second baseman must also cheat several steps closer to first if she has not already shaded that way anticipating a bunt with the runner on first. The second baseman breaks on the pitch and runs on a straight line to the inside of the base, placing the side of the left foot against the base. Because the second baseman will be taking the throw, the first baseman moves in as if covering a bunt and acts as a decoy, enticing the runner to take a bigger lead. The first baseman then ducks or moves to the side as the catcher makes the throw.

The first baseman may take the pickoff throw when she is playing back and when the pickoff is not prearranged. On called plays, the defense must be clear about who is taking the throw. The first baseman must indicate to the catcher and the second baseman that she is taking the throw. The right fielder is the backup for the play and should have already shaded slightly to the line because with a runner on first a bunt is expected. When the second baseman breaks on the pitch, so does the right fielder. They move together. It is critical that the right fielder reach the proper position on time.

The player covering the base, either the second baseman or the first baseman, takes the base away from the runner by standing at the back of the base. When the defensive player takes this position, the runner must go a greater distance outside the base path, making it more difficult to return to the base and touch the back corner. The defense thus has more time to make the play. The baseman takes a position on the infield side of the base with the heels even with the back of the base and the body in the base line (see figure 7.6). The player gives a target at the inside corner of the base about knee high. When she sees that the throw is on line, she drops down on the right knee to block the base as she catches the ball (see figure 3.14 on page 54). The runner will be diving back, not sliding.

If a right-handed player has not blocked the base runner off the base and the runner is going behind her, the player should turn counterclockwise to make the tag at the back of the base (see figure 7.7). Although this means turning her back to the runner, she has more time and distance to apply the tag and easier coverage of the back corner, which is where the runner is going. Should the runner break to second (delayed steal), teammates must loudly call "Going" because the player's back is to the runner. A left-handed player can more easily make a tag on the runner because the glove is on the same side as the runner. She can simply turn toward the runner to apply the tag. But when it is a close play and the runner is going behind her, she should use the technique of turning to the base to gain valuable time.

Advanced teams might try a fake pickoff at first. The goal of the fake is to have the runner going back to the base as the bunt is executed. The runner loses many steps if she is going the wrong way when the bunt is put down. With a runner on first, the second baseman runs two to three steps toward first as if setting up a pickoff, then stops not too far from her basic defensive position. To avoid being pulled too far out of

Figure 7.6 Position for receiving the pickoff throw at first base.

Figure 7.7 Right-handed player making the pickoff tag at the back of the base.

the basic position by the extra steps, the second baseman can quietly shift two to three steps toward second base as the pitcher approaches the rubber. The defense can occasionally use this play to inhibit the runner. If the play is used too often, the runner will not believe a pickoff is really on.

Pickoff at Second

The shortstop, second baseman, or center fielder can take the pickoff throw to second. By using different players the defense can catch the runner by surprise and make it difficult for her to know whom to watch. Another advantage of having several options is that one player may be closer to the bag and able to get there more quickly. For example, if the shortstop has pulled closer to third to protect against a steal of third or to be in better fielding position against a big pull hitter, the second baseman can more easily cover second. The catcher must know which player will be covering so that she can throw to a target. The infielders should signal to the catcher which player is covering the bag. Often the shortstop will act as a decoy by standing closer to third base, allowing the runner to take a bigger lead. Then the second baseman sneaks in behind the runner. If the shortstop will be making the play, she should back up several steps out of the runner's line of vision. Beginners may use only the second baseman because the runner and second baseman are on opposite sides of the bag, reducing the chance that one will interfere with the other. The center fielder must always back up the throw.

The center fielder can really surprise the runner by coming in from behind to make the pickoff. If this play is called, one of the other outfielders must shade toward center to get to a backup position behind second base. Should a wild throw occur, this outfielder is the only one who can stop the ball.

The receiving position for all receivers is between the runner and second base. The left foot is slightly ahead of and against the third-base side of second, the hips are down, and the body is well balanced. The player catches the ball and drops to one knee using the leg to block the base (see figure 7.8). For a full description see "Blocking the Base" in chapter 3, page 54.

Figure 7.8 Shortstop making the pickoff play at second base.

Pickoff at Third

On the pickoff at third, the third baseman or shortstop takes the throw. This is often a called play initiated by the coach to get an aggressive runner. A misplay here means that a run scores, so some teams never attempt a pickoff at third, considering it too risky. When the third baseman is back near the base, she takes the throw. Of course, when the third baseman is at the base, the runner will usually not take a big lead, making a pickoff less likely to succeed.

The shortstop comes in behind the runner when the third baseman is pulled in. If the third baseman moves in as if to field a bunt, the runner will be drawn farther off the base. When assuming the ready defensive position, the shortstop should cheat a little toward third so that she can get there more quickly. She must be careful, however, that the shift does not give away the pickoff attempt. The shortstop should not play deeper because doing so would increase the distance to third and she is not in the runner's line of vision anyway.

Communication is essential. Everyone must know who is covering the base. The left fielder backs up third for an overthrow. The receiver takes a position at the front corner of the bag and gives a knee-high target on the inside of the base line to establish a throwing lane. Both feet are on the infield side of the base with the right foot on the front corner of the base. Care must be taken to avoid hitting the runner with the throw because she will then usually score.

When the defense suspects a squeeze, the catcher should call for a pitchout and try to strand the runner. The third baseman must be well in front of the bag to encourage a good lead but not so far in that the offense calls off the squeeze. A pitchout allows the shortstop to break early to cover third.

Game Philosophy

When should the defense use a pickoff? Although sometimes the coach calls it, an alert catcher always looks for the opportunity. It is definitely a boost to the defense when the play works. A successful pickoff can demoralize the offense, often changing the momentum of the game. The element of surprise contributes to the chance of success. A team should not overuse the play.

The defense should consider several points in deciding whether to attempt the pickoff play:

- Does the defense, particularly the catcher, have the ability to make the out?
- Is the pitcher struggling so much that getting an out is a high priority?
- Is the runner off the base far enough to get the out?
- Would it be useful to set a pattern to keep aggressive base runners closer to the bag?
- Is the runner slow in returning to the base and not very alert?
- When the offense may be putting on a bunt, steal, or hit-and-run, does the base runner take an extra step?
- Is the field soft with poor footing?
- On the first pitch of a first-and-third play, the defense can pitch out to see what runners are doing. They should look to get the runner at third.

A team must always consider the game situation:

- Number of outs. With two out is the runner likely to score? If not, the defense should not risk the chance that an error will score her.
- What is the ability of the next batter? What are the chances of getting the batter out and ending the inning there? An error on a pickoff play can be costly.
- What is the count? With two strikes and two outs, the focus should be on the batter. The pickoff should be called when the pitcher is ahead on the count.

- What is the philosophy of the opposing coach? Does she or he like to run? How aggressive is the runner likely to be?
- How important is the runner? If she is not that important, the defense should go after the batter.

The pickoff throw should not be made when the catcher does not catch the ball cleanly, when the runner is not far enough off the base to have a chance of getting her, when no one is covering the base, or when there is no play. Any misplay on the pickoff attempt gives the runner an opportunity to advance, so the defense should not risk a throw unless they have a legitimate chance of being successful. A fake throw may hold the runner. The defense can also fake covering the base, driving the runner back by running behind her.

With multiple runners the defense must be careful about throwing behind the runners and providing an alert lead runner the opportunity to advance. They must not use the pickoff too often because the chance for error increases and the play slows the game.

Coaching Points for the Pickoff

- Make sure that the catcher and adjacent infielders know who is taking the throw.
- Don't waste the throw. Throw only if there is an opportunity to make an out.
- Use a look or a fake throw instead of throwing when doing so will hold the runner close.
- The receiver should take the base away from the runner when time permits.
- Use the element of surprise to pick off the runner. An out is not always the result of a quick release or the strongest arm.

STEALS

When a base runner goes to the next base on a pitch or throw, it is scored as an "attempted steal." Catching the runner stealing requires not only a quick, accurate throw from the catcher but also a total team effort. Good communication is necessary to alert the defense that the runner is going and to make sure it is clear who is covering the base.

Straight Steal

When a runner attempts to steal second, the shortstop takes the throw because she can face the runner and the runner will not interfere with the throw. The runner would be in front of the second baseman trying to get to the bag. On an attempted steal of third, the shortstop must take the base if the third baseman is up well in front of the base. The third baseman would not be in a position to see the runner, and it would be difficult for her to retreat on a full run and make the play. The third baseman may take the throw when playing back close to the bag, but she must clearly indicate to the catcher and shortstop that she is covering the bag.

The shortstop will either break with the runner and go directly to the base or wait to see if the ball is hit and then play it if it comes her way. The coach will usually dictate the philosophy used. If the runner likes to steal, the shortstop will often go with the runner. If the batter is a good contact hitter and the hit-and-run play may be on, the shortstop will hold her ground and play the ball. The second baseman then covers second for a possible double play. A pitchout frees the shortstop to go to the base immediately and not worry about the ball being hit.

The receiver must get to the base quickly. Ideally, she should be waiting at the base for the throw. She then applies the tag and takes the base away from the runner. See chapter 3 for specific techniques.

Delayed Steals

On a delayed steal the runner steals not on the catcher but on a throw. The runner takes her lead and steals on the throw back to the pitcher or a throw to another base. She might also take a slightly longer lead than normal to draw a pickoff attempt and then break on a throw behind her. When the runner breaks, the defense must yell loudly that she is going so that the player with the ball can react and make the throw to the base the runner is advancing to. If the base runner is caught between bases, the defense uses the rundown techniques described later in this chapter.

A delayed steal should never occur. The catcher must carefully watch all base runners and return the ball to the pitcher only after chasing the runners back to their bases. The catcher can do this by simply looking in their direction, by bringing the arm up as if to throw, or by taking a step in their direction. The catcher should never throw behind a runner who is far enough off the base to attempt a steal on the throw. Instead, she should throw ahead of the runner to keep her from advancing and chase her back. With multiple runners, attention must always be on the lead runner. The catcher should throw to pick off a runner only if she has a real chance of success. A throw may provide the opportunity for another runner to steal on the play.

RUNDOWNS

The purpose of the rundown (sometimes called a pickle) is to make an out on the runner caught between the bases. Should the defense fail to get the out, they must make sure that the runner does not advance a base. Three or fewer throws should be enough to get the runner. Using only a few throws cuts down the potential for error and gives any other base runners less time to advance. If a team needs more than three throws, they have not run hard enough at the runner to make her commit in one direction. The perfect play retires the runner without a throw. Players should execute the rundown with confidence and a belief that it is the runner who is in trouble.

When a runner is caught between bases, the player with the ball should run hard at her to make her commit to a direction. The direction should not be to the advanced base; the defensive player should chase the runner back to where she was. Therefore, the first throw must be ahead of the runner. To throw, the player holds the ball up (visible to the receiver) as if throwing a dart (see figure 7.9). The arm should not go back past the ear. The thrower should not fake because she could lose her grip and might fake out the receiver.

The throwing path is not on the base path where the ball might hit the runner and be difficult for the receiver to see.

Figure 7.9 Dart throw for rundowns.

The throw should never go over the runner. Throws should be shoulder high and on the diamond side of the base path because more backup is available. The throw is made with moderate speed when the receiver calls "Now." The receiver should give a target with the hands together slightly above the shoulders.

As the receiver catches the ball, she steps toward the base runner to close the distance and get closer for the tag. If possible, the tag is made with two hands to secure the ball and to permit a quicker release if there is another runner. The receiver must be two to three steps in front of the base when catching the ball. She should take the base away from the runner so that the runner's dive won't allow her to reach the base before the tag. If the runner is running toward the defensive player, the tag is made with a bent arm using a bullfighter's motion, as if using a cape with a charging bull. Using this motion protects the arm and the ball, and by avoiding a collision, the player can go quickly after other base runners. She comes up ready to throw.

The fielders' rotation is to follow the throw and go to the end of the opposite line. The fielder runs outside the base path and never crosses it. She must not stay on the base path where the runner can run into her and get an obstruction call. Two players should be in each line, preferably infielders because they are more experienced playing the base (see figure 7.10). On rundowns between first and second, the catcher, first baseman, second baseman, and shortstop are usually involved. But if the catcher has to stay at home because other runners are on base, then the pitcher, right fielder, or center fielder will join in. Between second and third, the first baseman, second baseman, shortstop, and pitcher or left fielder are usually in the play. Between third and home, the catcher, shortstop, first baseman, and third baseman usually make the play, although sometimes the pitcher or left fielder becomes involved.

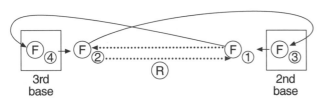

Figure 7.10 Rundown rotation and positioning.

Coaching Points for the Rundown

• Get the runner in three or fewer throws.

• Throw ahead of the runner first to chase her back.

• Throw with the motion of a dart thrower on the signal "Now." Keep the throw on the inside of the base path.

• Tag with your arm bent like that of a bullfighter.

• Rotate by following the throw and going to the end of the opposite line.

• Stay out of the base path and out of the runner's way unless you have the ball.

• After tagging the runner come up ready to throw.

FIRST-AND-THIRD SITUATIONS

The first-and-third play is one of the most difficult to defend, and it is challenging to run offensively as well. What the defense does is determined by the reaction of the runners, and the runners try to react to the defensive sets. For this reason the following section describes both the offensive plays and the defensive options.

With runners on first and third, the goal of the offense is either to score the runner from third or to advance the runner from first to second so that two runners are in scoring position. The offense will often sacrifice the runner between first and second, taking the out if the runner at third can score. The goal of the defense is to keep the runner at third from scoring and to hold the runner at first. Should the runner attempt to go to second base, the defensive goal is to get her out without letting the run score.

The best plans of either the offense or defense can go awry. Because of the risk involved, the defense may decide not to give the opponent the chance to win or tie the game on the fielders' ability to execute this play. Many coaches would rather have a hit decide the game and choose to ignore the play entirely or use a simple plan. The key to success for either the defense or the offense is to be fundamentally sound. The team that capitalizes on this play is the team that can run it without making mistakes.

Offensive Base-Running Options

The offense will use a first-and-third play in the following situations:

- Both base runners have speed and ability on the bases.
- The offense is struggling, and the team needs to make something happen.
- The defense is jittery.
- A weak hitter is at the plate.
- The team is facing a strong pitcher who is in control.
- It is late in the game with at least one out.

Two common setups can occur. With a runner at third the runner at first might execute a straight steal. But she may have arrived at first by a walk and simply continue to second. The defense must be prepared to react to both situations.

Runner at Third and Batter Walks.   After reaching first base the batter continues to second with no hesitation, even if the pitcher has the ball. The runner runs full speed to first and after making the turn to second slows to a trot. If it appears that no throw will be made to second, the base runner speeds up about 10 feet from second and slides hard into the base to avoid being caught by a surprise throw and tag. If a throw is made, the runner puts on the brakes and reverses direction, attempting to become involved in a rundown. If the defense runs the runner back to first, she may take off again on the throw back to the pitcher. Likewise, if the defense immediately throws to first base after the walk, the runner takes off on the first baseman's return throw to the pitcher.

Runner at Third and Runner at First Steals.   In this offensive play the batter takes a pitch, and the runner at first executes a straight steal. The runner stays alive and gets the defense to react so that she can take advantage of their defensive plan:

- If the ball is cut or not thrown to second base, the runner goes to second.
- If the ball is thrown through to second, the runner puts on the brakes and becomes caught in a rundown, giving the runner at third an opportunity to score.
- The runner can also use a delayed steal as the ball is returned to the pitcher.

The runner at third also reacts to the plan of the defense:

- If the ball goes directly back to the pitcher, the runner on third returns to the base immediately. She must stay there until the ball leaves the circle.

- If the defense is throwing to second and using a player to cut, the runner may draw the cut to ensure that the runner advances safely to second. The runner does not take a normal lead; she waits on the base until the catcher makes the throw. The runner on third then leads off hard (fakes a break) so that the defense assumes she is going and will execute a cut. The runner then immediately returns to the base because the player making the cut is looking for the opportunity to pick her off. If the runner on third takes a normal lead and then breaks a couple more steps, she will be so far off that the defense has a good chance of a pickoff.

- If the runner from first succeeds in becoming caught in a rundown, the runner at third reacts accordingly and goes for home when the opportunity arises. In this situation, the runner at third looks for the following:

  —The ball is in the fielder's glove, not in the throwing hand. The runner will gain a little time.

  —The infielder forgets about the runner.

  —The runner is being chased back to first by a right-handed thrower or to second by a left-handed thrower. The thrower will have to turn the feet and shoulders to make the throw home, and the runner can better see the throw coming. Runners should mirror each other with their leads. The closer the runner is pushed to first, the farther the lead runner can lead off; the closer the runner is to second, the closer the lead runner should be to third. If the runner at third becomes caught in a rundown, the other runner should attempt to get to third base.

- The runner may go home on the throw to second, making sure that the ball gets past the pitcher. The runner must have excellent speed and good reactions to challenge the defense in this manner. This play is used most often when the defense does not use a cut.

Defensive Options

The goal of the defense is to keep runners from advancing and get at least one out on the play. Primary attention must always be to the runner at third. Teammates must yell "Home" the instant the runner at third breaks. The defense gives up on the runner in the rundown to make sure that the runner at third does not score. If the runner on third gets too far off, the defender with the ball runs directly at her to get her to commit to a direction. Once one play has been made, fielders must be alert to a possible play on the other runner. All of these options can be used for walks and steals too.

Runner Caught in Rundown. Each of the following first and third plays can result in a rundown. The defense uses the regular rundown techniques to chase the runner back to first. The primary concern is still the runner at third, so players listen closely for their teammates to yell "Home" should the runner break. When that occurs, they direct all attention to the third-base runner. If the runner is hung out to dry between home and third, the player with the ball runs directly at her to make her commit to one direction. When in doubt the throw should go ahead of the runner to chase her back to third. On rundowns between first and second, the team should give up the rundown if the lead runner is threatening to score. In any rundown between first and second, the defense should tag out the runner quickly, being careful not to become tangled up in making the tag or otherwise being in poor position for a throw home.

Throw to Pitcher. When the defense runs this play, the catcher first looks to third after a walk to see if the runner can be picked off. If there is no sure play, the catcher returns the ball quickly to the pitcher in the circle. With the ball in the circle, the runner at third must return to the base. She cannot leave again (unless another play is made), so the defense can now ignore her. The pitcher watches the batter–base runner approach first base. If she continues to second, the pitcher moves to the back of the circle to be closer to second base. When the runner is 10 to 15 feet from second, the pitcher throws to the shortstop covering the base for the tag. The pitcher must throw early enough to allow for the runner's sudden acceleration into the base. The shortstop can help the pitcher's timing by calling "Now." The first baseman and third baseman remain at their bases in case a rundown follows. The pitcher then steps slightly off line to clear the throwing path home if the runner at third goes.

Throw to Second Baseman in Pickoff Position. This is a play option to use when the batter has walked with a runner on third. An advantage of throwing to a short second base is that the throw home is shorter and has more chance of getting the runner. The second baseman is in position for a quick tag that may surprise the runner, and her position on the base path may even discourage some runners from trying to advance to second.

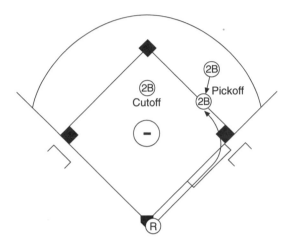

Figure 7.11 Pickoff and cutoff second base positions.

The second baseman takes a position on the base path about 15 to 20 feet from first base (see figure 7.11). The catcher has the option of throwing to the second baseman as the runner rounds first. The second baseman can apply the tag to the runner or hold the runner at the base if the throw arrives early. If the runner at third breaks for home, the defense must shout "Home," and the second baseman must forget the runner at first and go after the lead runner. The goal is always to get the lead runner. The throw goes to the catcher if the runner on third breaks for the plate. If the runner stops, the second baseman chases her back to third by running at her and then making the play at third.

Throw to Shortstop at Second Base. The catcher, after checking the lead runner, holds the ball to see if the batter continues to second. If the runner is advancing, the catcher throws to the shortstop covering second. The defense should use this play only if both players have strong, accurate arms and a slow runner is at third. The catcher does not throw down until the runner approaches second base. If the throw is too early, the runner will have time to stop and set up a rundown. This play is used most often with two outs.

Throw to Second Baseman in Cutoff Position. This difficult play requires many accurate throws. The defense must know what they are capable of. The second baseman takes a position in direct line from home to second and about 15 to 20 feet behind the pitcher's rubber (see figure 7.11). The body is sideways with the chest toward third base, which is the best position from which to make a throw home. The target is given to the catcher with the glove shoulder high. The catcher throws to the shortstop covering second base. The throw should be through the second baseman at a height where she can catch the ball easily. If the runner at third breaks for home, the second baseman cuts the ball and throws home. She must not watch the runner while making the catch. The second baseman focuses on catching the ball and relies on teammates to call for the cut by yelling "Home" or "Going." If the lead runner does not break on the throw, the second baseman fakes a catch and allows the ball to go directly through to the shortstop covering second to get the runner coming from first. A fake catch may stop the runner at third from thinking of going.

On a Straight Steal. If the runner on first executes a straight steal, the catcher's first look is always to third to see if the runner can be picked off. If there is no play at third, then the catcher throws to the shortstop or second baseman in the short or cutoff position, depending on the team's strategy. The catcher may also choose not to make a play and return the ball sharply to the pitcher.

The catcher has several options:

1. Pick off the runner at third.

2. Fake a throw to second and then attempt a pickoff at third, hoping to catch the runner leaning or breaking for home.

3. Throw to second base. The second baseman in the cutoff position cuts the throw if the base runner at third goes home as described earlier. The cut occurs if the defense yells "Going." If the runner does not break for home, the throw goes through to the shortstop for a tag or a possible rundown back to first.

4. Throw to second baseman in the basepath. The catcher keeps her body aligned as if she were throwing to second base but instead throws to the second baseman using the short second base option described earlier to set up a shorter return throw to home if the runner at third goes.

Other Considerations.   The defense must also be prepared for the possibility that the offense may bunt, slap, or run fake plays with runners at the corners. Scouting the opposition to know their tendencies will help, but the key is to be prepared for anything. Using a pitchout may help the defense set up the offense. If the offense chooses to play it safe and not steal, the defense should look for tactics like fake breaks that the offense may use in hopes of drawing throws and creating errors.

Sometimes the defense may be wise not to make a play. Some instances might be any of the following: (a) there are two out, (b) the batter is not a big threat, (c) the pitcher is in control, or (d) the runs are not that important. The defensive team may choose to make the opponent win with the bat rather than let them create their offense with base running and possible defensive errors. If the defense chooses not to make the play, they can try to bluff the runners into staying put. The catcher can fake a throw, or the team can use verbal cues to indicate that they are going for the runner. The coach may call "Get the runner if she goes" while signaling that the team will make no throw. Play-

Coaching Points for the First-and-Third Play

- Know the capability of your defense.
- Weigh the risks involved against the importance of the run at third and the value of keeping the other runner at first.
- Because young players find it difficult to decide quickly how to respond, the coach can call the play to be used after the pitcher throws ball three (in case of a walk) or, with a runner already on first, before the pitch.
- If the first baseman holds the ball at first base, it may discourage the runner from taking off for second after a walk or putout. Sometimes the umpire will call time if all players are standing still even though that is not the intent of the rules. The alert base runner may be planning to take off on the first baseman's throw back to the pitcher.
- Returning the ball quickly to the pitcher is the easiest defense because the runner at third must return immediately to the bag. The defense can ignore her and concentrate on the other base runner.

ers can also talk and bluff the runner and opposing coaches. Teams that vary both offensive and defensive strategies create an element of surprise that will often lead to success.

RELAYS

Relay throws are used when the ball is hit over or through the outfield and help is needed to get the ball to a base. Over a long distance two throws are more efficient than one and are always faster than a rainbow throw or a throw that bounces several times.

The shortstop is the relay for throws from the left fielder and center fielder. The second baseman is the relay for throws from right field. The exception is for balls on or near the foul lines. Then the third baseman or first baseman becomes the relay because they can more easily get in line with the fielder. If two players are in position where either could assume the relay and one has a significantly stronger arm, that player may be asked to make the relays when possible.

Distance between the relay and the target base depends on the strength and accuracy of the arms involved. A general rule is that the outfielder throws about 60 percent of the distance. The player making the relay moves with the outfielder until the outfielder stops, moving as if they were joined by a rope. As the outfielder bends to get the ball, the relay lines up in a straight line to the intended target.

Communication is vital. The relay must know where to throw the ball. Because the defensive team always wants to throw ahead of the runner or runners, one can usually assume that the throw will be going to third or home. The catcher and third baseman are in the best position to view the situation and need to yell loudly the commands of "Three, three" for third base or "Four, four" for home plate. They must make the call early so that the relay has time to line up properly. The player covering the base shouts "Right" or "Left" to help the relay player line up.

After the runner passes first base, an option is to have the first baseman back up any relays the second baseman is taking or cover second base so that the second baseman can back up the shortstop. The tradeoff is that the first baseman cannot act as a cutoff.

As the outfielder picks up the ball, the relay must wave her arms and yell so that the thrower can find her quickly. The relay doesn't stop calling or waving until the ball is on its way. She then turns sideways toward the glove to catch the ball over the throwing shoulder while moving sideways toward the infield. Being in motion eliminates the extra step needed for a hard throw. The relay moves toward the target, sees it, and throws.

Coaching Points for the Relay

- The outfielder should throw 60 percent of the distance.
- The relay moves with the outfielder as if they are joined by a rope.
- The catcher or third baseman calls for a throw to "Three" or "Four."
- The base player calls "Left" or "Right" to line up the relay with the target.
- The relay waves her arms and hollers until the outfielder releases the ball.
- The throw to the relay should be shoulder height. The relay turns sideways to catch the ball over the throwing shoulder while moving toward the infield.

CUTOFFS

A cutoff is used to intercept a throw to a base. Its purpose is to assist on weak throws or throws that are off line, or, if the throw is too late and the runner has already scored, to stop other runners from advancing. The cutoff is most commonly used on throws going home, and the first baseman is usually the cutoff. On balls hit near the left-field foul line, the third baseman may serve as the cut while still playing the base. On balls hit sharply to right field, the first baseman's first responsibility is to play first base.

The cutoff takes a position about 30 feet in front of the plate (near the pitcher's rubber) and directly in line with the thrower and the catcher (see figure 7.12). The catcher has the responsibility to position the cutoff by calling "Right," "Left," or "OK" until the cutoff is properly aligned. The thrower's target is home plate no matter where the cutoff is. The cutoff should wave both arms so the thrower has a better target. The cutoff should anticipate the upcoming play by noting the progress of the runners.

If the throw is off line, the catcher will call "Cut four" if the ball has a chance of getting the runner at home with the cutoff's help. If the catcher does not make the call but it is obvious that the ball needs help, the cutoff should take the initiative and make the cut. The cutoff should not make the cut if the throw is straight enough that the catcher can play it and get the out at home. Even if the throw appears slow or is bouncing, cutting it and making another throw takes more time. No call means that the cutoff should let the ball go through and pivot quickly away to allow the catcher to see it. The cutoff should fake a cut to stop other runners from advancing.

If the throw is too late, the catcher calls for the ball to be cut using one-word cues, such as, "Cut two, two, two" until the cut and throw are made. When "Cut" is called, the cutoff player should turn so the front shoulder points at the target as the catch is made. The cutoff catches the ball near the throwing shoulder for a quick release and looks for a play on the runner approaching the base called for by the catcher.

If the runner is not advancing home, the cut can be used to make sure that the ball doesn't get by the catcher. The call must be made well in advance so that the cutoff has time to react. If the cutoff has any doubt about whether to cut the throw, she should let the ball go through. The first effort must be to get any runner attempting to score.

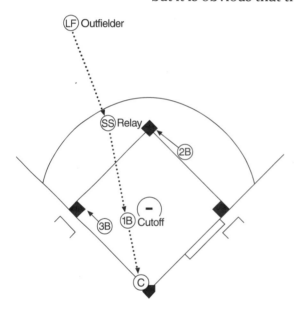

Figure 7.12 Cutoff position.

Coaching Points for the Cutoff

- The cutoff takes a position directly in line with the throw about 30 feet from home. The catcher calls "Left" or "Right" to help with alignment.
- The cutoff waves both arms. The thrower's target is home plate.
- The catcher calls "Cut" if the ball is off line or if the throw is too late to get the runner going home. She then calls the base to throw to.
- The cutoff player turns the front shoulder to the target as the catch is made.
- Do not cut a throw that is on line even if it will bounce several times.
- When there is no cut, the cutoff pivots away from the ball.

TEAM DEFENSE DRILLS

Use the following drills to work on team defensive skills.

Fielders should practice fielding bunts with both hands and with their feet in position to make the anticipated throw. Infielders should call "Bunt" loudly on the attempt and "Mine" when fielding the bunt to avoid any confusion about who will make the play. Start defensive players in their regular positions so timing and coverage are realistic. The first four drills focus on defending bunts.

Timing is critical when executing a pickoff. For pickoff drills ("Pickoff at First" and "Throw Through and Second-Baseman Cut"), have a pitcher throw pitches at normal speed. Fielders should start from their regular defensive positions so they can learn when they need to break on the pitch. As players' skills increase and throws become accurate, add baserunners so the defense can work on positioning and timing. These are also great conditioning drills for the runners.

Players must run full speed at the runner to make her commit, so work with your fielders to practice the dart throw at this speed. Use the progression of the next three drills to develop proper rundown techniques.

Relays must practice catching the ball sideways while moving to the target to save valuable time needed to get the runner—this can make the difference on close plays. Cutoffs are also quick plays that demand proper positioning and good timing. The last three drills work on these skills. Use base runners to help your fielders develop good decision-making skills and to create game pressure when practicing relays and cutoffs.

Roll Bunts

Purpose: To practice fielding bunts.

Procedure: Players assume defensive positions for fielding bunts. A coach stands behind the catcher and rolls balls onto the infield to be fielded as bunts. Players practice throwing to different bases.

Catcher–Third Base Exchange

Purpose: To have the catcher practice covering third when the third baseman fields the bunt.

Procedure: This drill requires two catchers, two third basemen, and one or two second baseman. The catchers, each with a ball, are behind home plate. A catcher rolls a bunt to one of the third basemen, who throws to the second baseman covering first. The catcher calls "I have third" and runs to cover the base. She receives the return throw from first base and applies a tag at third base. The catcher then runs home in foul territory while the second catcher and third baseman are executing the drill.

Pitcher and Catcher Throw Downs

Purpose: To have the catcher practice throw downs to the shortstop covering second and to have the pitcher practice fielding bunts and throwing to first.

Procedure: The drill requires a catcher, pitcher, shortstop, second baseman, and first baseman. Place empty buckets behind second base and first base. The pitcher and a coach each have a bucket of balls. The pitcher pitches a ball to the catcher in proper receiving position. The catcher should wear all gear to make the drill gamelike. On the first pitch the catcher throws down to the shortstop covering second. The coach, who is standing near the catcher, then rolls out a bunt, and the pitcher makes the play to first with the second baseman covering. The shortstop and second baseman both begin in their regular defensive positions so that base coverage is realistic. When players catch balls at the bases, they immediately drop them in the nearest bucket so that the drill can proceed rapidly.

Bunt Around

Purpose: To practice bunting and bunt defense with two stations on one infield.

Procedure: Set up two bunt defenses, each using half the field. Use second base as a second home plate and third base as another first base (see figure 7.13). The pitchers are back to back with one pitching to home and one to second. Bunters are in a line at each home plate. They bunt and run to first with the defense making the play to the first base on their half of the field. Runners continue running to the other bunting line. To keep the drill going, use only one bat at each plate.

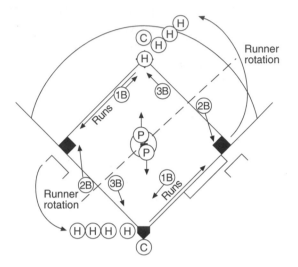

Figure 7.13 Bunt around drill.

Pickoff at First

Purpose: To have the catcher work on pickoff throws to first off pitched balls. The second baseman works on timing as she takes the pickoff at first.

Procedure: A pitcher pitches to the catcher with the second baseman in the normal starting position for a pickoff (several steps deeper while shading toward first). The second baseman breaks on the pitch in time to be at first base to receive the catcher's throw.

Variations:

- Add runners (wearing helmets) who work on leadoffs while the second baseman works on positioning and blocking runners off first.

- Add a shortstop. Runners alternate diving back, executing delayed steals, and performing straight steals to keep the defense honest. An extra second baseman calls the cues for the defense, that is, "Going."

Throw Through and Second-Baseman Cut

Purpose: To practice throw throughs by the catcher to the shortstop covering second and the second-base cut and throw home.

Procedure: The drill requires a pitcher, catcher, shortstop, and second baseman. On the first pitch the catcher throws through to the shortstop covering second. The ball is returned to the pitcher. On the second pitch the second baseman moves to the cutoff position behind the pitcher's rubber, cuts the throw, and throws home. Players continue to alternate between the two plays. Both throws from the catcher should be at one height so that the second baseman can cut the ball if the runner breaks and the defense calls "Home." Players begin in regular positions to work on timing and make the drill gamelike.

Variations:

- Add runners to work on timing.

- The second baseman cuts and throws to the third baseman covering third.

Rundown Dart Throw

Purpose: To practice the dart throw for relay and rotation.

Procedure: The drill uses three players. Two players in a line are facing one player. A player at the head of the line has a ball and runs toward her teammate ready to use a dart throw. The receiver calls "Now" and closes the gap when receiving the ball. She rotates to the end of the opposite line behind the receiver. Players run at medium speed. This is a good warm-up drill at the beginning of practice.

Full-Speed Dart Throws

Purpose: To improve accuracy of relay dart throws when running at full speed as needed in a game.

Procedure: A player faces a partner about 20 feet away. The thrower runs hard for three or four steps and makes an accurate dart throw to the receiver, who closes the gap and makes an imaginary tag. Players retreat to starting positions, and the partner repeats the drill going in the opposite direction. The focus is on running hard and making accurate throws.

Rundowns With Runner

Purpose: To practice defensive aspects of rundowns with a runner.

Procedure: Two lines of fielders take defensive positions for a rundown with a runner between bases. Have several runners ready to rotate in or have one runner who rotates to a defensive position after running. If the players are not on the diamond, number the bases so that the defense will know which is the lesser base. A coach throws a ball to the player at the front of one line. The defense may have to make a throw to get the ball to the player who can chase the runner back to the lesser base. The players then work on proper execution of the rundown, using only three throws to get the runner. The runner wins on the fourth throw and gets to rotate out.

Three-Player Line Relay

Purpose: To practice relay techniques and making accurate throws.

Procedure: Three players line up about 30 feet apart in a straight line. The middle player acts as the relay. While facing the relay, a player at one end drops the ball over her head. She turns and picks it up, locates the relay, and makes the throw. The relay waves and hollers until the ball is in the air. The relay throws to the third player, who repeats the drill in the opposite direction. The relay can move slightly off line to make it more challenging for the thrower to find the target.

Outfield Relay Throws

Purpose: To practice relay throws from the outfield.

Procedure: With the defense on the field and a runner at first or second, the coach drops a ball behind an outfielder. The defense executes the relay. The catcher calls for the play at third or home.

Variations:

- Add the cutoff.
- Practice gamelike situations with runners running from home, second, and first on fungoed balls. Practice execution of the cut.

Cutoffs and Team Defense

Purpose: To develop better decision making on the cutoff by executing the play with runners.

Procedure: A defensive team takes their positions. Alternate between starting a runner at first and starting a runner at second. A hitter or coach fungo hits ground balls to the outfielders, who field the balls and throw to the first baseman in the cutoff position. If a pitcher is part of the drill, she works on backing up third or home. The team practices cuts and throws to second and third. Emphasize making good decisions about the cut and making good throws all around. If the outfielder catches the ball in the air, the defense plays it out as a ground ball to avoid wasting time.

Variation: To practice relays as well as the cutoff, players can let the ball go through the outfield or the hitter can hit it over their heads.

8

Hitting

Hitting has been described as the most difficult task in all of sport. When a softball pitcher releases the ball, she is only 30 to 40 feet from the batter. The best pitchers can throw 65 to 68 miles per hour, which is equivalent to a 90-mile-per-hour pitch in baseball. At that speed the ball reaches the plate in .39 seconds. Factor in the various pitches that can be thrown (drop, rise, curve, change, and variations of those pitches), and the difficulty of hitting becomes obvious. Players aspire to a batting average of .300, which means that they fail to hit safely 7 times out of 10. Many find it difficult to get enough hitting practice. One estimate is that the average high school player practices hitting only 3 1/2 hours per season. Meanwhile, the pitcher is throwing over 200 pitches a day. To be good, consistent hitters, players must find a way to work on their hitting skills every day.

BAT SELECTION

The bat is an extension of the arms. It must be of a size and weight that the player can swing hard and easily control throughout the entire swing. Batters often use a bat that is too heavy, which leads to many mechanical problems. To determine whether a bat is too heavy, the player should grip it with one hand at the knob and hold it straight out parallel to the ground at shoulder height. If the bat waivers, or if she cannot hold that position for at least a minute, the bat is too heavy. As weight increases, bat control usually decreases. The shorter the bat, the more control she will have, but she will sacrifice power. The longer the lever, the more power she will have, though with less control. The bat must also be long enough to allow full plate coverage when she swings. Is the bat long enough that the player can hit a ball hard off a T placed low on the outside corner?

Most bats are built with a specific ratio of length and weight. Youth bats range in weight from 16 to 22 ounces and in length from 25 to 31 inches. College players usually swing a bat that weighs 22 to 26 ounces and measures no shorter than 32 inches. Most use a bat with a length of 33 or 34 inches.

Because the player will be swinging the bat many times, it must feel comfortable in her hands. The size of the player's hands will determine the thickness of the handle that she can grip comfortably. Comfort should be the guide. Barrel size and the location and size of the sweet spot are other attributes to consider. The bigger the barrel, the larger the hitting surface. The smaller the hitting area, the more bat control the batter will need to be successful. A bottle bat provides a large hitting surface. It is an excellent bat for bunting and for beginners. The sweet spot, or "center of percussion," is the place where contact with the ball gives the player a good feeling. When a player makes contact elsewhere on the bat, she will feel a sting or a hurt, and the ball will not go as far as it should.

The composition of the bat will help determine how far the ball will go when hit. New materials, with names that seem to change every year, allow manufacturers to make bats with very thin walls. The player just needs to be sure that the bat is stamped "Approved" for use in her league. The thinner the wall, the greater the trampoline effect. The bat gives at contact with the ball and propels it away faster. The greater the trampoline effect, the greater the distance the ball can go. Unfortunately, with use the bat loses some of its elasticity, and its performance declines. College players often get a new bat each year. If possible, the player should have a game bat and use an old bat for practice. Because of the thin walls the bats dent more often. Players should use softer balls for hitting practice when possible.

HITTING MECHANICS

Many philosophies are used in teaching players how to hit. Hitting coaches have their own ways of saying things, and many batters have distinctive styles. Through computer and video analysis, we are able to break down the swing and study the basic elements that successful hitters use.

Grip

When gripping the bat, the hitter applies pressure with the fingers, not the palms. She grips the bat where the calluses are. The bottom hand (left hand for a right-handed batter) controls the bat, and the top hand supports the bat loosely. The bottom hand grips the bat as a person would grip a hammer or a golf club (see figure 8.1). The top hand is placed against the bottom hand with the door-knocking knuckles (middle knuckles) of both hands in a straight line. The arms are not crossed. The bat is gripped loosely—no white knuckles here—and the wrists have flexibility. Some hitters curl the index finger of the top hand so that it only lightly touches the bat. For better bat control the player may choke up on the bat by moving both hands several inches up from the knob. Of course, a choke grip means a shorter bat and less power.

Figure 8.1 Hitting grip.

Hand Position

The hands start close to the body about three to four inches in front of the chest and between the shoulders. Both elbows are down, and the shoulders are tension free. Some players prefer a little movement back and forth with the hands and shoulders to keep them loose. We call this position the power position, or power alley.

Stance

The stance is the foundation of the swing. Both feet are pointed straight ahead toward the plate. The body is upright, and the hips, head, and eyes are level. The shoulders are basically level with the front shoulder aimed at the pitcher and slightly down. The batter then turns the front hip and shoulder back slightly (inward) toward the catcher. Weight is on the balls of the feet, and the feet are just two to four inches greater than shoulder-width apart (see figure 8.2 on page 156). The player jumps up and down and feels where her feet are when she lands. That position is the most balanced position. The feet are just outside the hips so that the weight is on the inside of the legs and feet. The knees are inside the feet and slightly bent. Weight is equally distributed. Good hitters have good rhythm. With her stance, can the player shift easily back toward the catcher and forward to the pitcher? If the feet are the correct distance apart, the hitter can easily make this shift. The volleyball knee drill on page 170 can help the player feel where her feet and weight should be.

Three types of stances describe the position of the feet (see figure 8.3 on page 156). All other elements of the stance described earlier remain the same.

Figure 8.2 The hitting stance.

- **Square stance:** The feet are the same distance from the plate. This stance permits the best plate coverage.

- **Open stance:** The front foot is two to three inches farther from the plate than the back foot. This stance produces a shorter swing and poorer coverage of the outside corner, but both eyes can see the ball better and the more compact swing allows the batter to make better contact.

- **Closed stance:** The front foot is two to three inches closer to the plate than the back foot. The batter will have more difficulty getting around on an inside pitch but will be better able to drive an outside pitch to right field.

Position in the Box. The batter's position in the box depends on the skills of both the batter and the pitcher. The best position is the one that gives the hitter maximum plate coverage as she adjusts to the type of hitter she is and the type of pitcher she is facing. The farther back the hitter is in the box, the more time she has to swing the bat. If the pitcher is very fast, the batter can move back to have more time to get the bat around. If the ball has a lot of movement, however, staying back allows the ball to break even more, adding to the pitcher's

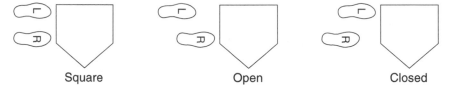

Square   Open   Closed

Figure 8.3 Square, open, and closed stances.

advantage. Against a slow pitcher, the batter should move up in the box if she is well ahead of the pitch with her swing. The up position also allows the batter to hit the pitch before it moves a lot. This position is particularly effective on drop balls.

If the batter crowds the plate, she will have good outside coverage but will have to be very quick to get the bat out in front for an inside pitch. Standing too far from the plate will make the hitter vulnerable to outside pitches and curves.

Focus. The player must see the ball to hit it. Players should have their eyes checked to be sure that they have the best vision possible. Both eyes are used in hitting. In the initial stance the head drops slightly and turns enough so that the back eye can see. The player should determine whether she is using the back eye by shutting the front eye and looking for the release point of the pitch with only the back eye.

The eyes can focus intently on an object for only a few seconds before the image becomes less clear. Using an eye shift helps the batter see the ball more clearly as the pitcher releases it. In the initial stance the batter uses a soft focus with the eyes relaxed. She focuses on the pitcher's chest or shoulders with a "soft," or general, focus. As the pitcher's hands separate, she shifts the eyes to the release point and goes from a "soft" focus to a "hard" focus while waiting to pick up the ball. The batter uses a look or glare that says she is going to attack the ball. She then tracks the ball all the way from the release to the contact point.

Stride

The stride is a step toward the pitcher with the front foot as the pitch is delivered (see figure 8.4). It serves as a timing mechanism for the swing. During the stride the batter must maintain balance. Therefore, the step is short—only three to four inches! The hitter does not want her center of gravity or head to move. The stride is a glide or slide forward toward the pitcher. The front toe opens slightly on the step, and the head moves little or not at all. During the stride the hips are cocked slightly, with the front shoulder, hip, and knee turned slightly toward the catcher. The player can think of her belly button as the lens of a camera that is pointed at the catcher. Weight remains on the inside of the back foot.

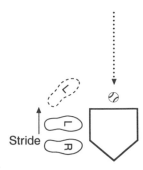

Figure 8.4 Hitting stride.

On the stride the weight stays on the back leg. The knee is over the back foot and does not turn. The player can practice the correct form by placing a chair against the back side of the back knee. She strides while making sure that the back leg stays in contact with the chair. When facing a pitcher the batter focuses on the release point during the stride. The stride must be consistent and to the same spot on every pitch, regardless of the pitch location, because the player starts the stride before she can identify what pitch is coming.

Timing determines when the batter steps. After the ball is released, she steps, allowing enough time to plant the front foot and complete the swing. She can still hit the ball if she steps too early, but she cannot hit it if she steps too late. Beginners often commit on the windup. As players practice and develop quicker hands, they learn to delay their commitment to the stride until they can clearly see the ball.

On the stride the hands go back to the launch position so that the bat is behind the back leg (see figure 8.5). As when using a hammer, a golf club, or a tennis racket, the player must first go back to get the stretch and power to go forward. In softball the hands go back only two to four inches. The batter cannot hit a ball above the hands, so the bat stays at the top of the strike zone. As the hands go back, they cock as if preparing to hammer a nail with the top hand. Cocking is not a hitch (i.e., a drop of the hands). The end of the bat will come close to the head, but the player must be careful not to wrap the bat around behind her. If the hitter takes the bat back too far, her body will twist and the shoulders will come off line. The arms are bent in a 90-degree position with both elbows pointed down. The head does not move, and the shoulders remain level. The hands stay close to the body. The closer they are to the body (and the center of gravity) the faster the body can rotate, producing faster bat speed.

Figure 8.5 Hand position during the stride.

Hip Rotation and Pivot

The batter strides first and then rotates the hips. These are two movements—a stride and then a pivot. The batter pivots hard on the ball of the back foot and drives the back

Figure 8.6 Hip rotation, pivot, and knob of bat to the ball during the swing.

hip hard into and against a rigid front side. It is a ballistic and aggressive rotational push forward. The back heel comes up, the foot releases, and the weight goes forward off the back leg. The back foot and back knee pivot toward the pitcher with the back leg in an L position (see figure 8.6). The body rotates around an imaginary pole running through the middle of the body. The belly button rotates from looking at the catcher to looking directly at the contact spot and no farther.

The batter must stay connected and flow into the ball as she sequentially unlocks her body parts. The back hip moves into the firm front side, then the hands follow and the bat lags behind. Note that the hands do not come forward with the hips and the bat is the last element. Weight shifts forward to the inside of the front foot as the hitter rotates the hips and pushes forward to drive into the ball. She must be in a balanced position to exert maximum force at contact. A straight line running down from the back ear to the pivot foot should pass through the shoulder, hip, and knee.

Swing

Good hitters have quick hands. The player must get the bat to the ball quickly. The bat travels the fastest route, in a direct line to the ball with no wasted movement. An inside-outside swing takes the bat directly to the ball (see figure 8.7). Coming around the ball with a sweeping movement takes too much time. Sweeping occurs when the batter straightens the arms before swinging.

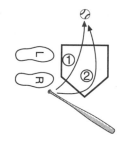

Figure 8.7 An inside-outside swing (1) versus a sweeping swing (2).

To perform an inside-outside swing, the player imagines a straight line from the pitcher to the catcher and keeps her hands always inside that line. Alternatively, the hitter can use the concept that the hands always stay between her and the plate.

As the hips pivot, the knob of the bat starts to move forward. The first arm movement takes the knob of the bat to the ball. The batter leads with the elbow and then extends the back of the hand and the knob forward. The movement resembles a karate chop with the bottom hand (see figure 8.8).

Both elbows stay bent until the last moment, when the bat head is driven forward. The top end of the bat stays close to the neck as long as possible. As the lead hand (knob) goes to the ball through the strike zone, the barrel of the bat lags behind. On the approach the barrel always stays above the hands. The batter swings the knob, not the bat head, then drives the bat barrel through the ball and whips the top hand through. The hitter should feel as if she is firing the bat at the ball.

The position of the wrists is critical to developing maximum power. The hands are at a 45-degree angle, and the wrist action is like the motion used to snap a flyswatter or towel. The batter does not roll the wrists or have the palm of the top hand up. Using either of these two methods to drive a nail with a hammer wouldn't work well, nor do they work well for batting. The batter wants quick hands and a whipping action to drive the ball. The swing must be tension free.

The player must not turn, or fly, the front shoulder open. She keeps the front shoulder down and pointed at the ball as long as possible. The hands can move without movement of the shoulders and head. The chin starts near the front shoulder and ends touching the back shoulder.

The batter should anticipate that each pitch will be a strike, starting to attack the ball on every pitch. It is easier to hold up than it is to start late.

Contact

The contact spot for a pitch down the middle is directly opposite the front hip. If the player were delivering a punch, she would want the recipient to be standing at this spot to receive the maximum blow. Contact for an inside pitch occurs sooner, in front of the body, and the hips must open earlier. On an inside pitch the batter should drive the back elbow into the body to get the hands out sooner and open the hips more quickly. For an outside pitch the contact spot is between the center of the body and the back hip, so the batter must wait on the ball. The hips stay closed until contact, and then the back hip drives through. The hands are well ahead of the bat head on an outside pitch. The batter must be patient and wait for the ball to come to her. By using good rotation of the hips, the hitter can hit just as hard to the opposite field as she does when pulling a pitch. The player must understand where to make contact with different pitches so that she can hit the ball hard at each location (see figure 8.9). This is what we mean when we say "Hit the ball where it is pitched."

At contact, both arms are bent close to 90 degrees and the bat is driven through the ball on a level plane. After the ball has left the bat, both arms are fully extended (see figure 8.10 on page 160). Both arms are straight, and the hitter should be looking down both arms and the barrel of the bat. The thumb and forefinger of the top hand are on top of the bat, and the V between them points directly at the contact spot. As full extension of the arms is reached, deceleration occurs and the bat loses speed. The hitter moves her head down at contact and feels her chest go to the ball while maintaining a firm and rigid front side. The action is like that of a boxer driving his back hand and body into an opponent. Because of the pivot the back foot and knee are pointing at the front leg. Most of the weight is transferred to the inside of the front foot and leg. The body is in a balanced position with weight on balls of the feet. The body flows into the ball.

Figure 8.8 The swing, just prior to contact.

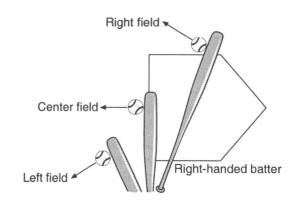

Figure 8.9 Contact points to hit the ball to left, center, or right field.

Follow-Through

In the follow-through, weight transfers almost completely to the front leg, but it remains on the balls of the feet. The body is upright and well balanced. The hitter must not fall back on the heels. The head is down, and the back shoulder almost touches the chin (see figure 8.11 on page 160). The front foot will open slightly after contact to about a 45-degree angle to the pitcher. This happens automatically; the hitter does not need to think about it. As momentum carries the bat behind the body, the wrists will automatically roll over, well after contact. The hitter should not think about rolling the

Figure 8.10 After contact, the arms are fully extended.

Figure 8.11 Follow-through position.

wrists. If she does, she will hit many ground balls and lose considerable power. She keeps both hands on the bat until the end of the swing. Some batters let go of the bat with their top hand after contact. A drawback of this habit is that the hitter may let go a little early and not fully use the upper hand to drive through the ball.

The hitter should not throw the bat after the swing because it might hit the catcher or another player. She should drop the bat straight down before she runs. If a player can't stop throwing the bat, she can carry it with her for a couple of steps until the habit is broken.

FRONT-FOOT HITTING

Some successful hitters are front-foot hitters. In this style of hitting, the batter shifts her weight to the front foot during the swing. Little weight remains on the back foot, so the back toe is often pointed down or dragged forward. The contact spot is out in front of the front hip, almost a foot farther forward than it would be if the batter were pivoting. A front-foot hitter is susceptible to change-ups. The advantage of this method is that the hitter can more easily keep the shoulders level and the front shoulder closed. A drawback of this method is that power comes from the upper body only. Many players choose to gain additional power from the hips by using the pivot.

Hitting Mechanics Checklist

Hands
- Line up the middle knuckles.
- Use the power position. The hands are three to four inches in front of the chest and between the shoulders. The elbows are down with no tension in the shoulders.

Stance
- Have your weight on the balls of your feet in a balanced position.
- Point your feet straight ahead.
- Position your knees between your feet and bend them slightly.
- Keep your hips level.
- Hold your head and eyes level.
- Position the front shoulder slightly down.
- Cock the front shoulder and hip slightly inward.
- Use soft focus on the pitcher's chest.

Stride
- Use a short, soft glide only three to four inches toward the pitcher.
- The front toe opens slightly and the hip stays closed.
- Do not move your head.
- Cock the front shoulder, hip, and knee slightly toward the catcher.
- Keep your weight on the inside of the back foot.
- Move your hands back three to four inches to the launch position.
- Cock your wrists.
- Shift to hard focus on the release point.
- Pivot on the ball of the back foot.
- Your back foot and back knee point to the pitcher.

Swing
- Bend your arms 90 degrees and keep the elbows down.
- Take the knob of the bat to the ball.
- Keep your hands inside the plate.
- The barrel lags behind, always above your hands.
- Cock your wrists at a 45-degree angle.
- Keep both elbows bent.
- Keep the top of the bat close to your neck as long as possible.
- Keep the front shoulder down, closed, and pointed at the ball.

Contact
- Keep your head and eyes down.
- At contact, arms are bent close to 90 degrees. The bat is driven through the ball on a level plane.
- Drive the barrelhead through the ball with the top hand.
- Keep your front side rigid and firm.
- Use a ballistic, aggressive, and rotational push forward.
- Transfer your weight to the inside of the front foot and leg.
- Your belly button points to the contact spot.
- Point the back foot and toe at the front knee in an L position.
- Imagine a straight line passing from your back ear through the shoulder, hip, knee, and pivot foot.

Follow-Through
- Your back shoulder almost touches your chin.
- Your front toe opens to 45 degrees.
- The bat carries behind your body.
- Your wrists roll over.
- Maintain balanced position.

Common Mechanical Problems

Check first for the following mechanical problems when a hitter is having problems. While each hitter has her own unique style, batters who are struggling will often have one or more of these mechanical breakdowns. Suggested corrections and drills to fix each problem are also provided.

Overstriding

Result

- Poor balance, dropping of the back shoulder, hitting under the ball.
- Poor weight transfer to the front leg so that the hitter lunges or weight stays on the back leg as the back side collapses (a backward C facing the catcher).

Corrections

- Put more weight on the front foot.
- Do not take a step. Just pick up the foot and put it down (widen the stance to start).
- Start with your feet closer together so that the distance is not as great when you finish.
- Use a stride tutor or similar inhibitor (stand inside two 13-inch tires) as you do drills.

Stepping Away From the Plate

Result

- The hitter strides away from the plate, and the hips open too early.
- The arm does all the hitting because the player cannot use her body to drive the ball.

Corrections

- Keep weight on the balls of the feet.
- Close your stance. Rotate the shoulders, front hip, and front toe in slightly.
- Put more weight on your front foot in the initial stance so that less weight transfer occurs on the step.
- Shorten your stride.

Drills

- The hitter can practice striding in the bullpen when the pitcher is throwing.
- Place a two-by-four behind the heels of the batter, extending straight ahead in the direction her foot should go. The batter hits off a T. The front foot should not step on or over the board.

- The batter hits outside pitches to right field off a T. To do this, she must stay closed to the ball.

Flying Front Shoulder

Result

- The front shoulder pulls out too early, which results in sweeping the bat because the arms are forced to reach.
- The head turns with the shoulders, resulting in poor eye contact.
- The hips open prematurely as the hitter pulls off the pitch. She thus cannot transfer weight into the ball.
- The hitter pulls the ball or misses it completely.

Corrections

- Aim your front shoulder at the ball.
- Exaggerate inward rotation in the initial stance to tuck your front shoulder in under the chin.
- Drive to the ball with your front shoulder.
- Keep your chin over the shoulder as long as possible.
- Focus on hitting from the back side, not the front leg. Keep weight on the back leg longer.

Poor Hip Rotation, Pivot, and Weight Transfer

Result

- The swing is slow and lacks power. The hitter becomes an arm swinger.

Corrections

- Concentrate on staying back and hitting with a quick, aggressive, and rotational move. Keep the weight on the back leg longer.
- Focus on standing tall and pivoting hard on the back foot.
- Keep a firm front side. Drive the back hip into the front hip.

- Maintain good balance at foot landing.
- Wait for the ball to come to you.

Sweeping Swing

Result

- A long arc to the ball produces a slow bat.
- Power is lost because the hands leave the power alley by the chest.

Corrections

- Keep your hands close to your chest and the bat by your neck as long as possible.
- Lead with the front elbow and concentrate on keeping the arms bent until you swing.

Drills

- Resistance swing
- Front-elbow drill
- Fence swing
- Self-toss up the middle
- Back-hand self-toss—hit with the front hand only

Upper Cutting

Results

- The back shoulder and hands drop as the bat approaches the ball.
- The back side usually has a backward C to the catcher.
- The player cannot shift weight to the front side.
- The hitter usually pops up or misses the ball completely (especially rise balls).

Corrections

- Lower your front shoulder slightly in the initial stance.
- Emphasize a "straight" or "tall" back side.
- Don't hitch (drop hands at start of swing). Make sure that your first hand movement is back and up, not down.
- When approaching the ball, keep the hands above the ball and the barrel above the hands.
- A drastic remedy is to start with the hands at chest height so that the only movement will be up.

Drills

- Double-Ts drills: The player swings over a back T.
- The player uses a high T so that hand movement is directly to the ball.
- Back knee down T drill.

Swinging Down

Results

- The hitter swings down instead of level.
- Every ball is driven into the ground.

Corrections

- Level the swing at contact. Drive straight through the ball.
- Don't let the top hand do all the work or roll over the top of the bat at contact.
- Emphasize having the front arm leading the bat to the ball with the knob going to the ball.
- Stay balanced with good rotation.

Swinging Too Late

Result

- The hitter does not get the bat head to the contact spot quickly enough. The ball is often popped up or hit weakly to the opposite field.

Corrections

- The hands must go back more quickly, just as a tennis player would move the hands in preparing to return a hard serve.
- Start the hands forward earlier. Be on time.
- Get the legs into the swing more aggressively.
- Eliminate extra bat movement. Take the knob straight to the ball.
- Use a lighter bat or choke up.

Swinging Too Early

Result

- The batter will pull the ball and hit it off the end of the bat.
- The batter will have trouble waiting on change-ups and curves.
- If the hitter transfers weight too early, she will lunge and lose power.

Corrections

- Understand contact spots. Have patience and wait for the pitch to arrive at the contact spot.
- Don't stride too early. React to the release of the pitch, not the pitcher's motion.
- Concentrate on driving the ball up the middle or to the opposite field.

(continued)

Common Mechanical Problems *(continued)*

- Close the stance and turn the front shoulder and hip slightly inward. Keep the front shoulder and hip in longer.
- Hit to the opposite field to force yourself to wait longer for the outside contact point.
- Have a tosser or pitcher fake toss or release to see whether your stride occurs on the arm motion or after seeing the pitch.

Not Driving Through Ball

Result

- The ball is pushed, not driven, and it does not explode off the bat. Power is limited.
- The hands get too far ahead of the bat, causing the barrel to lag too far behind.

Corrections

- Lead with the knob of the bat and swing the knob, not the bat head.
- Keep the barrel above the hands with the wrists cocked. Whip the top hand through.
- Make sure your hands are at a 45-degree angle to permit a powerful whipping action. Fire the bat head at the ball.
- Use a quick, ballistic, and aggressive hip rotation.
- Stay connected. Flow into the ball as you sequentially unlock the body parts.

Drill

- The player hits a soccer ball off a T.

Not Seeing the Ball

Result

- The hitter swings and misses or makes poor contact.

Corrections

- Have your vision checked.
- Make sure that your eyes are open during the swing.
- Turn your head so that you can use both eyes. Keep your head level so that your vision is not distorted. Shut your front eye to check whether your back eye is in a position to see.
- See the ball while getting ready to attack.
- Make sure your head does not move.
- Is the front shoulder flying open and taking your head with it?

Drills

- Have the player bunt to the opposite side so that she must wait and can see the ball longer.
- Use the shadow drill to make sure that the head is not moving on the stride or swing.
- Toss drills: The player calls the color of the ball or a colored spot on the ball as she hits it.
- When using T drills the player looks inside the T after contact.

Poor Bat Control

Result

- The hitter is unable to control the path of the bat or keep the barrelhead above the hands.

Corrections

- Check your grip.
- Use a lighter bat or choke up.
- Don't overswing.
- Strengthen the arms, wrist, and hands.

Drill

- Strength drills—zone hitting

Poor Bat Speed

Result

- The batter is late to the ball.
- The ball does not explode off the bat.

Corrections

- Be real aggressive with the bottom half of the body.
- Check to be sure that the middle knuckles are aligned and that you hold the bat at the calluses of the hands.
- Use an inside-outside swing with the bat going directly to the ball.
- Use a tension-free swing with no "muscling up."

Drills

- Hum: The player should hum constantly as she swings to see if she is tensing up. A variation is to hold a potato chip in the lips and stay loose enough that it doesn't break.
- Underload drills: The player swings a lighter bat to develop quick-twitch fibers and faster reactions.
- Fungo-bat swings: The batter uses a fungo bat, baseball bat, or end-loaded bat to get the feel of whipping the end of the bat through the ball.

LEARNING TO HIT

The purpose of practice sessions is for players to learn and build confidence. Therefore, players must have opportunities for success. Hitters should start with the T and progress to soft toss, front toss, the pitching machine, and live pitching using the drills at the end of this chapter. Hitters must practice as much as the pitchers, working every day on their hitting skills.

Practice sessions should include both quality and quantity. Hitting is a learned reaction. Only after many repetitions will the elements of the swing become automatic. Players should break down the swing and isolate each element in practice to learn the fundamentals. They should work on their problem spots but recognize that repetition for the sake of repetition is useless. More is not always better. Every practice swing should have a purpose.

Learning results from feedback and evaluation. Players should strive to learn something from every swing, whether a good swing or a poor one. They should note what they did right and what was not perfect. They should then establish a goal for the next swing or drill and repeat until the skill becomes ingrained and automatic. Perfect practice makes perfect.

Players can't think when they swing in a game. The skill must be automatic, and they can achieve that only through repetition. The goal is to be consistent: to see the ball, to hit the ball, and to avoid thinking too much.

THE MENTAL GAME OF HITTING

Hitting is adjusting—adjusting to the pitch, the type of pitcher, the count, the umpire, and the situation. The mental game of hitting begins in practice. In a game, it begins on the bench, continues in the on-deck circle and on the approach to the plate, and reaches its greatest intensity when the batter steps into the batter's box.

Success requires discipline, concentration, and quickness. Successful hitters are always prepared and ready to hit. They learn from every swing, obtain immediate feedback, and make the adjustments necessary for success. Players should understand that the difference between a .200 hitter and a .300 hitter is only 1 hit in 10 at bats.

Hitting is an attitude. It is confidence. Players should believe that they are always going to get a hit. They let the pitcher know that they are the best and that the pitcher has her hands full. They never let up. If they are 4 for 4, they strive to go 5 for 5. Successful hitters visualize success. They see themselves getting the winning hit. They live for the moment when the bases are loaded and they step to the plate with the game on the line.

Good hitters are aggressive, prepared to hit every pitch. The batter should stride to every pitch with the intention of hitting the ball. She should hold up on the swing only when she recognizes that the pitch location makes it a poor pitch to hit. The adjustment to hold up the swing should be made at the last moment. To do this, the player squeezes the bat and tenses up, stopping the swing before the bat goes through the strike zone. The approach to the pitch is "Yes, yes, yes, no" or "Yes, yes, yes, yes." If the batter does not prepare to swing at every pitch, she will not be able to pull the trigger when she really wants to swing. Hitters should focus only on the ball, not its location over the plate. If the ball is around home plate and the hitter is confident that she can hit it, then she should go after it! Players should focus on their strengths and jump on any mistakes made by the pitcher.

Hitters should know their best pitches to hit and their hitting zone. They should understand their strengths and hit their pitch. Good hitters consistently hit balls within their hitting zone (strength area), whereas weak hitters hit too many pitches in their weak area.

The Count

The pitcher is trying to get ahead in the count by throwing the first pitch for a strike. If she gets the strike, the next pitch will not be as good. The pitcher hopes the batter will chase the ball or that the umpire will call a strike if the pitch is close to the plate. The best pitch batters will likely see is that first pitch! Yet how many hitters take the first pitch with the justification that they want to see what the pitcher throws or that they want to get comfortable? Hitters can watch the pitcher warm up to see what she throws and become comfortable before that first pitch.

Hitting sometimes seems as difficult as winning the lottery. Our odds improve with three attempts, or chances, compared with one or two. So batters should get their money's worth by using all three opportunities. If they swing and miss, at least they can gather information to make adjustments on the next swing (too fast? too slow?). Hitters learn nothing by taking a good pitch and only decrease the odds.

If the pitcher is behind on the count, batters should expect to see the pitcher's best control pitch, usually a fastball, right over the plate. They should be ready to jump all over this pitch! With a runner on third and less than two out, batters should look for a drop ball. The pitcher does not want to throw an up ball that can easily be hit in the air. Batters should try to think like a pitcher as they look for a pitch to hit. The pitch selection charts in chapter 6 (tables 6.1 and 6.2) offer valuable information about what the pitcher and catcher are thinking and how they plan to set up the hitter. Pitchers generally establish a pattern during a game. By looking for this pattern, batters know what pitch to expect. If they know what pitch is likely to be coming, they can more easily recognize and adjust to it.

Umpire's Strike Zone

The size and shape of the umpire's strike zone may require hitters to make adjustments for the pitcher they are facing. If the umpire has a wide strike zone, the hitters must move closer to the plate to hit the outside pitch with the sweet spot of the bat. Alternatively, they may choose to lay off that pitch completely. With two strikes and a high-pitch umpire, hitters must enlarge the top of the strike zone. A stubborn batter who refuses to adjust will strike out often and not be successful.

Two-Strike Adjustment

With two strikes the goal is just to make contact. Hitters should recognize that the pitcher will throw a marginal or waste pitch and that they have to make some adjustments. But they should not drastically alter their swing and stance. The goal is to avoid striking out and to put the ball in play so that the defense must make the out. Batters should expect no sympathy on taking a called third strike. Players can practice these two-strike adjustments in the batting cage:

- Move closer to the plate to protect the outside corner and be able to reach outside pitches to drive to the opposite field.
- Enlarge the strike zone and swing at anything close to a strike. Don't let the umpire call you out.

- Wait on the ball to see it more clearly.
- Focus on just meeting the ball and using a compact swing to put the ball in play. Don't swing for the fence.

Slump Busting

Everyone has slumps. When a player is struggling, she should fine-tune her mechanics, not perform a complete overhaul. Slumps often start in the head, beginning with a loss of confidence. A mechanical breakdown can also lead to bad days.

Here are some suggestions for breaking a slump:

- The player should try to see the ball better and longer. She should concentrate on hitting the ball up the middle or to the opposite field.
- Opening up the stance can help. An open stance shortens the swing, and the head position makes it easier to keep both eyes on the ball.
- The player can choke up for better bat control.
- Self-examination of her mental approach may be useful.
- The player should relax and avoid overswinging.
- The player can work on her mechanics off a T.
- A day off may permit the player to get away from the pressure.

Game Situations

Hitters have a job to do in each at bat. While in the hole, they should review what situations are likely to arise and prepare mentally for those possibilities. The situation, position of the base runners, and the score will dictate the batter's goal. Although batters cannot control whether the batted ball is a hit or an error (unless it is a home run), good batters do have some control over where they hit the ball and what type of hit they make—bunt, ground ball, fly ball, and so on. Some common situations are listed in table 8.1 on page 168.

The Defense

Smart hitters survey the defensive setup and try to hit the ball where the defense is weakest. For example, if the outfield has shifted radically, expecting the batter to pull the ball, she should step back from the plate so that pitches are farther away from her body. More pitches are now outside, making it easier to take a pitch to the opposite-field gap created by the shift. If the outfield is playing so deep that the hitter cannot possibly hit the ball over their heads, she can choke up on the bat and drop the ball in front of the outfield. When the infield moves in on top of the batter, she looks to drive the ball by them.

BATTING-T DRILLS

A batting T is essential equipment in the development of a hitter. The T makes it possible to break down the elements of hitting into the most fundamental form. Hitters can spend many hours alone working with a T to develop and groove the swing. They start with high pitches first. The hands must go directly to the ball. Develop proper mechanics and when they become automatic, move to lower pitches.

Table 8.1
Situational Hitting

Situation	Outs	Goal	Pitch to look for
Leadoff batter	None	Get on base	Use disciplined strike zone
			Look for a pitcher's mistake pitch
			May take one strike looking for a walk
Runner at first	None	Avoid double play,	Ball low in the strike zone that
		force-out, and line drive	batter can bunt down
		Usually use a sacrifice bunt	
Runner at second	None	Advance runner	Pitch batter can hit behind runner:
			for right-hander, an outside pitch,
			for left-hander, an inside pitch
	Two	Score runner	Ball to drive hard through the infield
Runner at third	Less than two	Score runner with a ball	Expect a low pitch
		through the infield	Ball to hit hard though the infield
		or a deep fly ball	or an up pitch to hit for
			a deep fly ball
Runners at first and third	One	Avoid double play and score the run	Ball that batter can hit hard
		If runner stealing second,	For right-hander, an inside pitch,
		hit at shortstop	for left-hander, an outside pitch
No runners on	Two	Extra-base hit	Ball in hitting zone
			that batter can drive hard
Runner stealing and batter taking pitch	None, one, two	Protect runner	Move back in the box
			Point end of bat at catcher's eyes
Hit-and-run	None, one, two	Advance runner with possibility of reaching base	Any pitch that batter can hit on the ground

Batting Ts are available in a wide range of prices. ATEC has an excellent, durable T that is available with a rise-ball extension. Plastic construction cones also work well. For high pitches, the cone or T can be placed on a concrete block to make the ball high enough.

There are several important rules for using the T properly:

- Players should have a purpose for every swing.
- After the swing players should review their mechanics and get feedback from the results of the hit.
- After contact hitters look inside the T to make sure their head is on the ball and driving down.
- Players should use the T at all contact locations and at all heights in the strike zone.

- A high T is necessary to simulate a rise ball. Use T extensions or simply put the T up on a block.
- Place the T so that the ball is at the correct point of contact.
- Players should shift their eyes from an imaginary pitcher to the ball on the T before swinging to make hitting practice realistic.

No Stride

Purpose: To isolate and work on hip rotation and upper-body movement.

Procedure: The player steps to the spot where the front foot would be after the stride and starts in that position. She swings and concentrates on the pivot, hip rotation, and movement of the upper body. She drives the front shoulder to the outside corner of the plate. She keeps the head down and looks inside the T after contact. The goal is to hit a hard line drive off the T.

Variation: Put a target on a fence (a square of tape or a paper plate) for players to attempt to hit. They should avoid lifting their heads to watch the flight of the ball. They start 10 feet from the fence. As the players move farther back, it becomes more difficult for them to hit the target because the degree of error is magnified. It is like shooting at the moon. The trajectory may be off only a degree here, but out there it is miles off.

Two Stride

Purpose: To practice the stride and check for balance.

Procedure: The batter take her stride with the hands going back to launch position. She freezes and holds that position to review stride length, foot position, hand position, and balance. If all is correct, she repeats the stride and this time swings to hit the ball off the T. If she recognizes a problem, she repeats the stride and does not swing until all is correct.

Long T Hitting

Purpose: To allow players to see the outcome of their hits.

Procedure: Set up a T at least 30 feet from the net so that batters can see where the ball goes—ground ball, fly ball, pulled ball, and so forth. When a batter is close to the net, every hit looks good. The T can also be set up at home plate so that players can see the results and work on the contact spot for opposite-field hitting.

Soccer Ball

Purpose: To learn how to drive through the ball.

Procedure: Place a soccer ball on a T. If the T is an open tube, place a small bathroom plunger in the T to hold the ball or use a traffic cone and a plunger. The batter hits the soccer ball hard off the T. If she does not drive through the soccer ball, it will not explode off the bat.

Balance Beam

Purpose: To check balance during a swing.

Procedure: The hitter stands on a two-by-four or with both feet on the inner edge of a tire while hitting off the T. A hitter with good balance can stay on the beam throughout the swing.

Back Knee Down

Purpose: To develop upper-body strength and quickness. The drill helps the player stop lunging by eliminating lower-body movement. The drill can reduce upper cutting. It emphasizes keeping the barrel above the hands and using correct timing.

Procedure: Use a low T for this drill. The hitter kneels on a towel with the back knee at a 90-degree angle, keeping the shoulders on a level plane. The drill can also be done off a soft toss. The player sees the bat hit the ball.

Tomahawk Hitting

Purpose: To develop proper wrist action at contact.

Procedure: The hitter kneels with the back knee bent. Set the T for a high pitch. The player uses a bat and hits down on the top half of the ball using a tomahawk action. The player can perform the same action with one hand using a very small bat (a fisherman's club is the right size and shape).

Volleyball Knee Drill

Purpose: To emphasize keeping weight on the inside of the legs and using a short balanced stride.

Procedure: The hitter holds a deflated volleyball between her knees while completing the swing.

Bingo

Purpose: To develop a level swing and proper mechanics by offering instant feedback.

Procedure: Position two Ts at the same height with one directly behind the other. The batter drives the back ball into the front ball. The farther apart the Ts, the more difficult it is to hit the front ball because errors are magnified. The path of the hit provides instant feedback on the mechanics of the swing. If the hitter misses to the left, she has an outside-inside swing. If the hitter misses by going above, she is dropping her back shoulder. When successful, the hitter should yell "Bingo."

In-Out T Swing

Purpose: To develop an inside-outside swing.

Procedure: Place one T behind another with the back T higher than the front one. The distance between the Ts should be about three feet. The batter hits the ball off the front T without making contact with the back T. Using an inside-outside swing the batter will miss hitting the back T and receive instant feedback that she is swinging correctly. If the batter extends the arms and sweeps the bat, she will hit the back T.

Command T Drill

Purpose: To practice using the same stride while adjusting to different contact spots.

Procedure: Set one T at the contact spot for an inside pitch (front inside corner) and one for an outside pitch (back outside corner). As the hitter plants the front foot, a partner calls "In" or "Out." The batter hits the ball called for by the partner.

Variations:

- The hitter performs the drill with the eyes shut.

- On her own, the player hits the inside ball and then the outside ball, feeling the difference between the swings. This exercise develops muscle memory.

TOSS DRILLS

These drills are useful because they do not require a lot of space or expensive equipment. You can use rubber softballs, old balls, and Wiffle balls and hit into a fence, carpet, curtain, or cage. A good toss is essential for toss drills to be productive. The toss should be firm and level with moderate speed. To increase the accuracy of the tosses, place balls on the ground as targets to mark the contact spots.

Be safe! Make sure that the tosser is in a position where a ball or bat cannot hit her. Tosses are made from a kneeling or standing position, depending on the drill (see figure 8.12 on page 172). Beginning players should toss from the side. More advanced players can toss from a 45-degree angle in front of the hitter. The tosser should use a backswing with the toss so that the hitter can key her timing off the arm.

Back-Hand Wiffle Toss

Purpose: To emphasize the pivot and keeping the hands and back elbow close to the body.

Procedure: The tosser stands at a 45-degree angle in front of the hitter. She tosses Wiffles to the hitter's midsection. The hitter does not have a bat. From the stride position the hitter pivots and catches (or hits) the ball with the back hand at a spot opposite the belly button.

Figure 8.12
Tossing technique.

Location Toss

Purpose: To learn to adjust to the contact spot for three pitches—inside, middle, and outside.

Procedure: The tosser is in a kneeling position and tosses balls to the three spots where the batter should make contact. The tosser calls the number of the spot where she will toss the ball as she tosses it ("One" for inside, "Two" for middle, "Three" for outside). The hitter makes contact at that location, saying "Hit" on contact.

High Toss

Purpose: To learn to keep the barrel above the ball.

Procedure: The tosser throws from a standing position. The hitter hits tosses that are high inside and high outside.

Back Toss

Purpose: To practice keeping the hands inside the ball and driving the barrel through the ball.

Procedure: The tosser stands behind the batter. The batter turns her head slightly to track the ball. The toss should be on an inside-out path. The batter must wait on the ball, make contact out in front of the plate, and then drive hard through it.

Two-Ball Toss

Purpose: To adjust to hitting balls at different locations and develop quick adjustment and vision tracking.

Procedure: The tosser, kneeling, throws two balls at the same time from one hand and calls which ball to hit. The tosser throws balls of different sizes or colors. She calls top or bottom, small or big, or a color.

Front Bounce

Purpose: To develop timing.

Procedure: The tosser stands about 15 feet in front of the hitter. The tosser throws a tennis ball overhand, bouncing the ball up into the strike zone in front of the plate. The hitter uses the bounce as a trigger, or timing mechanism, to signal when she should take the hands back to launch position and begin the stride.

Self-Toss Up the Middle

Purpose: Proper mechanics are required to hit a ball up the middle. This drill allows the player to groove her swing and receive instant feedback about her mechanics on every hit. The self-toss also forces the elbows in and develops the proper flick of the wrists.

Procedure: The hitter self-tosses and tries to take every ball up the middle. The hitter tosses the ball up with the bottom hand while resting the bat on the back shoulder. The toss should be to the contact spot and no more than a foot above it; using both hands to grip the bat, the player hits the ball as it descends. To avoid chasing balls the hitter can stand three to four feet from a fence and hit into it. Hit into a mat or use Wiffle balls to protect the fence. Alternatively, she can stand at home plate and attempt to hit all balls over second base. She then repeats the drill, going from second base to home.

Front-Screen Toss

Purpose: To practice reacting to live underhand pitching.

Procedure: A screen standing about 15 feet in front of the hitter protects the tosser. The tosser throws both inside and outside at all heights. To simulate a change-up, the tosser loops (arcs) some of the tosses and forces the hitter to wait on the ball. The hitter takes a normal swing, hitting the ball where it is pitched. She should drive outside pitches to the opposite field and pull inside pitches.

Quick Hands

Purpose: To develop quick hands, the backswing, and a compact swing.

Procedure: The tosser stands in front of the batter and behind a screen about 15 feet in front of the hitter. The batter starts with the bat pointing at the tosser and must quickly get the hands back and forward to hit the tossed ball.

Snapbacks

Purpose: To develop a small stride, compact swing, fast hands, and arm strength.

Procedure: The tosser stands on the side of the batter or stands in front of the batter behind a screen. The tosser tosses balls to one contact spot in rapid succession, not allowing the bat to come to rest. The batter does not have time to adjust to different locations so the tosses should be consistent. The tosser throws 6 to 10 balls in a row. The hitter hits each ball hard, using a full swing.

Thunderstick

Purpose: To learn to see the ball better at contact.

Procedure: Using a very narrow bat for hitting and bunting forces the batter to look intently at the ball at contact. To make bats to use with baseball and golf-size Wiffles, cut broomsticks or doweling to bat size and tape the handles. Use the thunderstick to hit or bunt Wiffles off a soft toss.

Dotted Ball

Purpose: To practice making an aggressive approach to every pitch while being able to hold up after receiving information that says "Don't swing."

Procedure: Four circles, each the size of a quarter, are marked on several balls. Some balls have red circles, and some have green circles. The tosser hides the colors. The hitter strides aggressively, prepared to hit every toss. She hits the green dotted balls and holds up on the red ones by squeezing the bat and tensing up.

Hold Release

Purpose: To make sure that the hitter steps only when she sees the ball, not on the windup.

Procedure: A pitcher or tosser uses a regular windup but occasionally holds on to the ball and does not release it. The hitter should not step until the ball is released and she really sees the ball.

MACHINE DRILLS

Machines permit players to get many practice swings. Enough real pitching is never available. Machines can also be set up so that batters can work on particular pitches. Machines are most effective when they are inconsistent, just as pitchers are. Batters must learn to adjust as they must in the game. The feeder can add to the realism by varying the tempo of the feeds.

In Close

Purpose: To develop quick reactions to the ball and a small stride.

Procedure: The hitter stands about 30 feet from the machine. Set the machine to throw at the regular speed used at the normal distance. The hitter must react quickly after seeing the ball and use her normal swing, focusing on getting the bat out quickly.

Execution

Purpose: To develop the ability to execute on the next pitch.

Procedure: The feeder signals a specific play to the batter, who is hitting off a machine. The batter then steps into the box and executes. This drill makes hitting practice gamelike and allows players to practice signals.

No-Pull Drill

Purpose: To learn to wait for the outside pitch and drive it hard to the right side.

Procedure: The pitch is outside, and the goal is to hit all balls to the right side of the cage or machine. The contact spot is over the outside back corner.

Hitting Game

Purpose: To heighten competition and pressure in hitting practice.

Procedure: Players hit off a pitching machine in a cage. The batter scores no points for ground balls or for hitting the roof of the cage, three points for hitting the ball up the middle, and two points for hitting the side of the cage. The feeder and hitter compete against each other, getting 10 strikes each. Use a scorecard.

HITTING MECHANICS DRILLS

Hitting is a very complex skill. Coaches should use drills that break down the mechanics of the swing so hitters can isolate specific components. Repeat the drills until the action becomes automatic.

Wall Stride

Purpose: To learn to keep the front foot closed during the stride and to learn the contact spot.

Procedure: The player stands perpendicularly to a wall. She strides against the wall, keeping the foot closed, and brings the bat slowly forward to the contact point. (The bat is parallel to the wall.) This is the contact spot for a ball down the middle.

Shadow Drill

Purpose: To learn to keep the head still during the stride.

Procedure: The sun must be behind the player so that she can see her shadow. She places a ball on the shadow of her head. She takes her step and makes sure that her head does not move off the ball.

Stride to Launch

Purpose: To take the stride and hands back repeatedly so that doing so becomes automatic.

Procedure: The player assumes a correct balanced stance. She strides and takes the hands back and up slightly to launch position. The stride toe turns open slightly to the pitcher. The player does not swing. She repeats the stride many times.

Ball Kick

Purpose: To emphasize making a good pivot with feedback.

Procedure: The player places a ball against her back heel and works on knocking it away with a hard pivot.

Front-Elbow Drill

Purpose: To learn the action of the front arm when hitting.

Procedure: The hitter assumes the batting position without a bat. A partner stands in front of the hitter and extends a flat hand for a target at elbow distance. The hitter drives her elbow to the partner's hand and after contact straightens the arm and flips the wrist forward (palm down) as if hitting. She repeats the motion many times.

Glove in Armpit

Purpose: To practice keeping the back elbow down and in and the barrel up. The drill helps prevent sweeping the bat.

Procedure: The hitter places a glove under the lead arm and swings, keeping the glove there. The glove should not drop until the follow-through.

Resistance Swing

Purpose: To feel the various elements of the swing and develop muscle memory of swing components.

Procedure: The drill uses a partner or a bat handle attached to a fence with surgical cord. The batter assumes the batting stance. The partner stands behind the batter, holds the top of the bat with both hands, and offers resistance as the batter strides and swings all the way through. The partner walks around the hitter, allowing the full range of motion and applying only the amount of resistance that permits a correct swing. The batter feels the importance of keeping the hands in close, using an inside-outside swing, rotating the hips, and transferring her weight to produce power.

Bat on Neck

Purpose: To develop a compact swing by eliminating sweeping and dropping of the hands.

Procedure: The hitter starts with a bat on the shoulder and against the neck and keeps it there through her hip rotation. The bat leaves the neck only when she throws it to the contact spot.

Fence Swing

Purpose: To groove an inside-outside swing.

Procedure: The batter stands parallel to a fence slightly farther away than one bat length. She swings without contacting the fence and stays balanced with weight on the balls of the feet. She must not cheat by leaning back. Using a net instead of a rigid fence is less intimidating. The player repeats the swing many times at moderate speed to groove the swing.

Mirror Drill

Purpose: To understand, analyze, and evaluate the swing.

Procedure: The batter uses a full-length mirror to view her swing. Facing the mirror, she works on the first movement with or without a bat. The front shoulder is slightly down. She takes the lead elbow to the ball, then the knob. The hands start close to the chest for the inside-outside swing. The batter uses a side view to check the stride, with the hands going back to launch position (no swing). She uses many repetitions to develop an automatic response. She swings and checks to see that she has a quiet head, correct shoulder angle, level hips, and the proper pivot. The batter can check alignment and balance using the plumb line from the shoulder to the foot.

Line-Drive Cord

Purpose: To learn to keep the hands up and stop looping.

Procedure: Wiffle balls are strung on a cord that is then attached to two fences or poles and tightened so that the line is taut. For ease in setting up the cord, use clips or hooks on the ends of the cord and a turnbuckle (available at hardware stores) so that you can tighten the cord after it is attached. The balls all start at one end. The batter hits the Wiffle balls to the other end, keeping the hands above the cord. This is an excellent training tool for slappers who hit and then follow through down the cord.

Tracking

Purpose: To practice using a hard focus to see the pitch as it approaches the contact spot. The drill helps batters recognize strikes and the spin of pitches.

Procedure: The batter tracks the ball all the way from release to the contact spot, tracking off a machine or a pitcher in the bullpen. The batter identifies the location and makes a ball or strike call. If a pitcher is throwing, the batter calls out the pitch type as soon as she recognizes the spin.

Underload Swings

Purpose: To develop quick hands and quick-twitch fibers by training at a faster speed.

Procedure: Hit Wiffle balls off a soft toss using an underload bat. Just as runners improve speed by running down hills, hitters can use the underload theory to increase swing speed by using a lighter bat or a hitting stick that allows faster swings. A hitting stick can be made from a broomstick (or doweling). Foam pipe insulation is taped on the upper half to create the barrel. The hitting stick should be used to hit only Wiffle balls. Using a shorter bat and shortening the lever also increases quickness.

Strength Drills

Purpose: To increase strength in wrists and hands. The player uses a weighted or heavy bat and increases the weight as she becomes stronger. She does sets of 10.

Procedure:
1. Zone hitting: The hitter assumes the proper stance with pivot and swings the bat in the strike zone. She breaks the wrist back and forth 10 times at each of nine contact locations—high pitches that are in, down the middle, and outside, and the same series for pitches that are waist high and low. The total is 90 wrist swings.
2. Windshield wiper: With the arms extended in front of the chest, the hitter holds the bat head up. She rotates the wrists and bat back and forth like a windshield wiper. She keeps the hands at shoulder level.
3. Pullovers (for the triceps): Holding the bat with both hands, the hitter drops the bat directly back over her head. She then "throws" the bat forward with the bat head leading, keeping the elbows in during the throwing motion.
4. Bat raises: The hitter holds the bat at her side with the barrel pointed down. Keeping the arm at her side she raises the bat head using only the wrist.
5. Wrist circles: With the arm extended straightforward at shoulder level, the hitter makes wrist circles 10 times in each direction and then repeats with the other hand.

9

Bunting and Slap Hitting

Bunting plays an extremely important role in softball. Executing the short game is essential to a team's offensive strategy, and it adds excitement to the game. One of the most thrilling plays in the game is scoring a runner from third with a suicide squeeze. Everyone on the team should be proficient at the bunting game. Too many games are lost because someone could not get a bunt down. A team that bunts well wins games. Bunting is not as difficult as hitting, and it is easier to practice.

The left-side running slap is designed to give the batter a running start before hitting the ball. Because the batter is taking a swing at the ball, it is considered a hit, not a bunt. This distinction is important because a foul on a third strike with a slap is not an out as it is with a bunt. This chapter discusses both the slap hit and the bunt because the starting position in the box is the same and because the slapper should first learn to bunt before adding the slap. Because defenses are getting more sophisticated, a successful slapper must be able to drop a bunt when the defense is back and hit it through (slap) when the defense is in tight.

Why bunt or execute the slap? These offensive strategies can add variety to your offense, help advance runners while avoiding the double play and force-out, get the batter on base, help break an offensive slump, put pressure on the defense and take advantage of their weaknesses, and help your hitters against an overpowering pitcher.

SACRIFICE BUNT

The purpose of the sacrifice bunt is to advance a runner or runners with the expectation that the batter will be out; hence, it is called a sacrifice. The batter gives up an out for the good of the team. The batter's concern is to bunt the next strike and put it down so that the only play is at first. The sacrifice bunt is usually used with a runner on first and no outs and with the tiebreaker. When using the international tiebreaker rule, each team begins the tenth and subsequent innings of a tie game with a runner on second base. The runner is the batter who made the last official out in the previous inning. Usually, the visitors will attempt to sacrifice bunt the runner to third in hopes of getting at least one run. The home team will also usually bunt unless they need more than one run to win and feel they cannot afford to give up an out.

The sacrifice bunt requires the least movement of any bunt. The basic position of the bunter is at the front of the box so that any bunt directly down is in fair territory and will not bounce off the plate. Because the defense is anticipating most sacrifice bunts, the batter does not need to worry about turning early and giving it away. The bunter turns as the pitcher separates her hands so that as she attempts the bunt, her shoulders are not moving. Turning early also gives the batter time to read the defensive positioning before directing the ball.

An offensive option to use with the sacrifice bunt is the bunt-and-run. The runner goes on the pitch, and the batter bunts the ball. The batter's goal is just to advance the runner. The advantage is that the batter does not have to worry about placement because the runner has a head start on the defense. The batter must protect the runner, however, if the pitch is bad. The batter should stay in the box and try to distract the catcher or block her view.

Stance

The batter must make sure that her feet are not outside the batter's box when pivoting and when making contact. The weight is on the balls of the feet with the knees slightly bent and a slight bend at the waist. Keeping the weight forward will also help the batter get out of the way of a wild pitch. She should maintain good balance. Batters use two types of stances when putting down the bunt.

- **Squared stance**—The batter steps with the front foot to the outside line of the box and then steps forward with the back foot so that both feet are in a side-stride position parallel to the front line of the box (see figure 9.1). The feet are shoulder-width apart. Beginners often use this stance because it is easier to get the timing correct and be stationary at contact.
- **Pivot stance**—The batter pivots on the balls of both feet, turning the belly button toward the pitcher. The shoulders and hips are open to the pitcher. The feet stay in basic hitting position (forward-back) with the back foot moving a couple of inches closer to the plate for better balance (see figure 9.2). The batter is in a better running position, has better outside plate coverage, and is in a better position for a slap and hit.

Hand Position

As the bunter pivots, she has two options for holding the bat. Either of these techniques can be paired with either of the two stances described earlier. Players should experiment to find which stance and hand positions are most comfortable. Beginners will usually start with the square stance and hands apart for better bat control. As players become more skilled, they should move their hands together and try the pivot stance. The most important thing is for players to be comfortable and find out what works best for them.

- **Hands apart**—In this technique the bottom hand grips the bat with the knuckles up and the palm toward the ground. The top hand moves up the barrel to grip the bat just above the tape as if shaking hands with the bat. The top hand grips the bat in the fingertips, away from the base of the fingers, leaving a V-shaped space

Figure 9.1 Squared stance with the hands apart and the bat level.

Figure 9.2 Pivot stance with the hands together and the bat angled.

between the thumb and forefinger (see figure 9.1). The bat deadens the impact by sliding back into the V as the ball hits the bat, and the hand acts as a cushion. By holding the hands apart the bunter has better bat control.

- **Hands together**—In the second technique the hands are together in the hitting position with the top hand holding the bat loosely (see figure 9.2). This way, it is easier to slap and drive the ball, should the batter decide to attack the defense.

Bat Angle

The bat can be held level or at an angle. Again, these two techniques can be combined with either the square or pivot stances and with the hands apart or together. More advanced players usually hold their bats with some degree of angle.

- **Level bat**—The bat is held horizontally at the top of the strike zone (see figure 9.1). The only movement of the bat is down; the bat is always kept level. A disadvantage is that a bunt on the ball's bottom half will often be a foul pop-up to the catcher. The advantage of this technique is that the batter can more easily judge the strike zone—anything above the bat is a ball, and the batter never needs to extend above the bat to bunt the ball.
- **Angled bat**—The bat head is angled upward at about a 45-degree angle, and the bat head is pointed slightly toward the pitcher (see figure 9.2). The batter can more easily slash or drive the ball down. In addition, foul balls tend to kick more to the side, where the catcher cannot as easily make the out.

Contact Position

The bat is held in front of the chest and in front of home plate. The elbows are bent, pointed down, and slightly outside the body. The arms and shoulders are free of tension. The batter must be careful not to reach. Her head faces the pitcher, and her eyes are level. At contact, catch the ball with the bat, giving slightly with the bat and arms to soften the impact. Making contact with the end of the bat, rather than the sweet spot, will help deaden the ball.

To bunt a low pitch, the batter bends at the knees to lower the body while maintaining the same bat angle. She uses her legs as an elevator. As she lowers her hands and the bat, she makes sure that the bat head never drops below the hands.

The angle of the bat at contact will determine the direction of the ball. If the bat is square to the pitcher, the ball will rebound directly back to her. The bottom hand is the control hand. By pulling it forward or backward the batter can control where the ball will go. When a right-handed batter pulls the bottom hand back, the bunt will go toward third base; when the bottom hand is pushed forward, the ball will go to first. The adjustment of bat angle is not drastic. The batter should practice with a partner to learn the required angle. The partner tosses a ball, and the batter bunts alternately to each side of the tosser.

Right-handed batters will find it much easier to bunt an outside pitch toward first and an inside pitch toward third. For the best chance of success, players should bunt the ball where it is pitched. Only exceptional bunters should try otherwise. Bunters should not aim for the lines. They must allow for a margin of error and for the spin on the ball. The target should be in the area 45 degrees from the front corners of the plate. There is nothing worse than a well-executed bunt that rolls foul just as the runner slides safely to the base.

Coaching Points for the Sacrifice Bunt

- Bunt the ball! Admire it! When you see that the bunt is down and that the ball is out of your running path, then run!
- Don't drop your bat on the ball. If necessary carry it with you until you are well clear of the ball.
- If the first baseman fields the bunt and is waiting to tag you, stop and force her to come to you to apply the tag, giving the base runner more time to advance. Do not back up! Doing so is a dead ball, an automatic out, and the runners have to return to their bases.
- Focus on running in the running lane to avoid an interference call.

PUSH BUNT

The objective of the push bunt is to reach base safely. The push bunt is used to push the ball between the third baseman and the pitcher, or between the pitcher and the first baseman, hard enough so the shortstop or second baseman must charge the ball. The push bunt is most effective when the corners are playing in tight or are charging aggressively.

The starting grip and body position are the same as those used for a sacrifice bunt. Players choose the stance, hand position, and bat angle that are most comfortable. There should be no visible difference between the sacrifice bunt and the push bunt technique—hitters don't want to tip their intentions to the defense. With a push bunt, the grip tightens and both arms extend forward together to push the bat to the ball (see figure 9.3). The push of the

Figure 9.3 Push bunt.

bat is slightly down and through the ball to avoid line drives or pop-ups. The bunter may choose to take a short step into the ball while pushing it. However, she must be careful not to step completely out of the box or on the plate during contact—that's an automatic out. She moves quickly out of the box after contact. The location of the pitch dictates which side to direct the ball to.

SLASH, OR SLUG BUNT

The batter executes the slash, or slug bunt, by faking a bunt and then swinging away. The batter turns early, assuming a sacrifice-bunt position. The goal is to induce the corners to charge aggressively. The batter holds the sacrifice-bunt position long enough to get the corners to believe the bunt is on and to charge. At the last moment, when the ball is on its way, the batter rotates the shoulders and hips back slightly, being careful not to turn the rest of the body or head. The front shoulder comes to the chin. The backswing is about half of the distance used when hitting. If the hands are not already together on the rotation, the batter slides the lower hand up against the top hand to a hitting position. On the rotation she cocks the wrists back to prepare for making a chopping motion. She hits the ball down at the feet of the charging corner or at the gap between the corner and the pitcher. The batter does not use a full swing but a compact chop or slash down to bounce the ball. The element of surprise and the sharp hit down are what lead to success. The batter must be careful not to rotate too far back trying to take a full swing. The result is usually a late swing that produces a pop-up. An advantage of the squared bunt position is that it helps limit the backswing.

RIGHT-HANDED SNEAKY BUNT

An extremely effective bunt, particularly for a power hitter when the third baseman is playing back at the bag, is the right-handed sneaky bunt. The batter's body screens the third baseman's vision until the last moment, giving the batter a great jump.

The bunt can be executed with one or two hands. The batter assumes a normal hitting stance but at the front of the box. The bunter maintains the batting stance until the last instant, taking a stride forward exactly as if hitting away. On the stride, the top hand slides about halfway up the bat (see figure 9.4a). Weight is transferred to the front

Figure 9.4 Right-handed sneaky bunt. *(a)* Position during the stride and *(b)* at contact.

a

b

foot. (Some batters may also prefer to step back slightly from the plate with the back foot.) The batter drops the bat straight down, with the knob by the back hip and the bat head pointed toward first base (see figure 9.4b). The bat head is slightly higher than the knob. With weight on the front foot the body leans forward toward the plate. The player holds her head down to watch the ball meet the bat. Contact is made in one of two places—slightly behind the belt buckle or behind the back hip. The batter does not swing at the ball; by using just the wrist of the top hand, she gently taps the ball forward several feet in front of home plate. The bunter then runs hard to first base. If contact is made behind the hip, the ball will sometimes go behind the batter as she leaves the box. If the ball hits the batter immediately, she is still in the box, and the bunt is a foul ball.

LEFT-HANDED DRAG BUNT

To execute the left-handed drag bunt, the batter must use a normal hitting position to avoid telegraphing her intentions. This bunt is used to surprise the defense or when the corners are playing deep. The running start and closer position to first give a speedy lefty a real advantage. She waits for a good pitch and drops the bunt.

The front foot steps back to start the hands and body in motion (see figure 9.5a). The hands move upward to shoulder height as the foot comes back. As the bat begins moving forward, the hands move up the bat to a bunting position. The back foot then crosses over, ideally landing on the lines marking the front corner of the box. Weight

Figure 9.5 Left-handed drag bunt. *(a)* Step with the front foot to start the hands and body in motion and *(b)* grip the bat firmly and extend it with the bat head angled slightly forward at contact.

a

b

stays on the left foot after the crossover, and the head is on the ball. The hips and shoulders remain closed until contact is made. The batter must be careful not to open up or pull off the plate before contact because she will be vulnerable to an outside pitch or a change-up. At contact all momentum is toward the pitcher, not to first base. The grip is firm, and the bat is extended with the bat head angled slightly forward (see figure 9.5b). Most bunters should use both hands; it takes a lot of strength and bat control to bunt with only one hand. Contact is well in front of the body and the plate. Weight is on the left foot as contact is made.

The bunter should learn to angle the bat so that she can drag down either foul line as well as be able to drop the ball just in front of the plate. She looks for low pitches and goes with the pitch.

SQUEEZE BUNT

The two types of squeeze bunts are the suicide squeeze and the safety squeeze. The objective of both is to score the runner from third by surprising the defense. In the suicide squeeze the runner is going on the pitch, whereas in the safety squeeze the runner goes home when the ball has been bunted successfully.

In the suicide squeeze the count should be in the batter's favor so she can expect to see a strike. The batter and all runners must know the squeeze is on. The batter must know the signal and acknowledge that she has it. She then visualizes a successful squeeze before stepping into the box. She doesn't square to bunt until the last moment. She then pivots quickly into bunting stance. The bunter must put the bat on the ball to protect the runner if the pitch is one that the catcher can catch. If the batter can't bunt the ball, she should at least foul it off. She bunts the ball down, away from the foul lines, away from the catcher, and not too hard. A missed ball or a pop-up spells disaster.

The safety bunt is used to protect against a pitchout and when the defense has weak arms. The batter chooses the pitch to bunt. She has only one shot, however, because the element of surprise is gone after the first attempt. The runner goes on the result of the play. The batter feels less pressure because the runner waits to see if the bunt is successfully down. On a safety squeeze, bunting toward third base allows the runner at third to get a bigger lead because the third baseman must play the ball.

FAKE BUNT

In this play the batter acts as if she is bunting but doesn't touch the ball. The offense may use the fake bunt to distract or delay the catcher with runners stealing, to see how quickly the shortstop covers third with a runner at second, or to rattle the pitcher when the batter is taking a pitch.

Because the batter wants the defense to react without thinking, she must not commit too early. After showing the bunt, she brings the bat back out of the strike zone to avoid being called for a strike attempt. If the runner is stealing, the batter leaves the end of the bat pointed where the catcher's eyes will be when she stands. The catcher will then have to adjust to see the runner.

A fake bunt can be used in combination with other plays to confuse the defense further. A fake bunt and slap is effective with a hit-and-run. A fake bunt–fake slap–bunt will have the fielders bouncing around like yo-yos. A fake drag and hit is another variation. Here, the batter acts as if she is going to drag bunt and at the last moment cocks the wrists back and hits hard through the ball.

LEFT-HANDED RUNNING SLAP

A left-handed batter can get a running start before hitting the ball by using the left-side running slap. The lefty is already several steps closer to first. Adding a running start puts tremendous pressure on the defense to make the play quickly. The play often moves the defense out of position as well. To be successful, the batter should have good speed and the ability to put the ball in play.

The batter stands in her standard hitting position so that she does not tip the defense. The slapper must be in a position where the crossover step will put her on the lines of the front inside corner of the box. To execute the slap, the hitter runs first and hits second. She starts to move when the ball leaves the pitcher's hand. She must not anticipate the release. If she starts too soon, she will have to stop moving to slap the ball or will be way out of the box. The first step is a small jab step with the right foot, either forward or backward. The jab step acts as a timing mechanism. The left foot crosses aggressively over the right foot directly to the pitcher (see figure 9.6a). The left foot should land on the front line of the box on the inside corner. The right foot then opens slightly toward the pitcher. If the jab step is not used, the first step must include a pivot that opens the hips to the pitcher. The hips are square, but the front shoulder stays closed to permit total plate coverage.

a

b

Figure 9.6 Left-handed slap. Take a small jab step with the right foot, *(a)* then cross the left foot aggressively over the right foot directly to the pitcher so it lands on the front line of the box on the inside corner. *(b)* On the slap follow-through roll through the box and be in motion as contact is made.

The hands are held close to the body and high in the strike zone on the swing. The front side and front shoulder remain closed. The batter can use a choke grip for good bat control. The bat head is above the hands, which come forward with the crossover step. The batter must be careful not to drop her hands at the start of the swing. She hits the ball as the left foot lands on the front line. The swing is an inside-out swing. The knob is first, the head of the bat stays back, and the swing is down. The knob and hands stay inside the path of the ball. The hands are out in front. To hit to the left side, the batter should be late with the head of the bat. The batter contacts the ball behind her body and hits down into the ground to put the ball in play.

On the slap follow-through the batter rolls through the box, being in motion as she hits the ball (see figure 9.6b). She need not be moving fast; what is important is that she be in motion. The slapper continues running toward the pitcher after contact, being careful not to turn early to run to first. On the follow-through the bat is an extension of the right arm. The batter follows through with the bat in the right hand.

Batters should take the following steps to learn the slap:

1. Stand at the plate and catch pitches with a glove on the left hand to become comfortable catching the ball and seeing it from the left side.
2. Add the crossover step to the exercise of catching pitches.
3. Become proficient as a drag bunter.
4. Use the crossover step and hit off a tee. Draw a line to use as the inside line of the batter's box so that you can check alignment and make sure that the front shoulder stays closed. The hands should be even with the left foot and ahead of the bat, and the bat must have the proper angle at contact. Hit to the shortstop and the second baseman.
5. Run and hit off a T.
6. Run and hit off a machine.
7. Slap off a pitcher.

Coaching Points for the Slap

- Learn to bunt first.
- Avoid focusing too much on your footwork. Don't think feet! Think contact!
- Don't drop the hands. Keep the bat on the shoulder and the hands below if you can't correct the problem.
- Don't step away from the pitch or open your front side.
- Keep your feet under control. Focus on making contact, not on watching your feet.
- Work all pitches—high, low, in, out.
- If you are not getting the ball down, separate your hands on the bat or start with the bat at the one o'clock position.
- Use a fake slap and a miss to freeze the shortstop when a runner is stealing second or third. The shortstop will usually wait to play the ball on the slap and will be slow getting to the base.

MENTAL PREPARATION FOR THE SHORT GAME

The fun of the short game is the element of surprise. The offense can keep the defense guessing what they will do. Batters must not telegraph their intentions by changing their position in the box or by using a different hand or bat position. Bunters should execute on the first strike. If they turn to bunt, or run to slap, and don't execute, the element of surprise is lost.

As the batter approaches the on-deck circle, she should already know what the situation will likely call for. See table 9.1 for a review of several bunting situations. The player can start preparing mentally for the job she will probably be asked to do. Before stepping in the box she must know if she is bunting or slapping. If a signal is given, the batter should have no doubt about what her responsibilities are. If she has a question, she should not step into the box until she is sure. Time may be called if necessary, although doing so risks losing the element of surprise. The batter then visualizes executing the play successfully before she steps into the box. She must not visualize an unsuccessful effort. Players asked to bunt often have a tendency to tell themselves not to pop up the bunt. That image becomes the one they visualize. Coaches, too, must be sure to give positive instructions.

The mental preparation described in chapter 8 on hitting is important for the short game. Bunters must understand the umpire's strike zone, know what pitch to look for, and understand the count.

BUNTING AND SLAP-HITTING DRILLS

Pair up players to get many repetitions while working on bat control and ball placement. When partners are in close instruct the bunter to already be in a squared or pivot position, because there won't be time for her to turn her body to the correct position. For safety, use Wiffle balls when working on slug bunts and slaps. Always include drills in which players can bunt and then run to first to work on timing; bunters have a tendency in games to be in a hurry and run while bunting.

Table 9.1
Summary of Bunting Situations

Situation	Outs	Goal	Pitch to bunt
Sacrifice bunt	Less than two	Advance runner	Bunt next strike
Squeeze bunt	None, one, two	Score runner	Bunt or foul off next pitch
Safety squeeze	Less than two	Score runner	Bunt first strike
Bunt-and-run	Less than two	Advance runner	Bunt any strike and protect runner if a ball
Fake bunt	None, one, two	Rattle pitcher	Any strike
		Observe defensive coverage	If a ball, show bunt and then pull bat back
Knob bunt	None, one, two	Avoid strikeout	With two strikes when fooled by change-up and bat is out in front of body

Air Drill

Purpose: To evaluate and practice bunting technique.

Procedure: The coach calls a particular bunt, and the batter then assumes position in an imaginary batter's box. On the command "Ball" the batter executes the basic movement. The emphasis is on proper bat angle and contact spot, good balance, and using the legs to lower the body for low pitches.

Partner Front Soft Toss

Purpose: To develop bat and ball control while bunting. This drill allows many repetitions in a small area and in a short time.

Procedure: Players practice all bunting skills using any type of balls. One player tosses underhand to the bunter. The players should be about 15 feet apart. They use Wiffle balls when practicing chops, slashes, and slaps. The batter must already be in bunting position because there is no time to pivot.

Pepper

Purpose: To develop bat and ball control while bunting. This drill allows many repetitions in a small area and in a short time. This drill is a good activity to keep players warm while waiting for a game.

Procedure: Three or four players stand side by side and face a batter about 10 feet away. Players field and use an underhand toss to feed the batter, who executes all the short-game skills.

Variation: Play pepper with the hitter slapping the ball. All fielders are to the pitcher's right, and the batter tries to slap all balls to that area. She can slap standing still or with the run.

Machine Bunting

Purpose: To become proficient in all bunts.

Procedure: Facing medium-speed pitches to all locations, the batter executes all types of bunts. Tape or cones mark a target area. The batter rotates the body to bunting position on every pitch to develop timing and make the drill gamelike.

Variation: The batter must successfully execute 10 sacrifice bunts before she can go to the push bunt. After 10 successful push bunts, she moves on to the slash or sneaky bunt.

Bunting and Base Running

Purpose: To practice executing the sacrifice bunt and base running.

Procedure: Players form a bunting line at home, and running lines of three players are at first and third (see figure 9.7). On defense use a pitcher and catcher or a machine and several fielders to retrieve the balls. The fielders are close to home to field bunts and return the balls to the pitcher. The bunter must successfully bunt the first strike and then run to first in the running lane. Failure to bunt successfully or to stay in the running lane means that the player must continue running to right field as a penalty. If the bunter executes everything correctly, she joins the running line after touching first base. The runner on first goes when she sees that the bunt is angled down. On approaching second base she looks to see if third is open and hits the inside of the base on her turn. She then joins the line at third. The runner at third takes a lead in foul territory and breaks for home when she is sure the bunt is down.

Variation: Slappers slap the ball instead of bunting. Base runners go as soon as they see that the ball is hit down.

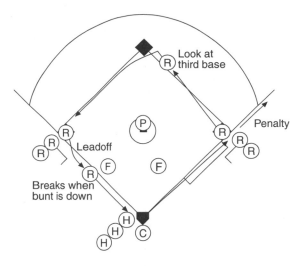

Figure 9.7 Bunting and base running drill.

Slapping Off Front Soft Toss

Purpose: To develop footwork and proper swing for the slap hit.

Procedure: The pitcher is 15 feet in front of the slapper and tosses easy pitches. The slapper does not move until the ball is released. The pitcher should hold on to some pitches to see if the slapper has started to move in anticipation.

Fence-Swing Drill

Purpose: To train the slapper to use the inside-outside swing and to lead with the knob of the bat.

Procedure: The player stands facing a fence one bat length away. She swings without making contact with the fence, leading with the knob and keeping the hands high. She does this with the eyes open and then with the eyes closed to groove the swing. The slapper adds footwork and continues running down the fence line after the swing, as she should on the follow-through.

Slap and Run Around Cone

Purpose: To practice running toward the pitcher when slapping.

Procedure: The slapper hits off a pitcher or machine. Place a cone two steps in front of the batter's box in line with the pitcher. The slapper must run around the cone before heading toward first base. The cone prevents the slapper from turning too early toward first.

Alternate Bunts and Slaps

Purpose: To eliminate telegraphing of the bunt or slap.

Procedure: A batter alternates executing drag bunts and slaps off a pitcher or machine. The emphasis is on keeping movements the same as long as possible. The pitcher or feeder calls "Bunt" or "Slap" when she recognizes what is coming.

10

Base Running

As base runners, players need to be aggressive and make things happen. Players with an aggressive reputation put pressure on the defense, forcing them to "worry and hurry," which in turn leads to errors on routine plays. To score, players must reach four bases safely with only three outs, so unless they can depend on extra-base hits to get home they will have to get something for nothing. By being aggressive they can get the team that extra base. Although speed is a great advantage, base runners also need good judgment to know when to go, proper technique to make the most of the speed they have, and an aggressive attitude that takes advantage of anything the opposing team offers. Players also need the ability to execute under pressure. This is one of the few aspects of the game that players can control. Unfortunately, it is often the least practiced.

Beginners will usually be controlled by the coach and told when to go and what to do. As players become more experienced, the coach usually gives them more freedom so that they can react on their own within the team's philosophy.

Players should practice base running whenever they have a chance. They can work on basic techniques on their own daily. During batting practice many opportunities are available to develop reactions and work on situations. Players should practice thinking for themselves.

IMPROVING SPEED

How important is speed? If a player can improve her speed to first by one-tenth of a second, her batting average should improve by 50 points. The average defensive play on an infield ground ball takes three seconds. The goal for the batter, then, is to be able to get to first in less than three seconds.

Everyone can get faster. Speed development should be a year-round conditioning activity. Players can study their running styles, perhaps by looking at videotapes showing them running to first and around the bases. They can have a track coach analyze their technique and make corrections. By practicing every day, the improved technique will become habit.

To improve speed, players need to learn proper running technique and concentrate on the following components.

- **Arm action**—The elbows are at a 90-degree angle and close to the body. The arms drive vigorously from the chest down past the hips. The player can think lip to hip or cheek to cheek. The thumb and forefinger touch lightly in a relaxed manner. The player drives the hands as if holding a hammer and pounding a nail just past her hips. The arms swing straight back and forth, not across the body. (Females tend to swing across the body.) The shoulders are tension free. The faster the arms go, the faster the legs go. To practice, the player should work only on arm action, starting slowly and increasing arm speed. She focuses on keeping the shoulders relaxed and using proper arm swing.

- **Knees**—The knees are lifted high to form a 90-degree hip angle, with the toes in upward position (full flexion at the ankle). Good flexibility in the hamstrings is required to get the legs up high. Stretches, especially toe touches with the knees bent, will increase flexibility.

- **Foot placement**—The feet are straight ahead with the instep touching the outside of an imaginary line going to the target. Running on the balls of the feet produces better spring and keeps the eyes from bouncing as much.

- **Body lean**—The head is up, and the body is tall (erect.) The lean is from the ankles, not the hips. Running is continuously losing balance and regaining it.

Pawing Action

The player stands sideways to a fence, working the leg farthest from the fence. She does a butt kick, then lifts the knee high with a forward stretch of the foot. The toes are pointed up toward the sky. She paws the ground with the ball of the foot, just brushing the ground, and then immediately goes back up with a butt kick. The pawing action is repeated continually. The player then performs the exercise with the other leg. The longer the feet are on the ground, the slower the player will be.

Being able to accelerate quickly is important in softball because of the short base paths. To improve acceleration players should do short sprints (five yards) as well as sprints starting from a prone position on the stomach. Players must honestly evaluate the weight they are carrying. At the racetrack a fast horse is sometimes handicapped by adding a five-pound weight to bring his ability down to that of the other horses in the field. If five pounds can affect a strong racehorse, what does excess weight do to you?

ON THE BASES

Speed on the bases begins with an explosion out of the batter's box. Players should then work on the techniques that can improve speed around the bases. They should try to reduce the number of steps required to circle the bases. At the same time they should always be looking for opportunities that get them to the next base and closer to the ultimate goal of scoring.

Out of the Box

To get a fast start, the player stays low, drives the elbows down, and explodes out of the box. She uses a good follow-through on the swing and shifts her weight to the front foot. The batter then pulls with the front foot instead of lifting it and replanting. Using the pull will improve quickness out of the box. The first step is then with the back foot.

To First Base

The player should develop the habit of running on or to the right side of the first-base line. She is out if she runs on the inside of the running lane and in the umpire's opinion interferes physically or visually with the fielder taking the throw at first. Halfway to first the runner takes a brief look to locate the ball and decide whether to run through the base or make the turn toward second (see figure 10.1). The runner turns only the head, not the shoulders.

On a close play the runner concentrates on a spot 15 feet beyond the base and runs through the base, being careful not to slow until after touching it. She touches the front of the base to reach it sooner. The runner doesn't lunge or leap at the base because doing so is slower and increases the chance of injury. A slide is used at first base only to avoid a tag, because sliding is slower than running through the base. The runner leans forward as she touches the base and at the same time turns her head toward the coach to see any signals and hear instructions. Players should always run hard, even on routine outs, and always

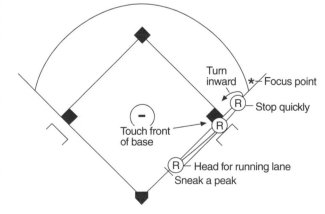

Figure 10.1 Key points on the run from home to first base.

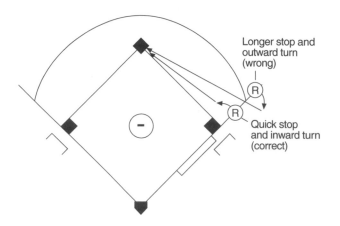

Longer stop and outward turn (wrong)

Quick stop and inward turn (correct)

Figure 10.2 A quick stop and inward turn decreases the distance to second base.

touch the base even if they think they are out. The defense may drop the ball or pull the foot. After touching the base the runner stops quickly, as close to the base as possible (see figure 10.2). Many runners go far beyond first base when stopping, increasing the distance to second base. They lose valuable time and may eliminate any opportunity to advance. The runner should put on the brakes by straightening up and planting a heel to act as a brake. She then lowers the center of gravity slightly by lowering the hips, maintaining good balance. The runner stops on or near the foul line, turns inward (toward the diamond), and locates the ball. The runner returns immediately to the base without making any movement toward second, but she should be ready to go to second on an overthrow or if the coach tells her to go. The runner should always follow the ball back into the pitcher's glove. Runners often do not see dropped balls or overthrows because they turn away from the play or fail to keep watching.

On a routine single the runner makes an aggressive turn and maintains a balanced position while locating the ball. Only when she can't see the ball does the runner look to the coach for help on whether to run through the base or make the turn. On balls hit up the middle or to right field, a runner saves time by making her own decisions.

Every time the batter strikes out, she should run to first base, making it a habit even if the rules say she is not entitled to run (runner on first and less than two out or catcher catches the ball). By running, the batter forces the catcher to react. By making it automatic, the runner never misses the opportunity to advance when the catcher drops the ball.

Leadoffs

The base runner should always use the same leadoff to avoid tipping off the defense about what she will be doing. The runner leads off aggressively on the release of every pitch to put pressure on the catcher and to be in position to take advantage of a dropped ball. A goal is to have the defense yell "Going" on every lead. The two basic leadoffs are the rocker start and the stationary start. Players should find the technique that works best and use it consistently at all bases.

Rocker Start. Also called the sprinter's start, this rolling start is the best leadoff because the body is already in motion as the ball is released. A further advantage is that it is more deceiving to the umpire because it is harder to judge exactly when the runner leaves the base. But an inexperienced umpire may react to the runner's movement and call an out, believing that the runner has left too soon although the back foot may still be in contact. Practice is necessary to develop the proper timing, and runners must study each pitcher's windup to get the maximum advantage.

The left foot is placed at the front edge of the base (facing the next base and farthest from home plate). The right foot is one step behind and to the side of the base so that the runner won't trip (see figure 10.3). Weight is over the front foot. Both elbows are bent in running position with the right arm forward. As the pitcher starts her movement, the runner shifts her weight to the back foot and switches the position of the arms by bringing the right arm back. She begins the motion back as the heel of the pitcher's back leg lifts up. (Another timing mechanism is any movement by the pitcher.) As the pitcher starts a downward motion (or lifts the heel of the other leg off the rubber), the runner should be in motion forward, simultaneously pulling down with the left arm and taking a step forward with the right foot. At release the runner pushes hard off the base with the left foot, using it as a sprinter would a starting block.

Stationary Start.   The runner cannot get an equivalent jump off the base starting from a stationary position. Another drawback is that the umpire can more easily judge when the runner leaves the base. The runner must be careful not to cheat by leaving early.

The runner is either in a forward-stride position with the arms in running position or in a sideways position with the arms hanging down a little lower, like those of a football lineman. The rear foot is on the edge of the base closest to the base the runner is advancing to (see figure 10.4). The runner assumes a well-balanced position, ready to react to the pitcher's movement. She pushes off the base when the pitcher's back heel lifts from the rubber. Doing this is quicker than waiting for the release, and the heel lift is easier to see.

Delayed Lead.   A more advanced leadoff, the delayed lead has the runner in motion when the bat meets the ball. When the ball is bunted or hit, being in motion is better than taking a leadoff, stopping, and restarting. The delayed lead can be used at first or third base with any lead except a straight steal. The runner tries to time the start so that she is leaving the base just before ball contact. She reacts to the ball as it approaches the hitter's contact spot. The goal is to be in full motion three steps off the base when the ball is bunted or hit. Then as the runner sees the bunt or hit angled down, she can continue to advance without losing a step or slowing down. If the ball is missed, the runner is no farther off the base than with a normal lead. (The delayed lead should not be used at second base because the runner should leave on the pitcher's release to take advantage of the five-step lead she should take there.)

Leadoff Distance.   At first base the leadoff should be one body length and one step (three steps). This leadoff allows for a step and a dive back on a pickoff attempt. At second base the lead should be five steps off the base because the runner is farther from the catcher. At third base the lead is three steps and always in foul territory so that any batted ball that hits the runner is a foul ball and not an out.

Figure 10.3   Rocker start.

Figure 10.4   Stationary start.

After the ball is hit, the runner adjusts the lead according to the location of the ball. When a ball is fielded or hit in the air, the closer the receiver is to the runner, the shorter the lead must be because the runner is more vulnerable to being put out. Conversely, when the ball is on the opposite side of the field, the runner can extend the lead. The runner should know how field conditions will affect footing and how far she can safely go. If the ground is soft or slippery, she should shorten her lead.

The base runner does not head back to the base until the pitcher has the ball. She never assumes the catch is made and always watches for an overthrow or a dropped ball.

Tagging Up

When a ball is hit in the air and caught with less than two out, runners who have left a base must return and tag before they can legally advance. Runners who have remained on the base or who have tagged it may leave again as soon as the ball is touched.

When possible a runner should watch the ball and the catch herself. She places the feet on the base for a good leadoff and turns her head to follow the ball. By making the decision herself, miscommunication between player and coach is eliminated and the player can react more quickly. (If the runner has to wait for the coach's command, a delay occurs until it all registers and the runner reacts.)

Runners should tag on all foul balls. Runners can advance only on a caught foul ball, so they should tag and be in position to go. If they can't tell if a ball is fair or foul, they should assume it is fair. At third base the runner should tag immediately on deep fly balls as soon as the ball is hit in the air. Should the ball be dropped or fumbled, the runner will score easily. At first or second base, the runner tags only if the fly ball is deep enough that she can advance on the catch and resulting throw. If the ball is very deep and it is obvious that she will advance easily, the runner should delay leaving a little to eliminate the chance of being called out for leaving early.

On shallow fly balls, runners (including runners at third) do not tag because they have no hope of advancing if the ball is caught. From a normal leadoff position, the runner has a better chance of advancing should the ball drop because she is closer to the next base than she would be if she had tagged. The runner leads off as far as she can while still being able to return if the ball is caught.

The goal of all runners is to score. They should be aggressive, go for extra bases, and anticipate. If it appears that the ball will not be caught, runners should be as far away from the base as possible and going hard to the next base. They should not tag up! If a fielder makes a spectacular catch, runners can scramble back. This principle applies everywhere except at third.

BETWEEN BASES

When a runner is between bases, she must always know where the ball is. She stays low, balanced, and ready to react forward or backward. She assumes a crouch position like a football lineman, with weight equally distributed, feet shoulder-width apart, and hips down. The runner doesn't lean or commit either way until the defense gives her a reason to go. The eyes are on the ball, and the arms hang loosely so that she is ready to react either way. When she goes, she uses the same footwork that she uses when fielding a ground ball to that side (see chapter 1, page 8). The first step is a jab step, and a crossover step follows. The runner pushes off hard on the jab step and drives with the elbows to increase acceleration.

The base runner should stay in the path of the thrown ball. Whenever possible she should interfere legally with the throw and make it more difficult for the defensive player to throw to the target. If the ball hits the runner, everyone should advance safely.

But the runner should not sacrifice speed. A straight line is still the fastest route between two points, so she should not veer too far off line.

Whenever possible, runners should avoid being tagged out by a defensive player. A base runner is allowed to leave the base path by three feet to avoid a tag. With multiple base runners, a player who can't avoid a tag should stop and make the defense chase her, giving the other runners time to advance. A runner going to first base may not back up to avoid a tag. If she does, she is out, the ball is dead, and all runners must return. Runners must attempt to avoid contact with the defensive player fielding the ball because that also results in a dead ball.

When the base runners must return to a base, they should always hustle back. A careless return can result in an out on a quick throw or when a defensive player blocks the base. Runners should be prepared to dive back on any pickoff throw. The dive back is normally to the back corner of the base farthest from the throw. But the runner must have an opening to get to the base. If the defensive player has blocked that corner, the runner must adjust to find an open corner. She starts the dive from a lowered body position using a swimmer's diving start. She takes a small jab step with the left foot toward the base, pivots to face it, and then lies out flat, reaching for the base with the closer hand. The arms and hands reach for the base just above the ground (see figure 10.5). The base runner should protect her fingers from injury by making a fist or half fist and protect her face by turning away from the throw. After touching the base, she keeps the tagging hand on the base, holds her position, and listens for the coach's instruction or the umpire's call so that she knows what the next move is.

If the runner returns standing up, she tags the corner farthest from the throw and leans slightly away from the receiver, being careful not to lean too much and lose balance when the tag is made. The baseman may push with the tag, hoping that the runner loses contact with the base and the umpire calls her out.

AROUND THE BASES

The shortest distance between two points is a straight line, and the goal is to take the shortest and quickest route possible. Players should count the number of steps they take from home to home and work to reduce that number. For a tight, efficient turn, the runner angles 3 or 4 feet to the right as she comes within 10 to15 feet of the base. This maneuver puts her in position to make the turn at the bag. She concentrates on the spot that she has to run at to make the correct turn and runs to it in a straight line. The desired turn is as close to a right angle as possible. She tries to hit the inside corner of first base and second base with the left foot. To produce a sharp turn, the runner leans

Figure 10.5 Diving back to the base.

Coaching Points for Base Running

- Read the ball off the bat. Focus on the contact spot.
- With none out be a little more conservative; with one out be more aggressive.
- Study the defense before and throughout the game. Know each player's arm strength and accuracy. Know the position of each defensive player when the ball is hit. Always look for something to take advantage of. Is the fielder off balance? Is the defense asleep? Are they making lazy throws?
- Review the situation and how you should respond to every swing and hit—number of outs, game situation, and defensive alignment.
- Don't hesitate. When you have made up your mind, don't change it—go hard.
- Advance on balls hit behind you if the defense is back and you have a good possibility for success.
- When forced to run to the next base, go hard and slide hard to break up the double play.
- Know the rules. Understand infield fly, interference and obstruction, delayed calls, and the third-strike rule.
- The shorter the throwing distance, the more vulnerable you are to being picked off. Adjust your lead to that distance.
- Never leave a base until you are sure the umpire has called you out.

to the inside of the base and dips the left shoulder as the right leg swings over the planted left foot. She does not shuffle her feet or break stride. If the right foot will hit the inside corner, she tightens the turn by exaggerating the inside lean and throwing her head and shoulder to the pitcher. At third base she uses the right foot on the inside corner to cut the distance going home.

If the ball is not in front of her as she approaches second base, the runner picks up the third-base coach to get help. About 15 feet before the base, she turns only her head, not the shoulders, to see the coach.

SLIDING

Base runners may need to slide in a variety of situations:

- to go full speed to a base without overrunning it,
- to avoid a collision,
- to attempt to avoid a tag,
- to break up a double play, or
- to knock the ball out of the fielder's glove.

Runners should slide on any close play. They must then quickly get to their feet to be ready to advance to the next base. Players must know how to slide and must practice sliding. Learning the proper techniques and practicing them will develop confidence and eliminate fear of sliding. The following sections describe several sliding techniques.

Bent-Leg Slide

Players should first master the bent-leg slide, the most basic slide. It is the safest slide and the foundation for the pop-up slide. The base runner goes straight to the base without losing any speed. She starts the slide approximately 10 feet (two to three steps) from the bag. The lead foot is extended, and the opposite leg is bent at a 45-degree angle and tucked under the knee of the forward leg. (Although either leg may be bent, it is best to tuck the left leg because it is easier to roll to the left and look to the next base.) The runner leans back, extends the arms out like an airplane, and extends the striding foot (preferably the right foot) toward the bag as if kicking a soccer ball (see figure 10.6). There is no leap or jump or loss of speed in the transition from the run to the takeoff. The arms are high and out to the side for balance. The takeoff leg (left) is bent and tucked under the knee of the forward leg.

The laces of the bottom foot face the base with the foot slightly off the ground. The top leg is slightly bent, with the kneecap facing up and the foot about six inches off the ground so that the spikes don't catch. Keeping the knee slightly bent allows the leg to give at impact and prevents locked-knee injuries.

The runner falls on her butt and the upper part of the bottom leg. She does not slide on the side of the knees or legs. The body slides horizontally to the ground and is often slightly turned toward the bent-leg side. The buttocks and the upper portion of the tucked leg should absorb the impact.

The arms and hands are thrown over the head or across the chest to protect them as well as lessen impact with the ground. The runner must be careful not to drag the hands on the ground. The chin is tucked to keep the head from hitting the ground, and the eyes are on the base. The back and shoulder blades are close to the ground, and the body stays low. The runner hits the base with the lead toe or heel.

Figure 10.6 Bent-leg slide.

Pop-Up Slide

To execute the pop-up slide, runners use the bent-leg slide, contact the base, and pop up to a standing position at the base ready to advance to the next base. This slide is used when sliding players realize that no play is being made or that the throw is well off target. The pop-up slide uses the same techniques as the bent-leg slide with these exceptions:

- The front leg is braced against the base at contact and the shin of the bent leg is simultaneously pressed against the ground. The runner throws her head, shoulders, and chest forward and upward, keeping the arms across the chest (see figure 10.7).
- Momentum will throw the body upward and pop the slider up to a sitting and then standing position.

To learn the pop-up slide, try these techniques.

1. The player should practice standing up from a sitting position without using the hands.
2. Lying flat in the bent-leg position, the player practices getting to a sitting position by bringing the arms to the chest while bending at the waist.

Figure 10.7 Pop-up slide.

Hook Slide

To avoid a tag, base runners can use the hook slide to slide away from the defensive player. The defensive position of the receiver and the position of the throw determine which side runners will slide to. The throw is generally to the inside, so runners will usually be going outside, away from the defensive player.

To hook slide to the right, the runner slides to a spot two to three feet outside and beyond the base. She starts the slide late and extends the right foot past the bag so that the left foot will hook the front corner of the bag's outfield side. The runner kicks the right foot forward and turns the ankle to the right so that the outside of the foot slides along the ground. She leans to the right and drops the right shoulder. The outside of the right calf and hip absorb most of the impact. The body is flat with the head up. The eyes must stay on the inside corner of the base. The left leg is straight with a slight bend at the knee as the sliding player reaches toward the corner of the base. She touches the base with the shoelaces of the back foot. The toe of the left foot catches the corner of the base, causing the leg to bend (see figure 10.8). As the runner slides, she pushes the left shoulder and left hip down to the ground to keep the body from rolling to the right. For a slide to the left, the footwork is reversed.

Figure 10.8 Hook slide.

Headfirst Slide

Because it allows all forward momentum of the run to continue, the headfirst slide is the fastest slide. But it has several drawbacks. It cannot be used to break up a double play. The runner cannot recover quickly to continue to the next base. It is dangerous because contact is made with the hands, and the head and arms are in a vulnerable position. And it should never be used at home where the catcher can block the plate.

To execute the headfirst slide, the player uses the same technique she used for diving back to a base. She runs full speed to within about 10 feet of the bag, bends forward, and dives low to the base. She bends the knees to get closer to the ground and uses a swimmer's start. The force is horizontal as she slides or glides along the ground. The sliding player swings both arms forward with the head up to look for the base. She arches the back slightly and slides on the lower stomach and upper thighs. The feet, elbows, and hands are off the ground, and the fingers are closed in a fist (see figure 10.9). As the play is made, the player protects her face by turning the head away from the action.

Figure 10.9 Headfirst slide.

Rollover Slide

Runners use the rollover slide to get around a defensive player who is blocking the plate. This maneuver is sometimes referred to as going backdoor. The runner slides on her back to a spot three to four feet outside and beyond the base. The left arm is extended out to the side. As the runner slides by the base, she pulls the left arm in sharply to the left side of the body and throws the right arm to the base, helping the body roll over to the stomach (see figure 10.10a). After completing the roll, she reaches for the base with the right hand (see figure 10.10b). This slide can also be done without the rollover. The base runner slides past the base and grabs it with the inside hand and arm, which are fully extended.

Learning to Slide

Players should learn how to slide in a grassy area free of debris and sprinklers. They should wear running shoes or just socks, not cleats. Long pants, sliding pads, knee and elbow pads, and gardening gloves will all help protect against abrasions. The base should be loose. A wet area near the base will allow players to slide easily.

Players can follow this progression when learning to slide:

1. Sit with the legs crossed and then extend the right foot (preferably). Lie down, grab the ears, and then extend the arms overhead, feeling the correct body position.

2. From a standing position, put the arms out like the wings of an airplane. Kick an imaginary soccer ball with the right foot. Then bend the left leg and sit down without the hands or legs touching the ground. (If necessary, coaches on both sides support the arms to help bear the player's weight as she first sits down.) Another option is for two coaches to hold a bat horizontal and chest high, supporting the bat at both ends. The player runs under the bat, grabs it with both hands (palm forward), and kicks her foot forward. Coaches lower the bat as the player gets into a sliding position.

a

b

Figure 10.10 Rollover slide. *(a)* Pull the left arm sharply to the left side and throw the right arm to the base and *(b)* reach for the base with the right hand after completing the roll.

3. Bend and tuck the left leg under the extended right leg, throw the hands overhead, and lie down. Carry grass or small rocks in each hand so that you are not tempted to use your hands to break the fall.

4. From a half-speed run, slide on a wet surface. Gradually increase speed and distance. Slip-and-slides, sheets of plastic, or cardboard can also be used as a sliding surface. The cleanest, softest, and safest teaching tool available is the Slide-Rite from Schutt Manufacturing.

5. Using a loose base on the infield surface will reduce the chance of a jammed ankle. The dirt in the sliding area should be loosened, and players should wear protective clothing.

Coaching Points for the Slide

- If in doubt, slide!
- Never change your mind once you start your slide.
- Slide to the base, not through the base, except at home.
- Check the infield surface before the game so that you can make the necessary adjustments. Is it hard? Soft? Are the bases level? Is home plate raised? Are corners protruding?

OFFENSIVE BASE-RUNNING PLAYS

Base-running plays are designed to give fast runners the opportunity to steal, to help protect runners with average speed, and to put pressure on the defense. The batter is asked to protect the runner or bunt and hit the ball in certain areas to create defensive challenges. Signals are given so that offensive efforts are coordinated and no one is caught by surprise. The only surprises should be to the defense. The following sections cover steals, the bunt-and-run or hit-and-run, squeeze plays, wild pitches, and rundowns. Because the actions of the base runners in first-and-third situations are determined by defensive strategies, those offensive plays are covered in chapter 7.

Steals

Base runners have a greater chance of scoring if they can get to the next base without using up an out! The steal is an effective way to get into scoring position. A runner at first base with two out must find a way to get to second. Not much can happen if she stays at first.

How aggressive the runners should be depends on the following considerations:

1. Score, inning, number of outs, and ability of the next batter. Runners must not take the bat out of the hands of a big hitter by being the third out of the inning or by vacating first base to set up an intentional walk.

2. The runners' capabilities—speed, quickness of reaction, and sliding ability. Runners should be realistic about their chance for success.

3. Condition of the base paths. Slow paths (wet, soft) will slow the runners.

4. The ability of the defense, particularly the catcher, to stop the runners.

5. Coaching philosophy. Do the players make their own base-running decisions?

The batter's job is to protect the runner on the steal. She moves deeper in the box to make the catcher's throw longer. If a runner is stealing third, a right-handed batter should also back away from the plate to hinder the catcher's view of third. The batter can further hinder the catcher's vision by beginning the swing and leaving the bat over the plate with the end of the barrel pointed at the catcher's eyes as she stands to throw. The batter can also create some confusion among the fielders by using fake slaps, fake bunts, and swinging and missing to freeze the defense and delay their base coverage. Even on a pitchout the batter must do her best to legally interfere with the catcher's attempts to throw out the runner.

Straight Steal. The steal is a good percentage play when the pitcher throws a lot of changes, when the catcher has a weak arm, or when the shortstop is slow to cover the base (particularly third base). The element of surprise is also a big factor in a successful steal.

The runner takes off for the next base when the pitcher releases the ball. The runner goes directly to the base and prepares to slide hard into the glove if she and the ball are arriving at the same time. The slide is away from the tag if the ball is already there. If the ball goes through, the runner must get up quickly and be ready to advance to the next base.

When the coach calls for a steal, the batter is usually asked to take the pitch and protect the runner. A full swing and a miss may help freeze the shortstop and give the runner an advantage of several steps.

Delayed Steal. The element of surprise is the key to success with the delayed steal. The base runner should look for a lazy pitcher who doesn't pay attention to the runners, a pitcher who becomes upset easily by her performance or by the umpire, a catcher who pays little attention to the runners, or a catcher who is aggressive and makes many throws to the base. The delayed steal may be called along with a take signal to the batter (the play is then definitely on), or the batter may be uninvolved and free to react to the pitch. In softball this play is rarely used at third.

The runner takes a normal lead and then breaks for the next base as the ball is released. She can use the delayed steal on the battery, on the defense, or on a throw behind her.

- To execute the delayed steal on the battery, the runner looks for a lazy return to the pitcher or a pitcher not looking her back. On the return to the pitcher, the runner goes as the ball leaves the catcher's hand.

- To use the delayed steal on the defense, the runner watches for the covering defensive player to vacate the base (walk away from the base) as the ball is returned to the pitcher. This often happens at second base, and an alert runner can easily reach the unattended base.

- The base runner can use the delayed steal on a throw behind her. She can set this up by taking a slightly longer lead to entice the catcher into making a pickoff throw. The runner breaks on the release of the ball to the base.

Double Steal. Two runners on base can use either a straight steal or a delayed steal. Signals should be used so that everyone knows what will happen. The double steal works best with no outs and a good hitter up. Even if the lead runner is thrown out, one runner is still in scoring position.

Slap-and-Steal. On the slap-and-steal the runner goes on the pitch. The batter shows bunt and then slaps the ball. This play forces the middle infielders to worry about both covering the base and playing the ball. With a runner at first a ball hit at the shortstop will keep her from covering second. Because the second baseman is moving to cover first base, second base is open. The batter would not want to slap to the shortstop with a runner on second because the runner should not try to advance on a ball hit in front of her. When used with a runner on third, this play becomes a suicide squeeze with the slap replacing the bunt. The goal of the slapper in that case is just to put the ball in play. A variation is to attempt to freeze the shortstop with a fake slap. The batter uses a late swing and misses the ball as the runner steals second.

Bunt-and-Run

The bunt-and-run, in which the run part really precedes the bunt, is useful against a tight defense to get a runner with average speed to second. A fast runner may get two bases on the bunt. The batter should be a good bunter. The runner leaves on the pitch as if stealing, and the batter puts the ball in play by bunting. An advantage for the bunter is that placement is not important; she must just get the bunt down. The runner goes hard, but she should try to see if the bunter has angled the ball down. She should also listen for the coach's help should the ball be popped up. An alert, speedy runner can often get two bases on this play if the defense fails to cover third immediately. As the runner rounds second base, she looks for third base to see if she can beat the defense there. If the pitch cannot be bunted, the batter should take the pitch. The play then becomes a straight steal. The batter does not want to pop up a poor pitch for a double play and must focus on protecting the runner

Hit-and-Run

The hit-and-run, which might more accurately be called the run-and-hit, is used with a runner on first or second. The runner leaves on the pitch, and the hitter's job is to make contact and hit the ball hard on the ground, ideally behind the runner. The batter must go after any pitch she can reach, not only strikes. If the batter cannot hit the ball, she should try to foul it off. If the batter cannot possibly reach the ball, she must do all she can to protect the runner. The runner must listen for contact, try to see if the ball is hit down or up, and listen for coaching help. She glances to home on the third or fourth step to try to pick up the ball.

The hit-and-run should not be used when a pitcher has poor control or when the count is in the pitcher's favor and the batter is not likely to see a good pitch. The play is most useful when the runner has average speed and the batter is a good contact hitter. The play can also be called with a power hitter at bat because the runner will have time to return on a long fly. The hit-and-run helps avoid a double play, puts pressure on the defense, and opens holes in the infield if the defense breaks to cover the runner. This can also be a good call when batters are overswinging (especially against a slow pitcher) or when a batter has lost her aggressiveness and isn't swinging.

Suicide Squeeze

One of the most exciting plays in softball, the suicide squeeze is used to score a runner from third. The element of surprise and the pressure the play exerts on the defense favor the offense. The play is usually called with one out when the count is such that the pitcher will be throwing a strike and has the control to do so. Miscommunication must not occur on this play, so the batter is usually required to give a return signal to confirm that the squeeze is on. The runner anticipates the pitcher's release to get a good jump, leaving on the pitch as if stealing home. The batter must bunt any pitch, rolling the ball away from the plate, preferably between the pitcher and the first baseman. If the pitch is at the batter, the batter must rock back and still put the ball down. If the batter is a good slapper, she may be asked to slap instead of bunt. She needs only to hit the ball down, although a high bounce to short or second gives the runner extra time. If the runner sees that the pitch is well out of the strike zone and that the batter has no chance of touching it, she should attempt to put on the brakes and get back. A pitchout can hang a runner out to dry.

Safety Squeeze

Like the suicide squeeze, the safety squeeze is used to score a runner from third. The difference is that the runner does not go until she sees that the bunt is angled down toward the ground. The best place to bunt is to the third baseman. She cannot see what the runner is doing, which adds to the pressure of making the play. Because the runner waits to see where the ball is bunted, she is not likely to be put out on a popped-up bunt or a missed pitch. The runner may be instructed not to go unless an error occurs on the play. A variation is for the runner to go after the defensive player fields the bunt and throws to first. This is a good call if the first baseman has a weak arm and the runner has good speed. The runner breaks when the ball leaves the fielder's hand, being careful not to be fooled by a fake throw. The safety squeeze puts less pressure on the batter because she can wait for a good pitch to bunt.

Wild Pitches

The aggressive, alert base runner watches the pitch all the way to the plate and anticipates where it will go. For example, a low ball that is headed down has a good chance of being a wild pitch or a passed ball. The alert base runner is ready to react to that pitch and advance to the next base if the ball bounds a safe distance away from the catcher. The runner cannot wait for a coach to tell her to go. She reacts immediately and slides hard into the next base. A runner who hesitates should stay.

Second-and-Third Play

With runners at second and third, the offense may have the runner at third going home automatically on any ground ball, whether no outs or one out and no matter where the ball is hit (except when it stays just in front of home plate and is picked up by the catcher). This is an excellent play because it puts pressure on the infield. If they make a mistake, a score results. If the defense gets the out at home, the offense is still left with the runners in the same spots—at second and third. The runner must slide hard at home, creating a difficult tag play as well as tying up the catcher so that she cannot easily make a play on the batter–base runner. The batter's responsibility is to hit the ball on the ground, toss the bat away from home plate knowing that the runner is coming home, and then try to get to second if the throw goes home. The batter–base runner automatically goes to second base unless stopped by the first-base coach. The runner at second goes to third as soon as she sees the defense throw home or to first. The runner from second should not be in a hurry because the play will be made elsewhere and she must not run into a tag out at short or third. If the runner at home is out by a mile, the offense still hopes to be left with runners at second and third. The worse case is to have runners at first and third. But if the defense makes a mistake or fumbles the ball, a run scores on what appears to be a routine ground ball.

Rundowns

If caught in a rundown, the runner should keep moving. She stays alive as long as possible, using quick changes of direction, head fakes, and changes of speed. She should stay as far from the throw as possible by changing direction as soon as the ball leaves the thrower's hand. The more throws the defense makes, the greater the chance they will make an error. If a player is the only runner, she might try to trip a hard-charging defensive player by dropping to the ground in front of her at the last second. The runner would then get up quickly and run the opposite direction.

The runner can also try to pick up a defensive obstruction call. She looks for a defensive player who has just thrown the ball and is still in the base path. The base runner runs into the player and alerts the umpire by calling "Obstruction." She should continue the play until she is sure that the call is made in her favor.

With two runners on base, the runner in the rundown tries to draw several throws to make time for the other runner to advance. If a runner is caught between third and home, the trailing runner should get to third base and the lead runner should try to go home. The lead runner should not attempt to go back to third because the other runner should be safely there. If the defense is playing on the trailing runner, she should try to gain time for the lead runner to make it home.

Should two runners end up on one base, one runner should remain tightly on the base. The runners should not create an easy double play by both leaving the base; let the defense chase one runner and get only one out.

On-Deck Batter

The on-deck batter has more to do than prepare for her at bat. With runners attempting to score, she takes a position behind home plate in direct line with the runner but out of the way of the catcher and umpire. She assists runners by telling them whether to slide or stand up and by directing them to one side of the plate or the other. She uses hand signals to indicate up or down and left or right, and she should use verbal cues as well. With a runner on third base she assumes an on-deck position closer to home plate than normal so that she can get to her position in time.

BASE-RUNNING DRILLS

Base runners must learn to react to the ball off the bat, the position of the hit, and the fielder's play and make many decisions on their own. Only through practice with gamelike situations can runners learn to react quickly and correctly. Use the following drills to help your players develop base-running skills. In addition, take every opportunity during batting practice to run the bases.

Home to First

Purpose: To practice techniques for running to first, including developing quickness out of the batter's box.

Procedure: This drill requires a batter, feeder, and five scattered defensive receivers. The remaining players rotate running to first. The first-base running lane needs to be drawn. The batter–base runner hits a ball off a soft toss or a machine and focuses on getting quickly out of the box. She heads to the center of the running lane. She takes a brief look and decides whether to make a turn for second or run straight through the base, pulling up short as soon as she hits the bag. The coach can use chalk lines or a cone as a reminder of when to look briefly at the play. The runner rotates to the first-base coaching box to see if the next runner touches the front half of the base. She then rotates to the end of the line at home.

Foul-Line Leadoffs

Purpose: To practice maintaining a balanced position after leading off.

Procedure: A pitcher uses second base as the mound and throws easily to a catcher near the pitcher's rubber. All runners are on the outfield foul line and use it as the base. They lead off on the pitcher's motion, take three steps, and assume a well-balanced position, ready to go either direction. They then react to the coach's command of "Back" or "Go." On "Go," they run three to four steps and then return to the foul line to repeat the drill. Run the drill on both foul lines so that runners become accustomed to watching the pitcher's release from both sides.

Leadoffs With Multiple Runners

Purpose: To practice leadoffs at each base. The entire team can practice.

Procedure: With a pitcher throwing to a catcher, runners at each base work on getting a good jump, taking three steps at first and third, and taking five steps at second. Several runners work at each base. Each group completes three leadoffs at a base before all rotate to the next base.

Watch and Take Advantage

Purpose: To practice holding the leadoff until the pitcher has the ball.

Procedure: A pitcher with a bucket of balls on the mound throws to a catcher. Runners form a line behind first base. The runner works on getting a good jump on her leadoff and then maintaining a balanced position until the ball is successfully returned to the pitcher. The catcher occasionally overthrows the pitcher or the pitcher drops the ball. The runner looks for the error and reacts by going to second.

Football Up and Down

Purpose: To develop the agility and quickness to escape a rundown.

Procedure: In staggered rows, players assume well-balanced positions as if between bases. The coach faces the players and gives hand signals to indicate the direction in which players move. The signals are right, left, down, and up. Players shuffle to the side on right and left signals. On the down signal they quickly hit the ground. Players should be absolutely flat. On the up signal they get up quickly to be ready to go again. In a rundown, players use the prone position to trip the defensive player.

First to Third

Purpose: To practice picking up the coach's signal when running from first to third.

Procedure: The drill uses a right fielder, second baseman (for relay), and catcher. Runners line up behind first. The coach fungo hits to the right fielder. The runner assumes a three-step leadoff before the hit. On the hit, the runner approaches second and looks to the third-base coach for the signal to stop or continue to third. If stopped, the runner makes an aggressive turn and finds the ball. She returns to the end of the line, and the next runner goes.

Sacrifice Fly With Runners

Purpose: To practice tagging at third on sacrifice flies with outfielders throwing home.

Procedure: The drill requires outfielders, a catcher, and runners at third. Fungo fly balls are hit in front of the outfielders. A runner at third base assumes a leadoff, tags, and then goes home on the catch. The on-deck batter moves into position to help. The runner can slide or swing wide of the catcher. The drill offers an opportunity for outfielders to work on throws under gamelike conditions. The drill can also be performed off ground balls. The runner rotates to the on-deck circle and then returns to the base-running line.

Variation: Add a runner at first so that the outfielder must choose whether to make a play at home or throw to second to stop the other runner from advancing.

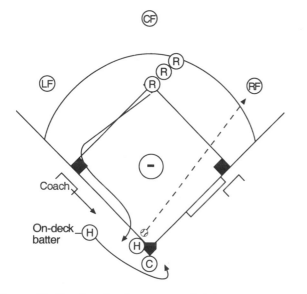

Figure 10.11 Scoring from second drill.

Scoring From Second

Purpose: To practice coaching the runner going home.

Procedure: Outfielders and a catcher take their positions, and the remainder of the team forms a line to run from second base (see figure 10.11). One runner is in the on-deck circle. The hitter fungo hits singles to the outfield. The runner is going all the way unless the third-base coach, who slides down the line to help, stops her. The on-deck batter moves into position at home to help the runner. The runner slides or swings wide (to avoid contact) as she approaches home. Runners rotate to the on-deck circle and then to the running line as the drill continues.

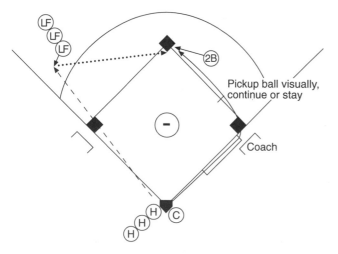

Figure 10.12 Stretching a single to a double drill.

Stretching a Single to a Double

Purpose: To practice making an aggressive turn at first.

Procedure: The drill requires three left fielders, a second baseman, and a catcher. Runners form a line behind home plate (see figure 10.12). A batter fungo hits a single near the left-field line. The batter takes an aggressive turn toward second. If the ball is not fielded cleanly or if the outfielder is not alert, the runner advances to second. The runner visually picks up the ball as soon as she rounds first; the first-base coach assists the runner.

APPENDIX A:

Defensive Skills Checklist

This checklist lists all the plays and skills used at each position. Players should review the list to make sure they are well prepared and feel confident about each item. Coaches can use this list to prepare practice and make sure they have covered everything before the first game.

Catcher
- [ ] Fielding bunts: throws to first, second, third
- [ ] Three throws to first: passed ball, bunt, pickoff
- [ ] Pickoffs
- [ ] Holding runners
- [ ] Throws to third with a right-handed batter
- [ ] Knee throws to bases
- [ ] Cutoff
- [ ] Rundowns
- [ ] Foul balls
- [ ] Playing the fence
- [ ] Pop-ups
- [ ] First-and-third play
- [ ] Force-out at home and throw to first
- [ ] Passed ball with a runner at third
- [ ] Blocking balls
- [ ] Framing
- [ ] Giving signals
- [ ] Blocking the plate
- [ ] Intentional walk

Pitcher
- [ ] Fielding bunts
- [ ] Squeeze play
- [ ] Pop-ups
- [ ] Fielding balls to the left side
- [ ] Covering home on passed balls
- [ ] Double plays
- [ ] Intentional walk
- [ ] Pitchout
- [ ] First-and-third play
- [ ] Backing up third and home
- [ ] Rundowns

First Base
- [ ] Tagging the base
- [ ] Tagging runners
- [ ] Fielding the bunt
- [ ] Working with the pitcher on bunts
- [ ] Working with the second baseman covering first
- [ ] Working with the second baseman on balls wide of first
- [ ] Throws to third
- [ ] Tagging first and throwing home

- [ ] Double plays
- [ ] Cutoff
- [ ] Short first base
- [ ] Pickoffs at first
- [ ] Coverage on intentional walks
- [ ] Throws from right field
- [ ] Pop-ups
- [ ] Playing the fence
- [ ] Foul balls
- [ ] Rundowns
- [ ] Relay from the right-field line

Second Base
- [ ] Covering first on a bunt
- [ ] Working with the first baseman on balls wide of first
- [ ] Double plays
- [ ] Pickoffs
- [ ] Fake pickoff
- [ ] Taking a charge
- [ ] Relay from right field
- [ ] Foul balls behind first
- [ ] Pop-ups
- [ ] Shallow flies to center and right field
- [ ] Rundowns

Shortstop

- ☐ Covering on steals (second and third)
- ☐ Covering second and third on bunts
- ☐ Pickoffs (second and third)
- ☐ Double plays from the pitcher, second, and first
- ☐ Relay from left and center
- ☐ Taking a charge
- ☐ Foul balls behind third
- ☐ Pop-ups
- ☐ Shallow flies to left and center
- ☐ Holding runners
- ☐ First-and-third play
- ☐ Fake throws (bluffs)
- ☐ Rundowns

Third Base

- ☐ Fielding bunts
- ☐ Squeeze
- ☐ Force-out at third and throw to first
- ☐ Holding runners and throw to first
- ☐ Fake throws

- ☐ Balls in the hole
- ☐ Double plays to second
- ☐ Covering third on a pickoff
- ☐ Pop-ups
- ☐ Playing the fence
- ☐ Coverage on intentional walks
- ☐ First-and-third play
- ☐ Rundowns
- ☐ Relay on the left-field line

Outfield

- ☐ Blocking balls
- ☐ Do or die
- ☐ Hitting relay
- ☐ Hitting cutoff
- ☐ Covering bases
- ☐ Playing the fences
- ☐ Throwing to bases
- ☐ Footwork: drop step, inside roll, outside roll
- ☐ Diving for balls
- ☐ Balls hit overhead
- ☐ Betweeners: outfield and infield
- ☐ Communication: infield and outfield

- ☐ Right fielder throwing to first to get runner
- ☐ Backing up bases
- ☐ Backing up other outfielders
- ☐ Backing up secondary throws
- ☐ Center-field pickoff at second base

Team Defense

- ☐ Rundowns
- ☐ Relays
- ☐ Cutoff
- ☐ Pickoffs
- ☐ First-and-third play
- ☐ Bunt defense
- ☐ Slap defense
- ☐ Double plays
- ☐ Cutting the run at the plate
- ☐ Bloop hits (Texas Leaguers)
- ☐ Bases loaded
- ☐ Steals
- ☐ Hit-and-run
- ☐ International tiebreaker (runner placed on second to start the inning)
- ☐ Intentional walks

APPENDIX B:

Offensive Skills Checklist

This checklist lists all the offensive skills and plays used in softball. Not all players will be able to execute all of the skills. Players should review the list to make sure they feel confident with the skills they will be using in a game. Coaches can use this list to prepare practice and develop game plans.

Hitting
- ☐ Contact
- ☐ Right side
- ☐ Hit-and-run
- ☐ Protecting the hitter
- ☐ Taking a pitch
- ☐ Two-strike adjustment

Bunts
- ☐ Sacrifice
- ☐ Push
- ☐ Slash (slug)
- ☐ Sneaky
- ☐ Drag
- ☐ Squeeze

- ☐ Safety
- ☐ Fake
- ☐ Knob
- ☐ Bunt-and-run

Running Slap

Base Running
- ☐ Out of box
- ☐ To first
- ☐ Rounding bases
- ☐ Between bases
- ☐ First-and-third play
- ☐ Second base to home
- ☐ Home to second base

- ☐ Second-and-third play
- ☐ Tagging
- ☐ Tag and draw throw
- ☐ Hit-and-run
- ☐ Bunt-and-run
- ☐ Rundowns

Sliding
- ☐ Regular
- ☐ Pop-up
- ☐ Hook
- ☐ Rollover
- ☐ Headfirst

Coaching at Home

Drill Finder

(continued)

About the Author

Judi Garman is one of the most successful soft-ball coaches in NCAA history. After establishing the softball program at Cal State Fullerton in 1980, Garman collected 913 wins and only 376 losses for a winning percentage of .708 and retired as the nation's winningest coach with more than 1,100 career wins.

During Garman's career at Cal State Fullerton, the Titans participated in postseason play 18 out of 20 seasons. Her teams won or shared eight conference titles and seven regional champion-ships. They won the NCAA championship in 1986; finished second in the Collegiate World Series in 1981, 1983, and 1985; finished third in 1982 and 1987; and fifth in 1995. While coaching at Golden West Junior College from 1975 to 1978, Judi's teams won four consecutive national titles.

She served as president of the National Soft-ball Coaches Association (NSCA) from 1990 to 1991. In 1993, she was elected to the NSCA Hall of Fame. In 1995, she was the recipient of the Woman of Excellence in Sports award.

As a player, Garman was a Canadian all-star outfielder and member of two Canadian national championship teams. She also was a member of the Saskatoon team that rep-resented Canada at the world championships held in Osaka, Japan, in 1970.

Now that she has retired from coaching, Garman maintains an extensive clinic-speak-ing schedule, spreading her softball knowledge around the world. Besides softball, she enjoys golfing, fishing, and snow skiing. She lives in Palm Springs, California and Aspen, Colorado.

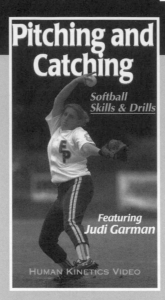